Mrs S. J. Ryan,
from Rob 1878.

BATTLES FOR THE UNION.

Captain Willard Glazier,

THE SOLDIER-AUTHOR.

I. Capture, Prison-Pen, and Escape.
II. Three Years in the Federal Cavalry.
III. Battles for the Union.
IV. The Roll of Honor.

Captain Glazier's works are growing more and more popular every day. Their delineations of military life, constantly varying scenes, and deeply interesting stories, combine to place their writer in the front rank of American authors.

SOLD ONLY BY SUBSCRIPTION.

Persons desiring Agencies for any of Captain Glazier's books should address

DUSTIN, GILMAN & CO.,

HARTFORD, CONN.

Willard Glazier

WILLARD GLAZIER

Battles for the Union:

COMPRISING

Descriptions of many of the most Stubbornly Contested Battles in the War of the Great Rebellion, together with Incidents and Reminiscences of the Camp, the March, and the Skirmish Line.

EMBRACING

A RECORD OF THE PRIVATIONS, HEROIC DEEDS, AND GLORIOUS TRIUMPHS OF THE SOLDIERS OF THE REPUBLIC.

BY

WILLARD GLAZIER,

AUTHOR OF "SOLDIERS OF THE SADDLE," "CAPTURE, PRISON-PEN, AND ESCAPE," "THE ROLL OF HONOR," ETC., ETC.

Illustrated.

DUSTIN, GILMAN & CO.;
PUBLICATION OFFICE, HARTFORD, CONN.;
BRANCH OFFICES CHICAGO, ILL., CINCINNATI, OHIO.
1875.

TO

THE MEMORY OF

My Sister Elvira,

THE CONSTANT COMPANION OF MY BOYHOOD,

WHOSE LAMP OF LIFE WENT OUT

ON THE DAY, AND AT THE HOUR OF MY CAPTURE BY THE ENEMY

AT NEW BALTIMORE, VIRGINIA,

In the Autumn of 1863,

AND WHOSE LAST WORDS WERE OF ME AND THE ARMY,

This Volume

IS AFFECTIONATELY AND TENDERLY INSCRIBED

BY HER BROTHER,

THE AUTHOR.

Preface.

IF there is anything of interest or importance in the history of war, it must naturally be found in the great battles which decide the issues of the controversy. The soldier turns to battle scenes for a record of his services and sacrifices. He cares but little for details of the camp and march, while he searches with avidity for the chapter which rehearses the story of his struggles and victories on the field of strife. The citizen and student of history look to grand combats, for the salient points in their chronology of events.

I have endeavored in this work to present in the most concise and simple form the great contests in the War for the Union. Should my late comrades in arms consider my pictures faithful, I shall feel more than compensated for the effort I have made to commemorate their glorious deeds.

WILLARD GLAZIER.

HARTFORD, CONN., AUGUST 22d, 1874.

Contents.

CHAPTER IV.

WILSON'S CREEK.

CHAPTER V.

BALL'S BLUFF.

CHAPTER VI

MILL SPRING.

CHAPTER VII.

PEA RIDGE.

CHAPTER VIII.

MERRIMAC AND MONITOR.

CHAPTER IX.

NEWBERN.

CHAPTER X.

WINCHESTER.

CHAPTER XI.

FALMOUTH HEIGHTS.

CHAPTER XII

PITTSBURG LANDING.

CHAPTER XIII.

WILLIAMSBURG.

CHAPTER XIV.

SEVEN PINES.

CHAPTER XV.

FAIR OAKS.

CHAPTER XVI.

MALVERN HILL.

CHAPTER XXI

ANTIETAM.

CHAPTER XXII.

CORINTH.

CHAPTER XXIII.

FREDERICKSBURG.

CHAPTER XXIV.

MURFREESBORO OR STONE RIVER.

CHAPTER XXXVII.

FORT PILLOW.

CHAPTER XXXVIII.

COLD HARBOR.

CHAPTER XXXIX.

FORT WAGNER.

CHAPTER XL.

CEDAR CREEK.

CHAPTER XLI.

WAYNESBORO.

CHAPTER XLII.

BENTONVILLE.

CHAPTER XLIII.

FIVE FORKS.

CHAPTER XLIV.

THE SURRENDER.

Illustrations.

CHAPTER I.

FORT SUMTER.

First Causes.—United States Property Seized.—Uprising of the North. —The Little Band at the Nation's Outpost.—From Moultrie to Sumter.—The Landing at Night.—Moultrie in Flames.—Star of the West.—No Help Yet.—Alone to Defend the Old Flag.—Starvation Ahead.—Communications Cut Off.—No Surrender.—The Bombardment.—Terrific Cannonading.—The Barracks on Fire.—Not a Biscuit Left.—Out of Ammunition.—Wigfall and his White Flag.—Sumter Surrenders on its Own Terms.—The Defeat a Glorious Victory.

FOR years the irrepressible conflict between slavery and freedom had been proclaimed by the wise and disbelieved by the unthinking. For years the storm cloud, which in 1861 broke over the nation's head, had been slowly gathering with ever accumulating wrath. Some near-sighted but well-intentioned people supposed that the lightning could be extracted from the threatening cloud by sending up the 'Compromise' kite, with its hempen string of 'Mason and Dixon's Line,' but the guns of Sumter undeceived them. Those guns awoke the nation from its fancied repose and echoed, not only over Charleston Harbor, but along the Atlantic coast and through the entire North.

With a grand and unanimous uprising not paralleled in history, the men of the free North flocked around the nation's standard and offered their lives and fortunes in its defence.

The people, before dormant, awoke suddenly to find that they had been sleeping on the edge of a crater whose boiling lava of injustice and slavery threatened to engulf them.

At the nation's outpost, in Charleston Harbor, alone with his little band, Major Robert Anderson awaited, behind the embrasures of Fort Sumter, the first attack of the insurgents.

"The property of the General Government south of the Potomac, with the exception of Fortress Monroe, Fort Sumter, Fort Pickens, and the Tortugas, had been successively seized by the authorities of the states within which they were situated."

"The three forts that then defended Charleston Harbor were Fort Moultrie, of Revolutionary fame, on Sullivan's Island; Castle Pinckney, near the city; and Fort Sumter, a new structure on an island in the channel, commanding all the approaches to the city. It had been erected by the Federal Government at considerable cost, and was not yet so far complete as to receive a garrison. The place was calculated for one hundred and forty-six guns and a war garrison of six hundred and fifty men. The only force that the Federal Government had for these three forts was a single company of artillery in Fort Moultrie, under command of Major Anderson." In December, 1860, his garrison, occupying Fort Moultrie, found it difficult to strengthen, and as the authorities at Charleston grew hourly more threatening, Major Anderson, on his own responsibility, abandoned the place for Fort

Sumter, where at ten o'clock on the night of the twenty-sixth his force disembarked from row boats.

"A few men were left at Moultrie under Captain Foster to cut down the flag-staff, spike the guns, burn the carriages and dismantle the place."

As the flames went up from Moultrie, Charleston saw what had happened and great excitement spread to that city and throughout the country. The action of Major Anderson was lauded at the North and denounced at the South.

But his new position at Fort Sumter was of doubtful advantage. He could not be surprised here as at Moultrie, but his communications were cut off and there was a prospect ahead of being starved out, unless help arrived. Help was sent by our Government, but the vigilant Charleston authorities, ever on the alert, prevented the landing of supplies and reënforcements.

Fort Moultrie was repaired and garrisoned by the insurgents, and on Sullivan and Morris Islands new batteries were built.

Troops were tendered to the Governor of South Carolina by three of the slave-holding states, and the palmetto flag waved over the post-office and Custom House at Charleston. The streets of that city were patrolled by the military; the telegraph was under censorship and the efforts of the authorities were directed toward getting possession of Sumter.

Major Anderson and his hero band worked steadily on, strengthening the Fort as best they could. Around them, battery after battery arose, each one cutting off more surely their hope of succor.

Their stock of food rapidly lessened, despite its most economic distribution.

On January fifth, 1861, the steamship "Star of the West" left New York with supplies and two hundred men for Fort Sumter, and arrived off Charleston bar at one o'clock on the morning of the ninth. The lights of the steamship had been extinguished to insure greater safety, but as the "Star of the West" passed over the harbor bar, a steamboat lying in wait, recognized her and signalled ashore. At a distance of half a mile from Morris Island, she was fired upon by a shore battery. Raising a large National flag at her mast-head she swept on, the Rebel shot over-reaching her, until at last, having got her range, two cannon balls took effect—forward and amidships. As she proceeded on her way, two steamers, having in tow an armed schooner, approached from Fort Moultrie, evidently intending to cut her off. The choice was one of capture or destruction, and the supply ship therefore put about and returned to New York.

Major Anderson and his artillery company had watched the approach of the "Star of the West," withholding meantime his fire upon the land batteries because he could not believe the act authorized by the state, and not knowing that the ship was coming to their relief. "He immediately dispatched a message to Governor Pickens denouncing the act as one of war and threatening that unless it was disavowed he would not permit any vessel to pass within range of his guns." Major Anderson afterwards referred the matter to his Government and requested that Lieutenant Talbot, bearer of despatches, might have facilities extended to him for his departure.

On April twelfth, 1861, the Rebels demanded the

BOMBARDMENT OF FORT SUMTER.

surrender of Fort Sumter. Major Anderson replied that "his sense of honor and his obligations to the Government would prevent his compliance" with the demand. At half-past four o'clock on the morning of the twelfth, the National flag was fired upon and the war of rebellion inaugurated. The heavy batteries of Mt. Pleasant and Cummings Point, a floating battery in the harbor and Fort Moultrie all poured in their red rain of shot and shell on the devoted heads of the patriot band in Sumter. For two hours this terrific bombardment was received without a reply, while crumbling walls tottered around them and exploding shells fell thick and fast.

Calmly, at half-past six o'clock, these men numbering less than a hundred, sat down under this fiery tempest to breakfast on their last biscuit. Afterwards they prepared heroically to resist the attack of an army of ten thousand, aided by an overpowering array of batteries.

The company was divided into three reliefs, and Captain Doubleday with Lieutenant Snyder in charge of the first relief, opened the return fire. The enthusiasm of the men was very great, and they remained steadily at the guns until relieved. The Columbiads and sea howitzers on the parapet were disabled, and the firing in that quarter became so intense that the men were withdrawn to the casemates.

It also became impossible to work the barbette or upper uncovered guns. A sentinel cried out "shot" or "shell" at every discharge of the enemy's guns and the men were thus enabled to obtain shelter.

For thirty-six hours was this unequal contest waged.

From the dawn of Friday morning until near the close of Saturday afternoon an incessant storm of fire fell upon the doomed fort. The wooden barracks inside were fired by the hot-shot batteries of the enemy. An eye-witness gives this vivid description of the scene:—

"The fire surrounded us on all sides. Fearful that the walls might crack and the shells pierce and prostrate them, we commenced taking the powder out of the magazine before the fire had fully enveloped it. We took ninety-six barrels of powder out and threw them into the sea, leaving two hundred barrels in it. Owing to a lack of cartridges, we kept five men inside the magazine, sewing, as we wanted them, thus using up our shirts, sheets, blankets, and all the available material in the fort. When we were finally obliged to close the magazine and our material for cartridges was exhausted, we were left destitute of any means to continue the contest. We had eaten our last biscuit thirty-six hours before. We came very near being stifled with the dense, livid smoke from the burning buildings. Many of the men lay prostrate on the ground, with wet handkerchiefs over their mouths and eyes, gasping for breath. It was a moment of imminent peril. If an eddy of wind had not ensued, we all, probably, should have been suffocated.

"The crashing of the shot, the bursting of the shells, the falling of walls, and the roar of flames made a pandemonium of the fort. We nevertheless kept up a steady fire."

The shells and ammunition of the upper service magazine exploded, destroying the tower and sending the upper part of the building flying in all directions. Three times the fort had been on fire, the men being unable to extinguish it the last time. Owing to the proximity of the flames, the powder barrels, though covered with wet blankets, were in danger, and all but four were thrown into the sea.

The flag-staff had been hit nine times, and at last it was cut down and placed upon the ramparts with the torn flag nailed to it.

As twilight approached, General Wigfall, formerly a Texas senator, came to the fort in a skiff, bearing a white flag fastened to his sword. Kettell reports the conversation which occured.

He said he came from General Beauregard, the flag of Sumter being down.

"It is up again," replied Lieutenant Davis.

General Wigfall then said,

"You are on fire, let us stop this: there is a white flag, will any one wave it from the embrasure?"

One of the officers replied,

"That is for you to do if you wish your batteries to stop."

General Wigfall then held out the flag when Corporal Bringhurst was directed to hold it for him. The Corporal did so, but the shot continued to strike around him. Lieutenant Davis then said,

"If you request that a white flag be shown here while you hold a conference with Major Anderson, it may be done."

General Wigfall then addressing Major Anderson, said:

"I am from General Beauregard. You have defended your flag nobly, sir: on what terms will you evacuate the fort?"

Major Anderson replied, "General Beauregard is already acquainted with my only terms."

"Do I understand that you will evacuate upon the terms proposed the other day?"

"Yes, sir, and on those conditions only," was the reply.

"Then, sir," said Wigfall, "I understand Major Anderson that the fort is to be ours."

"On those conditions only, I repeat."

"Very well," said Wigfall, and he retired.

The conditions were that the men should take all their company and individual property, their side and other arms, that their torn flag should be saluted and taken with them, and that they should march out in their own way and at their own time.

The terms were agreed to, and on Sunday morning at about nine o'clock the men were formed in line, and marched out while the cannon boomed over the bay in salutes to the stars and stripes, and the band played "Yankee Doodle" and "Hail to the Chief." A cheer went up from the patriotic band as the old flag was lowered, after which they boarded the transport Isabel which took them to the United States ship Baltic, in the offing, whence they were carried to New York.

Thus gloriously fell Fort Sumter. Can history furnish us nobler examples of men, who in the face of starvation worked more manfully at their guns in defence of their country's flag, nor yielded while there was a cartridge left to fire, or material left to make one?

During this terrific bombardment no life was lost on either side,—a fact to be wondered at.

From statistics gathered from the Charleston Mercury of May third, the Rebels during this cannonading, threw into and upon the fort, two thousand three hundred and sixty-one solid shot, and nine hundred and eighty shells from fourteen batteries. At the fiftieth discharge of guns in giving the salute of one hundred guns to the National flag, a Union soldier was killed by its accidental explosion, and several others were wounded.

Major Anderson and his men were received at the North with the honor due to heroes. They had covered their names with a glory which could not fade away, and while country is loved and bravery chronicled, these names, clothed in light like the stars of heaven, can never pass from patriotic remembrance.

CHAPTER II.

BIG BETHEL.

General Butler at Fortress Monroe.—Decides to Attack the Rebels at Big Bethel.—Plan of Major Winthrop.—Crossing the Hampton River at Midnight.—Colonel Duryea joined by General Pierce.—Fatal Mistake of Colonel Bendix.—The Confederates Retreat from Little Bethel.—Battle of Big Bethel, and fall of Major Winthrop.—Gallantry and Death of Lieutenant Grebble.—Official Report of the Battle.

EARLY in the month of June, 1861, General Benjamin F. Butler, commanding a Federal force at Fortress Monroe, received intelligence that the Rebels were fortifying themselves at an unimportant village known as Little Bethel, twelve miles from the fortress, and that five miles beyond this point, at Big Bethel, they were intrenching themselves in a still stronger position. Thus established, with the latter point as a base, they were continually issuing from their stronghold in marauding parties, making prisoners the friends of the Union, and impressing their slaves into the Southern service. General Butler decided to break up these Rebel encampments, and at once prepared a secret expedition for the consummation of his purpose.

The first step in this movement was to ferry his troops across the Hampton River at Hampton, as the enemy had previously burned the bridge. Ten flat boats were found, capable of conveying one hundred and fifty-seven men each, including oarsmen. Men from the Naval Brigade were thoroughly instructed in the management of these boats, and at twelve o'clock on the night of the ninth of June, with carefully muffled oars, Colonel Duryea, commanding the troops from Fortress Monroe crossed the river and marched to Newport News—a small town at the mouth of the James River, where he was joined by Brigadier-General Pierce with two regiments of his command which had been encamped at this point. The united forces now moved silently on towards Little Bethel.

The expedition was well planned in every particular, and is said to have been chiefly the work of Major Theodore Winthrop, approved by General Butler, and but for an untoward accident not unusual with a citizen soldiery, undisciplined and inexperienced on the field of battle, would have proved eminently successful to the Federal arms. The march of our columns was to be so timed that the commanders could form a junction and make a concentrated attack upon Little Bethel just at the dawn of day. We were then to pursue vigorously the routed and flying rebels to Big Bethel, and without giving them time to recover from their surprise, charge their batteries at that point.

In order to be secure against any accident which might naturally be anticipated in the darkness, no regiment was to commence an attack without first giving the watchword, and in order that they might recognize each other easily in daylight a white badge was worn on the left arm. For a time every thing went well and all were confident of success, but as ofttimes before

> "The best laid plans of men and mice
> Gang aft aglee."

At a point described as the Cross Roads by those who participated in the expedition, Colonel Bendix with his regiment and a section of light artillery, had taken position with instructions to guard and hold the crossing at all hazards. The Unionists continued to move silently on towards Little Bethel. The light of day now began to dawn upon the advancing columns. The Third New York Infantry just then came cautiously moving along in the dim twilight and fog of the morning, on the road from Hampton. General Pierce and Colonel Townsend with their respective staffs rode together, in advance of the main column. These mounted officers, in the uncertain and flickering light of the morning, presented the aspect of a large body of cavalry.

It was well known that there was no cavalry with the Union force, hence it was not strange that Colonel Bendix should imagine that Rebel cavalry was about to assail his rear, and immediately opened fire upon them with his artillery, at the distance of five hundred yards. It was well for our men that the road was lower than the level of the land on either side, and was bordered by stone fences. Three men were nevertheless killed and eight wounded by the discharge. General Pierce thus unexpectedly assailed, fell back and dispatched couriers to Fortress Monroe for reinforcements.

Colonel Duryea, who had stationed Colonel Bendix

at the intersection of the roads and who was himself advancing on the road to Little Bethel, alarmed by the cannonading in his rear, also retraced his steps. Daylight soon revealed the sad mistake of Bendix. But the Rebels encamped at Little Bethel heard the firing, took the alarm, and without having seen the Federals, fled, panic stricken, to their reserves at Big Bethel. General Pierce now pressed vigorously forward and quickly destroyed the camp at Little Bethel which had been deserted less than half an hour before he reached it. The Union columns then pushed briskly on, five miles farther to Big Bethel, where the enemy was found to be in position to receive them, posted in full force behind their batteries. It was perhaps not wise under the circumstances to order an assault. The Unionists were depressed by the unfortunate accident which prevented their surprising the Rebels. It was ten o'clock in the morning; the troops had not slept for thirty hours, had marched nearly twelve miles, and half the distance in a scorching sun. Still, it was thought best to make an attack, as it would have been humiliating indeed to have returned to the fortress without firing a gun at the foe. For upwards of two hours our troops fought with a determination which would have been creditable to veterans. Facing a storm of shot and shell from rifled cannon and masked batteries, they drove the Rebels from their first line of intrenchments, when other and more formidable batteries opened upon them and forced them to retire from the unequal contest. The retreat was conducted in good order, Duryea's Zouaves covering the rear of the retiring columns in the most gallant manner, keeping the enemy in check and picking off from the pursuing lines of the exultant Confederates the more reckless and daring who ventured in advance of their comrades.

The Federal officers deported themselves with great coolness and intrepidity. It is generally conceded that the enemy brought into this action between two and three thousand infantry, with from fifteen to twenty pieces of artillery. The Federal loss was about forty killed and wounded. The loss of the enemy is not definitely known, but is supposed to have been somewhat less than ours, from the fact that they were protected by earth works, while we assaulted their works from an open field. Our forces retired in perfect order to Hampton, where they were met by General Butler, and subsequently transported in flat boats to Fortress Monroe. The failure of the expedition was a great disappointment to the administration and country, and its conduct was for this reason criticised with much greater severity than it merited. The Rebels were so frightened by our attack that they abandoned their works and hastened the following day to Yorktown. The gallant Major Winthrop who is credited with the original plan of the expedition, fell in this engagement, while leading his men in a charge upon a redoubt. Noticing some hesitancy in the advancing lines, he dashed to the front, shouting, "Come on boys! one charge and the day is ours!" This was his last command, and noble words were never more fitly spoken. A drummer boy connected with a North Carolina regiment seeing so fair a mark, borrowed a comrade's musket, took deliberate aim and discharged its contents into the breast of the daring Major, who fell mortally wounded, nearer to the enemy's works than any other man.

Lieutenant Grebble also distinguished himself in this action, and sealed his devotion to the cause of the Union with his life. Unlimbering his gun he moved towards the enemy, slowly firing as he advanced until he arrived within two hundred yards of a masked battery. He had but eleven men to work his gun, and yet with this handful of braves, he faced the deadly fire from the rifled cannon of the foe which had scattered our infantry and left him without support. This single piece of artillery was so efficiently worked that he silenced all in the Rebel battery except one. The enemy, crippled and suffering from the persistent and unceasing blows of the young artillerist, made a sortie, thinking doubtless that they could entrap or drive him from his position. "Now Charlie," said the gallant lieutenant, to Captain Bartlett, "I have something to fire at. Just see how I can make them skedaddle." He gave them three or four charges of grape and they fled back to their intrenchments in confusion. After repulsing the sortie he was left with but five men. Addressing Corporal Peoples, he said, "All I can now do will be of no avail. Limber up the gun and take it away." At this moment a ball from the enemy's intrenchments struck him in the head and his body fell lifeless to the ground.

General Butler in his official report, commenting on this adventure says, "I think in the unfortunate combination of circumstances and the result which we have experienced, we have gained more than we have lost. Our troops have learned to have confidence in themselves under fire, the enemy have shown that they will not meet us in the open field, and our officers have learned wherein their organization and drill are inefficient."

CHAPTER III.

BULL RUN.

Date of the Battle.—Military Talent Displayed on Both Sides.—General Beauregard in Command of the Confederate Forces.—Expectations of the North and South Concerning the Result of the Battle.—The Division Generals Engaged.—Slow Progress of McDowell's Army.—Heavy Skirmish at Blackburn's Ford.—Sluggishness of Army Movements.—Patterson's Failure to Engage Johnston.—Hostilities Commenced.—Attack of Confederate Batteries on Burnside's Brigade.—Struggle for the Hill beyond Warrenton Turnpike.—Colonel Hunter Severely Wounded.—Success of the Union Arms up to Three o'clock P. M.—Confederate Reënforcements Turn the Scale.—Panic of our Forces. They Break and Fly in Confusion.—The Union Army a Mass of Fugitives.—Disastrous end of the Battle.—Patterson Blamed.

THE Field of Bull Run and the Plains of Manassas will never lose their interest for the imaginative young or the patriotic old; for on this field and over these plains are scattered the bones of more than forty thousand brave men of both North and South, who have met in mortal combat and laid down their lives in defence of their principles.

On the twenty-first of July, 1861, was fought the battle of Bull Run, the first of a long series of engagements on these historic plains. The battles of Bristoe, Groveton, Manassas, Centreville, and Chantilly succeeded in 1862, and in the summer and autumn of 1863 followed the cavalry actions at Aldie, Middleburg, Upperville, and New Baltimore.

No battle ground on the continent of America can present to the generations yet to come, such a gigantic Roll of Honor. Here also was displayed the best military talent, the keenest strategy, and the highest engineering skill of our civil war. Here were assembled the great representative leaders of slavery and freedom. Here, Scott, McDowell, Pope, and Meade, on the Federal side, and Beauregard, Johnston, and Lee on the Confederate side, have in turn held the reins of battle and shared both victory and defeat.

The action which resulted in the fall of Fort Sumter developed extraordinary talent in the Rebel General P. G. T. Beauregard, and brought him conspicuously before the Confederate Government. Called for by the unanimous voice of the Southern people, he was now ordered to take command of the main portion of the Confederate army in Northern Virginia. He selected Manassas Junction as his base of operations, and established his outposts near Fairfax Court House, seventeen miles from Washington.

General Beauregard's forces on the line of Bull Run, numbered on the sixteenth of July nearly forty thousand men and sixty-four pieces of artillery, together with a considerable body of cavalry. The threatening attitude of this force, almost within sight of the National Capital, led General Scott to concentrate the Union forces in that quarter with a view to meeting the Rebels in battle, and if possible, giving a death blow to the Rebellion.

Ludicrous indeed, in the light of subsequent events, was the general conviction of the hostile sections that a single decisive engagement would terminate the war.

Little did the Unionists then know of the ambitious designs of the pro slavery leaders, and still less did the uneducated, misguided masses of the South know of the patriotism, resources, and invincible determination of the North. On both sides there was great popular anxiety for a general battle to determine the question of relative manhood; and especially on the side of the South, from an impression that one distinct and large combat, resulting in its favor and showing conspicuously its superior valor, would alarm the North sufficiently to lead it to abandon the war. The New York Tribune, which was supposed at that time to be a faithful representative of the sentiment and temper of the North, said, on the nineteenth of July, 1861, "We have been most anxious that this struggle should be submitted, at the earliest moment, to the ordeal of a fair decisive battle. Give the Unionists a fair field, equal weapons and equal numbers, and we ask no more. Should the Rebel forces at all justify the vaunts of their journalistic trumpeters, we shall candidly admit the fact. If they can beat double the number of Unionists, they can end the struggle on their own terms."

A field for the grand combat was soon found, but its results were destined to disappoint both the victors and the vanquished. The South had looked forward to this field for an acknowledgment of its independence, the North for a downfall of the Rebellion.

At noon, on the seventeenth of July, the Federal troops, under the immediate command of General Irvin McDowell, struck tents and took up their line of march towards Fairfax, without baggage, and carrying three days rations in their haversacks. One division, under General Tyler, which had been encamped at Falls Church, marched to Vienna, while the main column, led by McDowell in person, moved direct from Alexandria to Fairfax Court House.

The head of General Tyler's division reached Vienna at sunset. The infantry turned into the fields, while the artillery took position on the hills. Near the railroad was a large woodpile, behind which the artillery took shelter when they fired upon an Ohio regiment passing in the cars. The wood was found convenient for bivouac fires, and the boys helped themselves to it without ceremony.

The force commanded by McDowell numbered about thirty-five thousand men, all of whom, with the exception of less than one regiment of the old regular army, were raw troops, who not only had never smelt powder, but were scarcely instructed in the simplest rudiments of the manual. Their knowledge of tactical evolutions amounted to nothing. The best portion of the troops were militia regiments, whose term of service would expire within four or five days, but who were nevertheless launched into the campaign with the vague idea that they had long enough to serve to accomplish the purpose of the expedition. This undisciplined and unstable mass was divided into five divisions, each consisting of two or more brigades, and was commanded as follows: First Division—Brigadier General D. Tyler, Connecticut Militia; Second Division—Colonel David Hunter, Third U. S. Cavalry; Third Division—Colonel S. P. Heintzelman, Seventeenth U. S. Infantry; Fourth Division—Briga dier General T. Runyon, New Jersey Militia; Fifth Division—Colonel Dixon S. Niles, Second U. S. Infantry.

Accompanying the army were fifty-five pieces of artillery, and an unnecessarily large train. Owing to the inexperience of the troops in marching, and the obstructions placed in the way of the retiring enemy, the progress of McDowell's army was exceedingly slow, and it was not until eleven o'clock of the eighteenth that General Tyler's division, forming the advance, entered Centreville, a small village seven miles northeast of Manassas Junction, and separated from it by Bull Run, which is a fordable stream flowing in a southeasterly direction into the Potomac.

From Centreville two roads diverge towards Bull Run, of which the more easterly and direct strikes the stream at Blackburn's Ford, not far from the Junction: while the other, known as the Warrenton Turnpike, takes a westerly course and crosses Bull Run at the Stone Bridge, four miles higher up. The village itself lies on the west side of an elevated ridge, and is capable of being strongly fortified.

Without waiting for the main body to come up, General Tyler immediately pushed forward a reconnoisance to Blackburn's Ford, where, rather unexpectedly, the enemy was discovered to be in large force. A heavy skirmish ensued, with considerable artillery firing; but the confederate position sheltered by dense woods, being considered too strong to be carried without developing a general engagement, the Federal troops were ordered back to Centreville, having experienced a loss of nearly one hundred men. That of the enemy was somewhat less. During the eighteenth and nineteenth, McDowell concentrated his army, with the exception of Runyon's Division, in and around Centreville, with a view of attacking the Rebels along Bull Run, and between this stream and Manassas Junction on Saturday, the twentieth. Here again, the dilatoriness which seemed to be inseparable from the movements of this army, manifested itself. The subsistence which should have been ready on the evening of the eighteenth, did not arrive until twenty-four hours later, so that the forward movement was postponed to Sunday, the twenty-first. The intervening time was occupied in reconnoitering Bull Run above and below Stone Bridge. By the evening of the twentieth McDowell had arranged his plan of battle, which, in general terms, contemplated a flank movement in force against the enemy's left wing, with feints on his right and center. As it was found impracticable to cross the stream at Blackburn's Ford or the Stone Bridge, on account of the steepness of the opposite bank and the obstructions accumulated by the enemy, he decided that the divisions of Hunter and Heintzelman should make the passage at Sudley Spring, two miles above the Stone Bridge, while Tyler demonstrated at the latter place in readiness to cross and support the main attacking column when occasion should offer. The division of General Miles was to be stationed as a reserve at Centreville. The Confederate forces were distributed on the twentieth along the right bank of Bull Run from Union Hill, two miles below Blackburn's Ford, to the Stone Bridge, and on that day comprised probably not far from twenty-five thousand men, under the command of General Beauregard. By the culpable, if not criminal negligence of General Patterson, Johnston's forces had been permitted to slip away from Winchester in the valley, and a considerable portion of them had already arrived with their commander. Although Johnston was the senior of Beauregard, he waived his privilege of assuming the chief direction of the Rebel army, upon seeing the dispositions made by his associate.

Our army being now prepared for an advance, received orders to move at two o'clock in the morning of the twenty-first. But neither officers nor men seemed to comprehend the fact that an encounter with the enemy would terminate their march, and so much time was consumed in getting ready to move and in the march itself, that the head of the column did not reach Sudley Springs until ten o'clock, a distance of eight miles from the starting point, whereas, according to McDowell's calculation, it should have been there three hours sooner. On arriving at Bull Run the men, being over-heated and thirsty, halted to fill their canteens, which was the occasion of more delay; so that when the advance brigade of Hunter's division, led by Colonel Burnside, debouched from the woods near Stone Bridge, it was past twelve o'clock. The tardiness of our troops in executing a flank movement, enabled Beauregard to withdraw his forces from Blackburn's Ford and concentrate them at the Stone Bridge. Beauregard was right in conjecturing that our troops in front of both places were not intending to make a serious attack, and the heavy clouds of dust arising in the direction of Sudley Springs seemed to indicate to him that beyond doubt the main body of our army was moving in that direction. He even projected a flank movement against Centreville, but through the miscarriage of an order failed to execute it.

The arrival of installments of Johnston's troops during the morning, increased Beauregard's force to nearly forty thousand men, now concentrated at Manassas Junction.

The action commenced at eleven o'clock A. M., by an attack of the Confederate batteries, well protected by woods, upon General Burnside's brigade, which for some moments was subjected to a severe fire. Colonel Porter attracted by the cannonading came up to the support of Burnside, with Griffin's battery and a battalion of regulars.

Burnside thus reinforced, pushed back the enemy beyond the Warrenton Turnpike, thereby enabling the brigades of Sherman and Keys of Tyler's division, to cross Bull Run a short distance above the Stone Bridge and take part in the engagement. This division, in accordance with the plan of the battle, had been manœuvering during the morning against the Stone Bridge, and one of its brigades commanded by Colonel Schenck still remained in position on the left bank of the stream. The remaining brigade under Colonel Richardson conducted the feint at Blackburn's Ford.

Colonel Heintzelman who crossed at Sudley Springs in the rear of Hunter, now came up with his division, and uniting it with our main force on the right bank of Bull Run, pressed the Confederates up the slopes of a hill beyond the Warrenton Turnpike where we were met by some well posted batteries which played with effect upon our advancing columns. The struggle for the possession of this hill was one of great determination, and our undisciplined troops, though fighting on unknown ground and against an enemy protected by woods and earthworks, showed decided pluck and considerable steadiness. Colonel Hunter having been severely wounded while leading the flanking column was succeeded by Colonel Heintzelman.

Inch by inch and step by step the Confederates were pushed back, yielding their ground reluctantly and making repeated attempts to disable or capture our artillery under Griffin and Pickett, which had been advanced to within a few hundred yards of their line of battle. Three determined charges were made upon the former, the horses of which had been killed or disabled. Their third assault was repulsed with great spirit, and they were pushed back behind their rifle pits. General Keys had in the mean time made a detour of the hill with his brigade, for the purpose of attacking the enemy on his right flank, and the sappers and miners had been put to work to remove the obstructions in front of the Stone Bridge, so as to allow the remaining brigade of Tyler's division to cross and co-operate with the main force.

Success had attended the Union arms up to three o'clock in the afternoon. The Confederates had been driven nearly a mile and a half from their original position, and their final disappearance gave our troops a few moments of much needed rest; in fact our army was so much exhausted by a twelve hours' march and several hours in line of battle that it was in poor condition to reap the fruits of victory. In his official report General McDowell says: "They had been up since two o'clock in the morning and had made what to those unused to such things, seemed a long march, before coming into action, though the longest distance gone over was not more than nine and a half miles; and though they had three days' provisions served out to them the day before, many no doubt either did not eat them or threw them away on the march or during the battle, and were therefore without food. They had done much severe fighting. Some of the regiments which had been driven from the hill in the first two attempts of the enemy to regain possession of it, had become shaken, were unsteady and had many men out of the ranks." On the other hand the Confederates had marched a comparatively short distance and fought under the advantage of knowing that every succeeding hour would add to their strength and would, as a natural consequence, comparatively weaken their enemy. Every train from the valley brought regiments or brigades from Johnston's command while no re-inforcements had been sent to the unsupported troops of McDowell, nor was it probable that any could be sent. Hence the situation of the Confederates even after they had been compelled to seek shelter in the woods, was really less critical than ours, for their supports were already upon the field. In fact the Rebel line of battle had barely retired from the open field when dense clouds of dust rising from the direction of the railroad, was an evidence of the arrival of fresh troops, and from their position on the hill our soldiers could perceive long and well ordered columns of infantry hastening up in the Confederate rear. It was whispered instantly from rank to rank that General Patterson had come to their assistance; and then the Plains of Manassas were made to ring with the hearty cheers of the Boys in Blue. The surprise and consternation may be imagined when our men heard still louder cheers breaking out along the whole Rebel front followed by a sharp fire from the woods on their right which rapidly extended to their rear. Patterson had neither come to their aid nor moved from his position, and the troops whose appearance had called forth such an outburst of enthusiasm were Johnston's remaining brigade under General Kirby Smith which arrived in season to turn the scale in favor of the Confederates.

The effect of this surprise upon our army was extremely disheartening. The first line recoiled before the fire of the enemy, and confused by vague apprehensions of being surrounded by overwhelming numbers, became panic stricken and fell into disorder. The example was contagious. Regiment after regiment broke and fled in confusion down the hill, the panic momentarily increasing, until the greater part of the but recently victorious army, had become a mass of fugitives rushing pell mell across the Warrenton Turnpike to the fords at which they had crossed in the morning, completely indifferent to the commands of their officers.

As our retreating columns approached Bull Run the miscellaneous crowd of teamsters and civilians on the other side who had not crossed the stream caught the infection and suddenly turned their faces towards Washington, notwithstanding the Confederates were some miles distant and from eight to twelve thousand fresh Union troops who had not as yet been engaged, were in readiness to withstand their attack. But the Rebels, whether too much exhausted, or intimidated by the firmness of our reserves, made no attempt to pursue their advantage, and beyond harrassing our retreat with a few squadrons of cavalry, contented themselves with occupying the field of battle.

Our losses, according to the official report of General McDowell, were four hundred and eighty-six killed, one thousand and twelve wounded, and thirteen hundred and four missing. Considerable artillery was abandoned during the retreat, including the batteries of Griffin and Rickets, which through loss of horses fell into the hands of the enemy at the beginning of the panic. The Confederate loss as reported by General Beauregard was three hundred and seventy-eight killed, fourteen hundred and eighty-nine wounded and thirty-five missing. On the Union side, Colonel Cameron of the Seventy-ninth New York Volunteers was killed, Colonels Hunter and Heintzelman wounded, and Colonels Wilcox and Corcoran were taken prisoners. The Confederate Generals Bee and Bartow were killed and General Kirby Smith wounded.

Thus ended the famous battle of Bull Run, of which more absurd stories have been told than of any engagement of modern times, and the result of which filled the Rebels with an inflated idea of their superiority and contempt for their enemy, for which they were shortly compelled to pay dear. Our army, fighting under many disadvantages and against overpowering numbers, was uniformly successful until their sudden panic; and the vigor with which they pushed the Confederates may be seen in the official reports of the killed and wounded, and in their utter failure to pursue our retreating columns. The chief cause of our defeat may be attributed to the stupidity of General Patterson, who should have engaged Johnston on the Potomac and thereby prevented his forming a junction with Beauregard at Manassas. Had Patterson attacked or followed Johnston the battle might have terminated very differently, and the struggle which was protracted through four bloody years have been closed in a single campaign.

CHAPTER IV.

WILSON'S CREEK.

General Fremont in Command of the Western Department.—Rendezvous at St. Louis.—Lyon in a Critical Situation.—The March at Night.—Out of the Streets of Springfield.—The Midnight Halt.—Camp Fires of the Enemy.—The Rebels at Breakfast.—Sigel adds an Unexpected Dish to their Morning Repast.—Panic and Flight.—Battle and Victory, followed by Confusion.—The Mistaken Troops.—"Our Friends are Firing Upon us."—Sigel's Disaster.—General Lyon at the Front.—They cannot Break His Lines.—Heroism and Bravery Conquer Numbers.—Lyon's Last Charge.—Victory and Death.—The Nation's Beloved Hero.—Rebel Army Routed and in Full Retreat.—Withdrawal to Springfield.

IMMEDIATELY after our repulse at Bull Run, General John Charles Fremont, a brave and accomplished officer who had distinguished himself in early life in an expedition to California, was assignedto the command of the Western Department, comprising Illinois and the states and territories lying between the Mississippi and the Rocky Mountains. General Fremont assumed command on the twenty-sixth of July, 1861, and established his head-quarters at St. Louis, making that point a place of rendezvous for the organization of recruits then arriving as reënforcements to his army. He also located a camp at Jefferson City for the reception and instruction of volunteers, and placed it under the command of General John Pope.

General Fremont put forth every exertion in his power to raise and equip a force for the rescue of the state from the grasp of the Confederates, who from the first, were determined to possess it. Regiments of undisciplined troops soon began to pour in, but there were neither arms nor equipments sufficient for them, and the situation was indeed critical. Cairo and St. Louis were both threatened by the constantly increasing rebel force near Columbus; while in southwestern Missouri the bold and intrepid Lyon, who had pressed on to Springfield, was in a critical position owing to the greatly superior force of McCulloch and Rains, who were advancing to meet him,—his own little army being in the meantime reduced by the expiration of the term of service of the Iowa three months regiments.

Fremont's force at St. Louis, undisciplined and but poorly armed, was hardly sufficient to withstand an attack from such a force as the Rebels could bring against it; and Cairo, a position of considerable importance in a military point of view, was defended by a handful of unorganized troops. If any reënforcements were sent to General Lyon they could not reach him in time to be of service, while their withdrawal would seriously endanger St. Louis and Cairo. He was poorly supplied with cavalry, he was one hundred and fifty miles from any railroad, and had no present hope of reënforcements. Had he attempted to retreat with such an army, it is highly probable that the entire force would have become disorganized and destroyed. Nor could he remain on the defensive at Springfield with an almost certain prospect of capture confronting him. Under this discouraging array of circumstances, General Lyon did not wait to be attacked, but determined to bring on the battle himself. His only hope lay in a bold stroke. He made it at the cost of his life, but his army was saved.

From the village of Springfield, Missouri, two roads lead outward—one to Fayetteville, Arkansas, southwestward, and one to Mt. Vernon, due westward. Both these roads cross Wilson's creek, five miles apart. Calling this five miles of Cross Road the base of a triangle, running along the stream, Springfield would be the apex, and the ten miles of highway leading from that village to the points of intersection with Wilson's Creek, would constitute the two remaining sides of the triangle. Looking towards Springfield on this base line at the creek, General Lyon was on the left, Sigel on the right, and the rebel army between.

It was the night of August ninth. Silently the force under General Lyon marched out of the streets of Springfield, and into the open country to meet the enemy, outnumbering them three to one. At one o'clock on the morning of the tenth they came in sight of the rebel camp fires, and halting cautiously, rested on their arms till day-break. General Lyon hoped by surprising the enemy in front and rear, to put him to rout and gain a victory which would extricate him from the difficulties of his situation. To accomplish this purpose he had divided his command in two columns—his own force taking the Mt. Vernon road to attack the Rebels in front, and the other column under the intrepid Sigel moving down the

Fayetteville road to surprise the enemy in the rear. Sigel had with him six pieces of artillery, two companies of cavalry, and several regiments of infantry. The term of service of the Fifth Missouri volunteers had expired, and Colonel Sigel, by his personal influence had induced them to re-enlist for eight days; but this re-enlistment had also expired on the day before the battle. Many of the officers had gone home, and a considerable portion of Sigel's troops were raw recruits.

At daybreak on the morning of the tenth, Sigel with his command came within a mile of the rebel camp and captured about forty prisoners—Confederates who were going out for provisions and water. Quietly the Union troops marched up the hills bordering Wilson's Creek and beheld below them the rebel encampment. The enemy were breakfasting. A well-directed shot from Sigel's artillery, sent directly into the encampment, was the first intimation they received of his presence. Surprised into utter disorder, they retreated panic-stricken down the valley. Our infantry pursued, forming in the camp so recently occupied by the enemy. But, recovering from the first panic the enemy formed in line of battle, opposing Colonel Sigel's little band with a force three thousand strong. Our artillery and infantry moved into the valley, and after a short engagement the enemy was driven from the field. During this time the sound of battle from the other end of the valley road, told Sigel that Lyon was there, and in order to aid him Sigel urged his troops up the valley, obtaining a position where any attempted retreat of the enemy might be cut off. He had taken one hundred prisoners, and everything looked promising, when by one of those accidents which no one can foresee, his temporary success was turned into disaster. The firing at the other end of the Cross Road had ceased, which led Sigel to the impression that Lyon was victorious and his troops in probable pursuit of the enemy. Large bodies of Confederates appearing to the eastward, and apparently retreating south, confirmed this idea, but owing to the gloom of the morning and the absence of all uniform it was impossible to distinguish Unionists from Confederates. At this juncture of affairs, Sigel received word that Lyon was advancing victoriously up the road, and the command not to fire upon the advancing troops, was given. Just as the soldiers of Sigel's command waved their flags in welcome to their supposed comrades in arms, a destructive fire burst upon them which covered the ground with the dead and the dying, and at the same moment a Rebel battery from the hill sent its scathing shot and shell down upon the bewildered Union ranks. Utter confusion resulted. The cry ran from mouth to mouth, "Our friends are firing upon us,"—nor could they be persuaded otherwise until the dead fell around them like leaves in autumn time. The horses were shot down at their guns, and death was reaping a terrible harvest. It would not have been strange if a panic had ensued under these circumstances among the best drilled troops, but most of these men were just from peaceful homes and had never before been under fire.

The disorderly retreat which now commenced cannot, therefore, be wondered at.

WILSON'S CREEK.

Five cannon were abandoned in the confusion, and the foe, with wild yells, came rushing on.

Colonel Sigel himself narrowly escaped capture in his efforts to arrest the rout. After this disaster it was impossible for Sigel to join Lyon with the remnant of his command, the enemy occupying the only road by which he could do so in time to make the movement of use. There was no alternative for Sigel but to withdraw his shattered ranks from the field as safely as possible.

Meantime General Lyon on the other road had encountered the enemy's pickets at day-break, which prevented the surprise from being as great as was that of Sigel. When Lyon reached the north end of the camp he found the enemy prepared to receive him, but he succeeded in gaining a commanding position at the north of the valley in which the camp was situated. Abbott describes this part of the engagement as follows: "Captain Plummer with four companies of infantry protected his left flank. The battle was now commenced by a fire of shot and shell from Captain Totten's battery and soon became general. In vain did the Rebel host endeavor to drive Lyon from his well chosen position. On the right, on the left, and in front they assailed him in charge succeeding charge, but in vain. His quick eye detected every movement and successfully met and defeated it. The overwhelming numbers of the Rebels enabled them to replace, after each repulse, their defeated forces with fresh regiments, while Lyon's little band found no time for rest, no respite from the battle. The Rebel host surged wave after wave upon his heroic lines, as billows of the sea dash upon the coast. And as the rocks upon that coast beat back the flood, so did these heroic soldiers of freedom with courage which would have ennobled veterans, and with patriotism which has won a nation's homage and love, hurl back the tireless surges of rebellion, which threatened to engulf them. It will be enough for any of these patriots to say, 'I was at the battle of Wilson's Creek,' to secure the warmest grasp of every patriot's hand.

"Wherever the missiles of death flew thickest, and the peril of battle was most imminent, there was General Lyon surely to be found.

"His young troops needed this encouragement on the part of their adored leader and it inspired them with bravery which nothing else could have conferred. His horse had been shot under him; three times he had been wounded, and though faint from the loss of blood, he refused to retire even to have his wounds dressed; in vain did his officers beseech him to avoid so much exposure. It was one of those eventful hours, which General Lyon fully comprehended, in which there was no hope but in despair.

"Again and again had the enemy been repulsed, only to return again and again, with fresh troops to the charge. Colonels Mitchell, Deitzler, and Andrews were all severely wounded. All the men were exhausted with the long unintermitted battle, and it seemed as though one puff of war's fierce tempest would now sweep away the thin and tremulous line. Just then the Rebels again formed in a fresh and solid column for the charge. With firm and rapid tread and raising unearthly yells they swept up the slope.

General Lyon called for the troops standing nearest him to form for an opposing charge. Undaunted, and ready for the battle they inquired 'Who will be our leader?' 'Come on, brave men,' shouted General Lyon, 'I will lead you.' In a moment he was at their head. At the next moment they were on the full run: at the next, a deadly storm of bullets swept their ranks, staggering but not checking them in their impetuous advance,—on—on they rushed, for God and Liberty; and in another moment the foe were dispersed like dust by the gale. The victory was entire; this division of the Rebels could rally no more; the army was saved; *but Lyon was dead!* Two bullets had pierced his bosom. As he fell one of his officers sprang to his side and inquired anxiously, 'Are you hurt?' 'Not much,' was his faint reply. They were his last words. He fell asleep to wake no more."

After Lyon's death Major Sturgis assumed command. His forces were exhausted with the long battle; they had had no water since the evening before, and could get none nearer than Springfield. A foe confronted them twenty thousand strong, and though one victory had been gained, another battle impended. Sigel's disaster was unknown to them, and when a heavy column approached from the direction in which Sigel's guns had been heard, bearing the American flag and wearing uniforms not unlike their own, they naturally supposed the force to be Sigel's. The advancing troops were allowed to approach unmolested.

Suddenly the Union banner was hauled down, the Rebel colors went up and at the same time a discharge of artillery from a hill near by, swept our ranks.

The fiercest battle of the day now commenced. But Major Sturgis and his command sustained the unexpected attack with unwavering firmness. The line remained compact, without a break, and though at times it seemed as though the brave little band would be utterly swept away, yet with muzzle to muzzle and almost hand to hand the unequal contest was waged. Suddenly, by an ingenious manœuvre, the reserve was brought upon the enemy's flank and in a short time the whole Rebel army was routed and in full retreat.

Not having sufficient force to follow up the victory Major Sturgis withdrew to Springfield, reaching that place at about five o'clock in the evening. The discomfited foé attempted no molestation. Their plans had been thwarted and their baggage train fired and destroyed.

Therefore in its *results*, the battle of Wilson's Creek may be counted a victory. It is probable that but for the natural mistake into which Sigel's forces were led, the complete rout of the entire rebel army under Price would have been effected.

Nor is it probable that an attack conducted in any other way by so small a force upon one so much larger would have been equally successful.

The results desired were obtained, but at what fearful cost! A nation mourned when Lyon fell. Said the New York *Tribune*, in an issue of that time. "Such honors were never before, perhaps, paid to so young a general.

"Funeral obsequies attended him from the battlefield where he fell, across one half a continent, taken up from state to state, from city to city, from village to village and carried forward for near two thousand miles, amid the tearful eyes, the bowed heads and the deepest expressions of personal sorrow of hundreds of thousands of grateful people."

Thus was the soil of Missouri again bedewed with patriot gore, and when the young of future generations shall search history for examples of sublime heroism, among those who died for the cause of Union and Liberty, surely no nobler instance can be found than that of Lyon at Wilson's Creek.

CHAPTER V.

BALL'S BLUFF.

Situation of Ball's Bluff.—The Hostile Armies on Opposite Banks of the River.—Reconnoitre at Drainesville.—Feint of Gorman's Brigade at Edward's Ferry.—Attack of the Enemy from the Woods.—Union Troops Exposed to a Murderous Fire.—Death of Baker.—Ineffectual Means of Transportation.—Attempts to Regain the Maryland Shore.—Troops Shot or Drowned in Crossing.—Defeat of the Union Arms.—Causes of the Disaster.

THE months of August and September, 1861, passed away without action on the part of General McClellan, who had been elevated to the command of the Army of the Potomac.

The battle of Ball's Bluff, which was fought on the twenty-first of October, just three months after the engagement at Bull Run, was an event that cast a profound gloom over the country, not only because of the defeat of the Union arms and the death of a noble and brave officer, but because of the disappointment which it caused to the hopes that had been excited through the growth and development of the army. Ball's Bluff is the name applied to a part of the bank of the Potomac east of the village of Leesburg. Opposite the Bluff and about one hundred yards away is Harrison's Island, a long narrow tract, containing about four hundred acres. Between this island and the Virginia shore the river is about two hundred yards broad, with an exceedingly rapid current. Between the island and the Maryland shore, the stream is nearly three hundred yards wide, but not quite so rapid. A few rods above the upper end of the island is a ferry across the Potomac known as Conrad's Ferry, and about an equal distance below the island is Edward's Ferry. The two hostile armies had for many months held the opposite banks of the river at this point. It was here that the Confederates had contemplated an irruption into Maryland to attack Washington. General Banks held the Maryland side of the river from Great Falls to Edward's Ferry; from that point to Conrad's Ferry was stationed the division of General Stone, with headquarters at Poolesville. Next in order came the force of Colonel Geary and then that of Colonel Lander. On the Virginia side the principal Confederate posts were at Leesburg and Drainesville. As it was important to ascertain the strength of the enemy at the latter place, General McClellan on the nineteenth of October, directed General McCall to make a reconnoisance in that quarter. McCall executed this order the same day and returned to his camp at Poolesville on the twentieth, reporting no enemy in Drainesville nor within four miles of Leesburg. In consequence of this report the following dispatch was sent to General Stone:—

"To Brigadier-General Stone,
Poolesville, Md.:

General McClellan desires me to inform you that General McCall occupied Drainesville yesterday, and is still there. Will send out reconnoisances to-day in all directions from that point. The General desires you to keep a good lookout from

Leesburg, to see if the movement has the effect to drive them away. Perhaps a slight demonstration on your part would have the effect to move them.

A. V. COLBURN,
Assistant Adjutant-General."

As soon as these instructions reached General Stone, he ordered the brigade of General Gorman to Edward's Ferry; detachments of the Fifteenth and Twentieth Massachusetts to Harrison's Island; and a section of a battery and the California and Tammany Regiments under Colonel Edward D. Baker to Conrad's Ferry. A feint to cross the river was then made by the force of General Gorman, in full view of the enemy.

At twenty minutes after one o'clock, on the morning of the twenty-first, Colonel Devens with five companies of the Fifteenth Massachusetts, accompanied by Colonel Lee with a portion of the Twentieth Massachusetts, crossed from Harrison's Island to the Virginia side and took position on the top of Ball's Bluff, which at this point rises abruptly some one hundred and fifty feet from the river. In order to draw attention from the movement of Devens, General Stone instructed Colonel Gorman to hurry two companies of the First Minnesota Infantry across the river and to send out a squadron of Cavalry on the Leesburg road. In the meantime General Stone, having received a message from Colonel Devens stating that he had found no enemy, ordered a battalion of the Fifteenth Massachusetts to cross and protect the flank of Devens, and Colonel Baker to be in readiness with his brigade to act as a support if necessary. Colonel Devans continuing to push forward, encountered a large body of

Confederate troops near Leesburg a few minutes after sunrise, and immediately fell back in good order to the Bluff. While waiting reinforcements and further orders he was attacked about noon by the enemy who opened fire from a concealed position in the woods.

The small Union force suffered greatly from this attack, being drawn up in an open field of about six acres and exposed on all sides to the fire of the Confederate sharpshooters. Detachments of the First California, Twentieth Massachusetts, Tammany Regiment, and four pieces of artillery had now crossed the river, and at twenty minutes after two o'clock in the afternoon, the skirmishing in front became very brisk.

Colonel Baker, having assumed command of the entire force, formed his line for action at four o'clock —the Fifteenth and Twentieth Massachusetts on the right, the Californians on the left and the Tammany Regiment and the artillery in the centre. Indications of a large Confederate force now became apparent although none were visible. These troops numbering not far from four thousand men pressing upon the little band of Colonel Baker with increasing vigor and more effective fire, induced a consultation among the Union officers which resulted in a determination to stand. A retreat was sure to result in disaster, as such a movement would bring them to the steep brink of the river, where the rapid descent only led to a small boat and a scow as a means of transport over a swift channel. To hold their ground until reinforcements could cross at Edward's Ferry and come to their aid, was now their only hope. Two companies being pushed forward, to feel the Confederates in the woods on the left, were met by a murderous fire which seemed to be the signal for an attack along the whole line of the enemy, who, readily discovering their superiority in numbers, closed in on both sides of the field with overwhelming force.

The gallant Colonel Baker fell dead while in the act of leading his men in a charge. Colonel Cogswell of the Tammany Regiment now assumed command, and as he found it impossible to hold his position attempted to regain the Maryland shore. Our troops retired in good order closely pursued by the Confederates. On reaching the river but one boat was at hand and that was swamped at the second crossing. After the boat went down no alternative was left but to swim or surrender. The majority chose the former course and throwing their arms into the river, dispersed, some up and some down the bank, and others on logs endeavored to reach Harrison's Island by swimming. In this attempt many were shot and more were drowned. The artillery was tumbled down the bank but was subsequently taken up by the enemy, together with some cases of shot.

Not more than nine hundred of our men returned to their camps, about half of the missing having been taken prisoners on the river shore. The Confederates, who were commanded by General Evans, admitted a loss of one hundred and fifty-five.

During the progress of the battle, General Stone was preparing to cross the river at Edward's Ferry, but desisted on the receipt of news announcing the death of Colonel Baker and the defeat of his command. Orders were then received from McClellan to hold the

Island and Virginia shore at Edward's Ferry, at all hazards. General Gorman at once proceeded to strengthen his position, and reinforcements came forward until there were nearly four thousand Infantry, with Ricketts' Battery, and a detachment of cavalry, on the Virginia shore, behind five hundred feet of intrenchments. Further intelligence caused a change of plan and the whole force returned to the Maryland side of the Potomac.

The principal causes of our repulse at Ball's Bluff were the selection of a miserable point for crossing the Potomac, insufficient means of transportation and lack of a definite object in venturing into a position where retreat was utterly impossible in the face of greatly superior numbers.

CHAPTER VI.

MILL SPRING.

Geographical Location of Mill Spring.—Encampment of Zollicoffer.—Occupancy of Logan's Cross Roads by Union Troops.—The Enemy Hedged in.—Starvation or Battle.—Zollicoffer Leads the Rebel Advance.—Colonel Fry Discovers a General's Uniform under a Rubber Overcoat.—The Fatal Shot.—Zollicoffer Falls.—Consternation and Rout of the Enemy.—A Deserted Camp.—Victory for the "Boys in Blue."

On the blue waters of the Cumberland, about twenty-five miles southeast of Columbia, and fifteen miles west of Somerset, is situated Mill Spring, Kentucky, made famous as one of the battle grounds of the war, and as the spot where fell the popular Confederate General Zollicoffer, shot dead by the pistol of Colonel Fry of the Fourth Kentucky Volunteers.

During the late autumn of 1861, and early winter of 1862, General Zollicoffer was encamped at Mill Spring, on the southern bank of the Cumberland. Resolving also to occupy the opposite or northern bank at Camp Beach Grove, he fortified the latter place with earthworks, and placed there five regiments of infantry, twelve guns, and several hundred cavalry, keeping at Mill Spring two regiments of infantry and a few hundred horse. About the first of January, 1862, the force was augmented by the brigade of General Carroll, from Knoxville,—General George B.

Crittenden having arrived and taken command a short time previous.

On the seventeenth of January, pursuant to orders from General Buell, General Thomas advanced and occupied Logan's Cross Roads, ten miles north of the Beech Grove Camp. The enemy was in a critical situation. Already on short allowance, their supplies of food promised to be cut off entirely. The surrounding country had been exhausted, and the supplies which might have come down the Cumberland from Nashville, were prevented by the Union forces stationed at Columbia. In every direction the roads leading outward into the more remote country were impassible. Added to this, General Schoepf held the key to the position fifteen miles to the eastward, at Somerset. Therefore, the only way out of this environment of difficulties which surrounded them, was to make an attack upon the Union forces at Logan's Cross Roads. The design was to attack our troops before the force at Somerset would be able to join them, and also before the reserve at Columbia could be brought up. In pursuance of this plan, on the nineteenth of January, the brigade of Zollicoffer moved in advance, followed by that of Carroll and the reserve, constituting a force of about four thousand infantry. Zollicoffer's command consisted of four regiments of infantry and four guns. Two Mississippi companies were deployed as skirmishers, marching one on each side of the road. About two miles from camp the Federal cavalry was encountered and driven in, and Zollicoffer rode confidently on, as he believed, to victory. A rubber overcoat disguised his uniform, but his features were too well known to prevent him from being a mark for the muskets of the "boys in blue." The fatal hour for him crept on apace, and as the Confederate General, surrounded by his staff, ascended a hill, he encountered the main body of the Federal troops. It was at this point that Colonel Fry of the Fourth Kentucky infantry, recognizing the Rebel leader, took swift aim with his revolver, and the fall of Zollicoffer attested the sure work of the pistol ball.

Constèrnation and disorder among the Confederate troops followed, and in the resulting confusion the Ninth Ohio charged with the bayonet, turning the enemy's flank and driving him from the field. Thus the Confederate forces fell ingloriously back to their intrenchments on the Cumberland.

The cannonade was continued until dark. In the evening the forces under General Schoepf at Somerset, came up, and on the following morning the cannonading was resumed with Parrott guns, the fire being directed in part against the ferry across Fishing Creek—a swollen torrent between Columbia and Somerset—to keep the enemy from crossing. Upon approaching the intrenchments it was discovered that the enemy had decamped during the night, abandoning everything,—twelve guns, with caissons filled, one hundred and fifty wagons, one thousand horses, and many stores. After crossing they had burned the ferry boats, so that pursuit was impossible. As they could not hold the camp they were obliged to abandon everything and retire to the most accessible point of supply.

The Union loss was thirty-nine killed, and two hundred and seven wounded. The Confederates lost one hundred and ninety killed, sixty-two wounded, and eighty-nine prisoners, besides the loss of General Zollicoffer and Baillie Peyton, and also a large number that were drowned while crossing the Cumberland.

The battle of Mill Spring was one of a series of engagements which resulted so successfully, that by March 1st, 1862, every Confederate soldier had left the State.

CHAPTER VII.

PEA RIDGE.

The Boston Mountains Camp.—Red Skin Re-enforcements.—Sigel's Ten-mile Fight.—The Long Battle-Line.—" War's Thunders and Flowers of Red Shot."—Sigel Frustrates McCulloch.—Struggle Between Osterhaus and McCulloch.—Bold Charge of Indiana Troops.—Re-enforcements.—Night brings a Suspension of Hostilities.—Battle at Sunrise.—Terrible Array of Union Batteries.—Two Hours of Iron Hail.—The Enemy Completely Routed.—Precipitous Retreat to the Boston Mountains.—Death of McCulloch.—Fearful Barbarities.—Burial of the Dead.—Elk Horn.

THE opening scenes in the drama of this battle slowly merged into view during the first days of March, 1862. The wild scenery of Northwestern Arkansas, where the rugged outlines of the Boston Mountains throw their shadows in the sun, constituted its shadowy back-ground.

Sterling Price and Ben McCulloch were there, having been driven from Sugar Creek, fifty miles away, by our forces. There, too, Earl Van Dorn's troops reënforced them, not only with the flower of the Southern chivalry but also with the dusky ranks of the Lo family—a body of Choctaw, Cherokee, and Chickasaw Indians under the leadership of Confederate Pike. Added to this, came also the division of McIntosh, making the powerful array of nine thousand Missouri State troops under Price, six Arkansas regiments under McCulloch, five Texan regiments under Van Dorn, and some three thousand Indians under Pike and McIntosh, aggregating between twenty and twenty-five thousand men. This force carried seventy guns, and Van Dorn was their chief. The Union General Curtis waited expectantly at Sugar Creek, a short distance south of Pea Ridge, preparing himself for the storm of battle about to break above his head.

Meantime, on March fifth, Sigel, then at Bentonville, ten miles away, received orders to join Curtis at Pea Ridge, and on the next day the command was promptly executed. But it was a hazardous and difficult achievement. Four Confederate regiments attacked his rear-guard, which consisted of the Thirty-Sixth Illinois, and Second Missouri. But the attack was useless, for these brave men cut their way through the solid living wall of Rebel soldiery and rejoined their comrades, though with a loss of twenty-eight killed and wounded and a number of prisoners. For the entire distance of ten miles Sigel contested every step of his advance. Supported by the infantry, his guns were halted, and the advancing Rebel ranks, unable to stand before the discharges of grape and shell from the effective aim of our artillerymen, broke and fled in confusion. Before the scattered ranks of the enemy could re-form, the guns of Sigel were limbered and the troops fell back into position behind another battery planted at the next turn in the road. This programme was continuously enacted for the entire distance of ten miles between Bentonville and Pea Ridge. At last Sigel arrived at the west end of Pea Ridge, where he formed a junction with the divisions of Generals Carr and Davis.

On the morning of the fifth of March, General Van Dorn moved forward with his command, taking with him four days cooked rations. He had decided to attack our rear and endeavor thus to cut off our base of supplies and reënforcements.

The Union position was on the main road leading from Springfield to Fayetteville, and General Van Dorn, leaving that road near the latter place and passing through Bentonville, entered the main road again near the state boundary eight miles north of Sugar Creek. A considerable body of Indians took position about two miles away on our right, to divert attention from the main attack in the rear, while a small force was left to make a feint upon our front. The first two divisions of the Union troops were commanded by Sigel, and the entire force was in four divisions under Colonel Osterhaus, General Asboth, Colonel Jefferson C. Davis, and Colonel Carr, respectively. When the intention of the enemy to attack our right and rear became apparent to General Curtis, he changed front so that his right wing which was at Sugar Hollow Creek, became his left wing under Sigel, while Carr at the head of Big Sugar Creek held the new right. The line stretched across Pea Ridge. It was early on the morning of the seventh, and Carr's division advanced to a point up the road within four miles of the Arkansas and Missouri State line, while the brigade of Colonel Dodge filed off from the main road east of the Elk Horn hotel, and Vandeveer's brigade passed a half mile beyond the hotel, taking position on the left of the road.

The enemy, sheltered by some woods, were posted

on a declivity in front of the Elk Horn house. Colonel Dodge now inaugurated the battle by opening fire on the enemy at that point, but he met with a prompt response. At the same time also, a battery from our lines sent its well-directed fire into the ranks of the enemy with great effect, but was sharply replied to, exploding two of the Union caissons. Nine o'clock had arrived and the whole line was engaged in the fury of battle. In a short time after this the enemy captured one of our guns, but the Ninth Iowa infantry supports coming up at this time discharged their fire with such vigor into the Rebel ranks that they were driven to the shelter of the woods. Repeated charges were made by the enemy, and another gun and caisson were captured, but the steady fire of our troops strewed the ground with their dead. Carr, holding an untenable position and overpowered by superior numbers, was compelled to retire until about four in the afternoon, when Colonel Asboth supporting him with two regiments and a battery, he was enabled to hold his ground for the night. The enemy were armed with double-barreled shot guns, loaded with ball and buck shot—an effective weapon at short range.

On the left wing McCulloch endeavored to form a junction with the troops of Van Dorn and Price, thus surrounding our army on three sides and cutting off our retreat. But the quick eyes of Sigel, detecting the movement, he ordered forward three pieces of flying artillery and a force of cavalry to take a commanding position and delay the movements of the enemy until our infantry could be brought up in position for an attack. But these pieces had hardly obtained their position when an overwhelming force of the enemy's cavalry swept down upon them, capturing our artillery and driving our horsemen. This movement enabled their infantry to reach in safety the cover of a dense wood where McCulloch encountered Osterhaus and a severe struggle ensued. Davis was now ordered to the support of the Union line, and the Third Iowa was sent forward to clear the timber; but the enemy were in great numbers, the ranks of our cavalry were broken, in disorder, and pursued, and we suffered the capture of three guns. But at this critical juncture Osterhaus and his Indiana regiments came up on the double-quick and sending a murderous fire into the enemy's ranks, charged immediately after with the bayonet. This bold charge put to rout the Indians and Texans, and the three captured field pieces were recovered. The command was then reënforced by General Sigel, and the action re-commenced with greater fury than before.

The heavy guns of the enemy were brought into position and an artillery battle took place which resulted in the retirement of the enemy in confusion, leaving the Union troops masters of this part of the bloody field. Night let fall her intervening curtain of darkness between the contending armies, with Union success on the left, defeat on the right, and the battle yet unfinished. At dark the firing ceased from all quarters and the exhausted soldiers slept upon their arms. Carr's division now occupied the center with Davis on the right, and Sigel still holding the left. Near the position occupied by our forces a hill rose abruptly to the height of two hundred feet, very precipitous in our front, but sloping gradually to the northward. On this eminence the enemy during the night had planted batteries which commanded our forces, and also at the right base of this hill, batteries and large bodies of infantry were posted. At the edge of some timber to the left, supports of infantry were disposed, while beyond the road, to the extreme left, were posted their cavalry and infantry.

At sunrise our right and center with their batteries, opened fire upon the enemy, while Sigel, having learned the exact position of the enemy's batteries, advanced with the left wing to take the hill, forming his line of battle by changing front so as to face the right flank of the enemy.

Sigel then ordered the Twenty-Fifth Illinois into position along a fence in open view of the Confederate batteries, which immediately opened fire upon them. One of our batteries, consisting of six or seven guns, several of which were rifled twelve-pounders was at once thrown into line one hundred paces to the rear of our advanced infantry, on a rise of ground.

The Twelfth Missouri then wheeled into line with the Twenty-Fifth Illinois on their left, and another battery of guns similarly arranged a short distance behind them. But the crushing array was not yet complete, for still another regiment and another battery wheeled into position, until thirty pieces of artillery, fifteen or twenty paces distant from each other, formed one unbroken line, with the infantry lying down in front. As each piece circled into position, its fire was discharged at the enemy, and the fire of the entire line was so effective as to silence every

Confederate battery, one by one. "Such a terrible fire no human courage could stand. The crowded ranks of the enemy were decimated, their horses shot at their guns, and large trees literally demolished; but the Rebels stood bravely to their posts. For over two hours did the iron hail fall, until one by one the Rebel pieces ceased to play. Onward crept our infantry; onward came Sigel and his terrible guns. Shorter and shorter became the range. No charge of theirs could face that iron hail or dare to venture on that compact line of bayonets. They turned and fled. The center and right were ordered forward, the right turning the left of the enemy and cross-firing on his center. This final position of the enemy was in the arc of a circle. A charge of infantry by the whole line completely routed them, and they retreated through the deep, impassable defiles of Cross Timber, towards the Boston Mountains, closely pursued by the cavalry."

The Union loss at this battle was two hundred and twelve killed, nine hundred and seventy-two wounded, one hundred and seventy-six missing. The enemy's loss was reported at two thousand. General Herbert, Colonel Stone, Adjutant General, and Colonel Price were taken prisoners. Ben. McCulloch, General McIntosh, and General Stark were among the killed. General Price was wounded.

On the ninth of March, General Van Dorn asked permission to bury the dead of the seventh and eighth. General Curtis granted permission, but in the letter accompanying it complained that in some cases the Union dead had been scalped and mangled. General

Van Dorn replied, expressing a desire to repress the savage horrors of war, and stated that numbers of Confederate prisoners who had surrendered, were reported to have been murdered in cold blood by the Germans. General Curtis replied that he had no knowledge of any such atrocities committed by German soldiers under his command.

A strange feature of this contest was the employment of the wild hordes of Indian tribes under the leadership of McCulloch and McIntosh. They rushed to the fray with savage war-whoops and hideous yells, and the cleft skulls lying in pools of blood after the battle, showed that their barbarian mode of warfare had not been forgotten. McCulloch met his fate on the first day of the battle, leading the advance on the left. A minie ball penetrated his left lung, and he died of the wound at about eleven o'clock that night. His career as a soldier was a checkered one. His military glory beginning among the assembled ranks of Texan Rangers on the banks of the Guadaloupe, twenty-six years before, now went down in blood. San Jacinto and Buena Vista had witnessed his bravery, but the field of Pea Ridge witnessed his fall, fighting against country—against liberty. It was a bloody engagement, lasting fifteen hours,—the greater part of two consecutive days being spent in battle. But northern Arkansas was cleared of Confederate troops, and the forces of Van Dorn and Price were sent to the support of Beauregard at Memphis.

CHAPTER VIII.

MERRIMAC AND MONITOR.

The Projection of the Monitor.—Ericsson's Visit to Washington.—The Merrimac Launched.—Arrival off Newport News.—Attack on the Cumberland.—Heroism of the Crew.—No Surrender.—Sublime Bravery.—Sinking of the ill-fated Frigate.—The Burning of the Congress.—Despair of the Fleet.—The Speck of Light on the Waves.—Arrival of the Monitor.—The Merrimac Again Appears.—The Strange Looking Antagonist.—The Fight Opens.—Fierce Conflict.—The Baptism of Fire.—Four Hours of Battle.—The Merrimac Signals for Help.—The Monitor Victorious.—Our Fleet Saved.—Cheers of the Multitude.

PERHAPS no single event of our last war decided issues of greater moment to the nation than the naval engagement between the Merrimac and Monitor.

Had the Merrimac been successful, every other craft on the high seas, at home or abroad, would have been at her mercy. Going about like some wild monster of the deep, with her iron tusk and her coat of mail, impervious to shot or shell, she could have destroyed whole fleets and sent them whirling to the bottom. New York city would have been unsafe,—every city on the coast would have been unsafe, and the probable ravages of this iron Leviathan can hardly be properly estimated. What *might* have happened but for the Monitor, who can tell? But the Monitor, Providentially—can we believe otherwise?—proved to be our David of the seas who slew the iron-clad Goliah and saved to us our navy.

Instigated and pushed forward by private enterprise, she was successfully launched in the face of all adverse prediction, and arrived off Newport News barely in time to arrest the Merrimac on her errand of wholesale destruction.

C. S. Bushnell, Esq., a capitalist of New Haven, Connecticut, learning of Captain Ericsson's plan for an invulnerable sea battery, was the prime mover in the building of the Monitor. That gentleman insisted on taking the model to Washington, in company with Ericsson, and submitting the new and strange diagrams to the Government Naval Board. After persistent efforts he was successful in obtaining a guarantee of payment when the Monitor should demonstrate her ability to do all that was promised concerning her.

The steam frigate Merrimac, scuttled and sunk at the burning of the Norfolk navy yard, was considered one of the finest ships in the American navy. She mounted forty guns and was estimated at four thousand tons burden.

"This magnificent structure was raised by the Rebels and cut down, leaving only the hull, which was exceedingly massive and solid. Over this they constructed a sloping shield of railroad iron, firmly plated together, and extending two feet under the water. Its appearance was much like the slanting roof of a house, set upon a ship's hull like an extinguisher,—the ends of the vessel fore and aft, projecting a few feet beyond this roof. The gun-deck was completely inclosed by this shield, and nothing appeared above it but a short smoke-stack and two flag-staffs. The weight of iron was so immense that the ship nearly broke her back in launching; but the fracture was repaired. The fact that such a formidable mailed battery was in preparation, was well known at the North, and her speedy appearance was daily predicted by the press."

On Saturday the eighth of March, 1862—the same day that Fremont fought the battle of Pea Ridge—the Merrimac steamed into the mouth of the James River from Norfolk, headed towards our blockading fleet off Newport News. The old passenger steamers, the Jamestown and Yorktown, plying formerly between New York and Richmond, and now refitted into Confederate war vessels, accompanied the Merrimac, and in her train came a retinue of armed tugs and other war craft. The frigates Cumberland and Congress, doing guard duty off Newport News, were anchored half a mile from shore as the Merrimac came in sight. Unmindful of the broadsides which the two frigates hurled against her iron sides, she steered straight for the Cumberland, and rushing upon her, struck her amidships, inflicting a death blow. Then, reversing her engine, she went back and making a second plunge, again struck the Cumberland in the same place, crushing through the whole side of the ship.

At the same time the guns of the iron-clad demon thundered destruction through the decks of the ill-fated Cumberland, strewing her floors with the dead, wounded, and dying. But her brave crew under command of Lieutenant George M. Morris, with a heroism which rose to the pitch of sublimity, still fought on, as long as a gun of the sinking ship remained unsubmerged. "One sailor with both his legs shot off, hobbled up to his gun on the bleeding stumps and pulling the lanyard, fired it, then fell back dead."

The heroic commander and the no less heroic crew proudly refused to lower the beloved stars and stripes to the flag of Rebellion, preferring to sink with the ship rather than surrender. Rapidly the noble Cumberland went down, her guns thundering as she sank, the last shot being fired from her deck while the gunner who pulled the trigger stood knee-deep in water. After the frigate was engulfed, "a few feet of her topmasts rose above the wave, and there the stars and stripes still floated, victorious in death." "The surface of the water was now covered with fragments of the wreck, and with hundreds of men swimming towards the shore, while from all directions, boats were pushing out for their rescue. About one hundred of the dead and wounded went down with the ship. While this multitude of men were struggling in the water, the steam propeller "Whillden," then lying under the guns of Newport News, not half a mile off, Captain William Riggins commanding, instantly put off in the face of the resistless enemy and rescued a large number who would otherwise have been drowned. Probably her humane errand saved her from the destruction to which she was exposed, since the moment after she had picked up the last man, a shot from the Merrimac passed through her boiler, thus emphatically ordering her away."

It had taken only three-quarters of an hour to dispatch the Cumberland, and the destroying demon in mailed armor, made the Congress her next object of attention.

That vessel being only partly manned was grounded while endeavoring to escape from the fatal clutches of the Merrimac, who came on, resistless as doom.

At a distance of about one hundred yards from the helpless Congress, the Merrimac discharged her terrible broadsides into the disabled ship, while the two Confederate gun-boats, the Jamestown and Yorktown rushed up on either side and added their rain of red-hot shot to that of the Merrimac. The dead and dying on the decks of the Congress were mingled in sickening confusion with dismantled guns and torn rigging. Her dry timbers took fire in three places, and, fanned by the fresh breeze, soon the billows of flame rolled above the billows of water. With her commanding officer killed and her wounded facing the prospect of death by the slow torture of burning, the Congress, at last, surrendered. But with horrible inhumanity, the Merrimac fired another broadside into her while the white flag was flying at her masthead.

The Congress burned until midnight when, the fire reaching her magazine, she exploded with a noise which shook the bay and sent the fiery fragments, like a thousand rockets, into the air.

The two remaining frigates of the fleet, the St. Lawrence and the Minnesota, were next in order of attack, and, strangely enough, they were both aground. But the Minnesota sent a broadside from her heavy guns into the Merrimac, at short range, and it was thought that some of the shot, entering her port-holes,

MERRIMAC AND MONITOR.

damaged her machinery, as she did not proceed with the attack.

Night was coming on and after some hesitation, the Merrimac steamed to her anchorage behind Craney Island.

The darkness that settled over Hampton Roads that night was nothing to the darkness of despair which wrapped the hearts of the fleet in its pall of gloom. The garrison at Newport News and Fortress Monroe could be dispatched as easily as the Cumberland had been, and even Washington might not be safe from the devastation which the Merrimac threatened. For no one knew whether she might not be able to ascend the Potomac. In an hour the strength of our navy and coast fortresses had crumbled before this single iron-clad—mistress of the high seas.

As the disastrous news was flashed over the wires through the North, consternation filled all hearts. No one knew where the ravages thus begun would end. It did not seem improbable that this single vessel might solve the problem of the war in favor of slavery and the South as against Union and liberty.

At about ten o'clock on that eventful Saturday night the anxious garrison at Fortress Monroe descried a singular looking craft approaching from the sea, towed by two small steamers. It resembled "nothing in the heavens above or the earth beneath or in the waters under the earth."

The raft proved to be the new Ericsson battery, the Monitor, in tow of the gunboats Sachem and Currituck. Only twenty-four inches of hull were visible above the water, and the small, round, revolving turret nine feet high, in the center of the battery, mounted only two guns. Beside her big adversary, the little Monitor appeared very insignificant, both in size and armament—her two guns being pitted against the ten carried by the Merrimac.

An eye witness gives the following vivid description of the scenes and emotions of that long-to-be-remembered Saturday night:—

"That morrow! How anxiously we waited for it! how much we feared its results! How anxious our Saturday eve of preparation! At sundown there was nothing to dispute the empire of the seas with the Merrimac, and had a land attack been made by Magruder then, God only knows what our fate would have been. The St. Lawrence and the Minnesota aground and helpless, the Roanoke with a broken shaft—these were our defenses by sea; while on land we were doing all possible to resist a night invasion; but who could hope that would have much efficiency? Oh! what a night that was; that night I never can forget. There was no fear during its long hours—danger, I find, does not bring that—but there was a longing for some interposition of God and waiting upon Him from whom we felt our help must come, in earnest, fervent prayer, while not neglecting all the means of martial defence He had placed in our hands. Fugitives from Newport News kept arriving; ladies and children had walked the long ten miles from Newport News, feeling that their presence only embarrassed their brave husbands. Sailors from the Congress and Cumberland came, one of them with his ship's flag bound about his waist, as he had swum with it ashore, determined the enemy should never trail it in dishonor as a trophy. Dusky fugitives, the contrabands came, mournfully fleeing from a fate worse than death—slavery. These entered my cabin hungry and weary, or passed it in long, sad procession. The heavens were aflame with the burning Congress. The hotel was crowded with fugitives, and private hospitality was taxed to the utmost. But there were *no soldiers among the flying host;* all in our camps at Newport News and camp Hamilton were at the post of duty, undismayed, and ready to do all and dare all for their country. The sailors came only to seek another chance at the enemy, since the bold Cumberland had gone down in the deep waters, and the Congress had gone upward, as if a chariot of fire, to convey the manly souls whose bodies had perished in that conflict, upward to heaven. I had lost several friends there ; yet not lost, for they are saved who do their duty to their country and their God, as these had done. We did not pray in vain.

> "The heavy night hung dark the hills and waters o'er,"

but the night was not half so heavy as our hearts, nor so dark as our prospects. All at once a speck of light gleamed on the distant wave ; it moved ; it came nearer and nearer and at ten o'clock at night, *the Monitor appeared.* 'When the tale of bricks is doubled, Moses comes.' I never more firmly believed in special providences than at that hour. Even skeptics were converted for the moment and said, 'God has sent her!' But how insignificant she looked ; she was but a speck on the dark blue sea at night, almost a laughable object by day. The enemy call her a cheese-box on a raft, and the comparison is a good one. Could she meet the Merrimac? The morrow must determine, for under God, the Monitor is our only hope."

Lieutenant J. L. Worden was in command of the Monitor, and reporting to the flag-ship Roanoke on his arrival at Fortress Monroe, received orders to lay by the Minnesota and guard her in case of a night attack.

Sunday morning, March ninth, dawned brightly over the serene waters of the Chesapeake, and shortly after nine o'clock, the Merrimac with her retinue of the previous day was seen approaching from the direction of Sewall's Point.

Instantly the Monitor put herself in fighting trim, the dead-light covers were put on, the iron hatches closed, and the officers took positions at their several posts. Lieutenant Green was in charge of the gunners, and Chief Engineer Stimers controlled the movements of the revolving turret.

The mammoth Merrimac confidently advanced and opened fire upon the Minnesota; but before a second broadside could be delivered, the little Monitor steamed out from behind the grounded vessel, and when at a distance of about half a mile, the order to fire was given, "The gun was aimed, the huge, iron pendulum swung aside, the men sprang to the gun-ropes, a momentary creaking of pulleys was heard, then a thundering report and a solid ball weighing a hundred and seventy pounds, was hurled against the mailed side of the Merrimac. The Monitor had uttered her maiden speech, and it was a challenge which no antagonist could venture to disregard."

The Merrimac staggered under this unexpected blow and pausing in her attack on the Minnesota, turned her attention to the little Monitor. Immediately, her ten terrible guns thundered their broadside against her diminutive antagonist, and when the smoke lifted and revealed the turret of the Monitor unharmed, and the stars and stripes still gaily floating aloft, the Merrimac rushed upon her to ride her down as she had done the Cumberland and Congress. But a different sort of craft grappled with her now and she found a foeman worthy of her steel. "Reserve your fire," said Lieutenant Worden to the gunners, "aim deliberately and do not lose a shot." The Merrimac struck the Monitor at full speed, but caused only a slight jar to the staunch little craft, as the iron prow of this mailed monster glided harmlessly over the nearly submerged hull of the Ericsson Battery. The Merrimac, however, received a severe gash as the sharp edge of the Monitor cut her coat of mail, and a bad leak was the result.

The contest now waxed fierce and heavy as the two vessels, alternately receding and approaching, poured their volleys of shot into each other in rapid succession, while the smoke of the terrible battle wrapped the actors in a dark and impenetrable cloud. With "muzzle to muzzle they hailed their heavy metal on each others sides." "Flash and thunder-roar burst forth incessantly from the tumultuous mælstrom of darkness, and solid balls weighing a hundred and seventy pounds, glancing from the armor, ricochetted over the water in all directions from one to two miles."

For four long hours this terrible duel on which the safety of a nation hung, continued, but when the smoke of battle lifted, it revealed the Monitor uninjured and triumphant, and the Merrimac pierced in three places, wounded unto death. Compelled to signal for help, she was taken in tow by two tugs who helped the crippled giant back to Norfolk.

Just as the Merrimac was firing her last shot Lieutenant Worden was struck prostrate by the concussion of a hundred-pound shot, which hit the grating just in front of his eyes, filling them with powder and minute fragments of iron. When he "revived from the stunning blow he had received," his first question was, "Have I saved the Minnesota?" "Yes," was the reply, "and whipped the Merrimac." "Then," he rejoined, "I care not what becomes of me."

When Lieutenant Wise visited the Monitor after the contest was ended, every thing was as serene on board the victorious craft as though nothing had happened. "One officer stood by the mirror leisurely combing his hair, another was washing some blood from his hands, while the gallant commander lay on a settee with his eyes bandaged, giving no signs of the pain that racked him."

Thousands of anxious spectators lined the shore from Newport News to Fortress Monroe, and from the Confederate fortifications across the James, watching with breathless interest the furious combat. "No tongue can tell the joy which thrilled the hearts of the National troops at the result. Cheer after cheer rose from the fleet and from the fortress, and rolled like reverberating thunder along the shores and over the bay."

The Merrimac had rendered her last service. She never recovered from the fatal blows dealt her by the guns of the Monitor, and months of repair did not restore her usefulness. But the brave little Monitor came out of this trial of fire unscathed. Of all the twenty-two shot which had struck her in every part, only one had produced a noticeable indentation.

This one, coming in contact with a huge iron beam, made a deflection in the beam of an inch and a half. A slight dent on the outside of the Monitor was the only evidence that the prow of the Merrimac had struck her in a vain attempt to ride her down.

The Rebels published no official account of the losses on board the Merrimac in this encounter, but a statement was made in the Norfolk Day Book, estimating their loss at nine killed and eleven wounded. The statement, however, was contradicted by some other Southern journals. Two or three million dollars worth of property was lost to the Government with the Cumberland and Congress, to say nothing of the loss of life.

Considering the fact that the construction of the Merrimac was known for months previous to her appearance, and that an accurate description of her was said to have been sent the War and Navy Departments, by General Wool, three weeks before she left Norfolk, on her mission of destruction, the apathy of the Naval Board is something to be wondered at. But the disaster which might have overtaken the nation through their negligence was happily averted by the private enterprise which launched the Monitor.

CHAPTER IX.

NEWBERN.

The City and its Connections.—Rebel Fortifications.—Assemblage of Gunboats at Hatteras.—The Advance Down Pamlico Sound.—Slocum's Creek Landing.—The Long March. The Forest Camp Fires.—Attack on the Outer Fortifications.—Impetuous Bravery of Union Troops.—Heroic Charge Through an Embrasure.—The Old Flag Floats Over the Captured Fort.—Entrance into Newbern. Ten o'clock and All is Well. Battle of the Fleet.—Brilliant Advance of the Gunboats.—All Difficulties Conquered.—Victory and its Spoils.—The Sabbath Bells.

NEWBERN is a city of about five thousand inhabitants, situated at the confluence of the Neuse and Trent rivers where the Neuse makes a broad estuary before entering Pamlico Sound. It is connected by rail with Goldsboro and Raleigh on the west, via North Carolina Rail Road, with Beaufort on the south, and is an important military post. The Confederates, appreciating this fact, had constructed in its defence fortifications of such strength that they imagined the Union troops had but to come within range of their batteries to be doomed to certain destruction. In order to capture this city and to act in concerted movement with the Army of the Potomac, General Burnside on the twelfth of March, 1862, had collected a formidable fleet and army at Hatteras and ordered all to be in readiness to start that night at the appointed signal. He delivered a brief and stirring address to the soldiers, asking their best efforts in this perilous enterprise, and in his order, he said,

"The General commanding, takes pleasure in announcing that the Army of the Potomac under General McClellan, is now advancing upon Richmond and was at the latest dates occupying Centreville, the enemy having evacuated all the advanced fortifications before Manassas, and those on the Potomac. He again calls upon his command for an important movement which will greatly demoralize the enemy and contribute much to the success of our brothers of the Potomac Army."

From Hatteras the fleet sailed south-westward down Pamlico Sound, entered the mouth of the Neuse and anchored upon the western bank of that river, within a few miles of Newbern. The defences of Newbern unquestionably had been well planned and well built. A line of water batteries commanded the river and, reaching inland, connected with them, were field fortifications to prevent the enemy from advancing by shore. Six miles down the river the guns of the lower fort threatened the daring intruder, and from that point back to the city there extended a continuous chain of forts and batteries. Near the city a fort mounting thirteen heavy guns and bomb proof, was so arranged as to command both the water and the only land approaches on that side. In fact, the entire area for several miles before the city, was filled with forts, earthworks, ditches, rifle pits, and all the other mechanical appliances of warfare.

On the morning of the thirteenth the troops were landed at a point called Slocum's Creek, sixteen miles below Newbern. Abbott gives the following description of the landing:—"The barges proceeded in regular battle array, regiment by regiment, towards the shore, every man ready to repel an assault, and the gunboats in the meantime shelling every spot in the vicinity where a foe might lurk. The men wading through the water held their muskets and ammunition under their arms to keep them dry. The barges grounded in the shoal water sixty yards from the shore. It was truly a picturesque scene, resembling a frolic rather than the dread realities of war, to see five thousand men with jokes and laughter and cheers, often up to their waists in water, and sometimes stumbling over some obstruction, all eager to see who would be the first to land. The ground was marshy; it had rained violently through the night; the path led through a fringe of forest draped in the funereal weeds of the Spanish moss. The wheels of the guns sank in the mire and were dragged along with much difficulty. A cold March wind swept over the drenched and shivering ranks, and notwithstanding all the endeavors to keep up good cheer, the hours were dark and dreary. Much of this suffering might have been and should have been avoided. One of the vessels contained a floating bridge to secure the landing of the soldiers dry shod. But the eagerness to get to shore very unwisely caused this precaution to be neglected or forgotten."

Until mid-day they marched along the marshy river banks without meeting the foe or any signs of one. At about that time however, they encountered some cavalry barracks, bearing evidence of very hasty leave-taking. Breakfasts, cooked, yet untasted, were left behind, and all the evidences of very recent occupancy were strewn about. But the Federal forces, with a great struggle in anticipation, did not stop to satisfy any idle curiosity regarding the *modus operandi* of Rebel cookery. Steadily they pushed onward, filling the road in a dense column two and a half miles in length,—the Twenty-fourth Massachusetts leading the van, and the Eleventh Connecticut bringing up the rear.

Suddenly, the order to halt and form in line of battle brought the column to a stand. Directly in front of them stood a long line of breastworks and batteries. A deep ditch extended along the front, and the flanks were protected by an abattis of felled trees. But, as a reconnoitering party sent forward soon learned, the guns to this extensive fort were not yet mounted, and peacefully our troops entered it and took possession, raising the standard of Liberty upon its ramparts. But with a march of yet eight miles before them, and unknown difficulties to overcome, the Union troops, after halting a few moments, pressed bravely on. Many dropped by the wayside utterly overcome with fatigue, and unable to go one step farther. Others lost their shoes in the mire and went forward with torn and bleeding feet. A drizzling rain set in which kept the men drenched to the skin and added greatly to their discomfort.

Night was swiftly approaching when a horseman from Newbern was arrested who communicated the news that Manassas was evacuated, and that McClellan was probably in hot pursuit after the retreating foe, and perhaps on his way to Richmond. At this joyful news, cheer after cheer broke from the lips of the men, and stimulated and alert they resumed their march. At six o'clock of that day the scouts came in, reporting a line of rebel fortifications a mile ahead. It was the beginning of a rainy twilight, and after the weary and toilsome day's march through the rain, wading oftentimes through mud knee deep, the order to "halt!" which now sounded through the ranks, was most welcome. They were in the midst of a forest of pine trees, and on either side of the road thousands of soldiers threw themselves on the ground for rest and sleep, with no shelter overhead save the pine trees and the clouds of a gloomy night. Some of them had lighted fires of the resinous pitch, and in every direction the flames leapt gaily up while the red reflection fell athwart the recumbent forms and faces of the sleeping soldiery, lighting up the whole scene with a weird and picturesque beauty.

Seven o'clock of the next morning found them, after having breakfasted, once more on the march towards Newbern. General Reno with the First Massachusetts had the advance, and marched by the side of the railroad track which connects Newbern and Beaufort. Slowly along the river the gunboats steamed, keeping pace with the marching men on the shore. Says Abbott, in his history of the "Civil War," "upon turning a curve in the road, they came in sight of a train of cars which had just come down from Newbern with reinforcements for the Rebels. On a platform car in front of the engine, stood a rifled cannon in position to rake the road. The Massachusetts men rushed forward at the double-quick at the same time pouring in such a volley of bullets upon the foe that they abandoned everything and ran for the intrenchments. The troops were immediately deployed in line of battle through the woods, and impetuously commenced an attack upon the formidable ramparts. The first cannon shot from the rebel battery passed through the body of Lieut.-Colonel Henry Merritt, of the Massachusetts Twenty-third, and he fell instantly dead. The Tenth Connecticut under General Foster, a very gallant body of men, occupied the extreme left, and under the most discouraging circumstances of position maintained the renown they had acquired at Roanoke. The whole line extended more than a mile. For an hour the battle raged in an uninterrupted storm of bullets and cannon balls from both sides, with no apparent advantage to either." As the battle waxed more and more fierce, our men approached to the very muzzles of the guns of the enemy's breastworks, until Lieut.-Colonel Clark of the Twenty-first Massachusetts made a brilliant dash at the head of four companies, and rushed full tilt on the double-quick through one of the embrasures.

The gunners, astonished at such daring, fled panic-stricken. The National flag was waved for one victorious moment over the heroic conquest, but as they were about to take the next gun, two rebel regiments swept down upon them and compelled them to retire. They were held at bay, however, only for a few brief moments, for in that time the Rhode Island Fourth came up and successfully assaulted the same spot, thus opening a door to victory through which their comrades speedily followed.

The charge of the Fourth Rhode Island led by Colonel Rodman, was said to be heroic. Directly fronting them a battery of five guns threatened annihilation, and in close proximity another battery of nine guns presented itself, protected behind rifle pits. On the double-quick they charged directly upon the deadly muzzles of these five guns, firing as they ran, and rushing through the parapet, immediately formed in battle array and successfully charged upon the remaining and most formidable battery. Thus both batteries and two flags were captured. The Eighth and Eleventh Connecticut and Fifth Rhode Island followed immediately in support, and the ranks of the enemy dissolved before their victorious entrance like banks of fog under sunbeam bayonets.

Quickly the Union standard went up over the captured works and then came a grand charge upon the enemy's left wing, by those still outside the breastworks. In utter confusion and headlong panic the Rebel foe was routed. With wild huzzahs the Union forces rushed over the ramparts discharging their firearms at the flying grey-coats, and almost immediately, over every bastion of the captured fort, the "old flag" flaunted its starry folds victoriously. Cheer after cheer rent the air from the exultant troops who had so heroically won the hard-fought and bloody field.

Every regiment and company had behaved valiantly, —every man was a hero. The Fifty-first New York, leading the charge under General Reno, won a proud reputation for bravery and valorous daring. The Fifty-first Pennslyvania came under the heaviest fire without wavering.

Inside the battery the dead and the dying commingled in revolting confusion with mangled corpses, dismounted guns, broken muskets, and stores of all sorts, blood-stained and trampled in the mire. It was a sickening spectacle and one in awful contrast to the joyful exultation of the victors.

But Burnside did not waste a moment of precious time in rejoicing over the spoils of victory but pressed on towards Newbern, taking advantage of the panic of the enemy.

Our forces pushed rapidly forward, meeting none to contest their advance. By early afternoon they had reached the eastern bank of the Trent only to find the magnificent bridge which spanned the river in one vast sheet of flames, and on the opposite shore the city in seven different localities, broke forth in conflagration. Both the railroad and county road bridge were fired as also a number of cotton batteries. Fortunately, two small steamers were found, abandoned by the enemy, and with these General Foster's corps was ferried across the river and took possession of the nearly deserted city. The soldiers speedily extinguished the fires, a provost marshal with a strong guard was appointed, and before nine o'clock at night order was restored, quietness reigned, and at ten o'clock the city and its inhabitants were wrapped in peaceful slumbers. It was a sleep which the exhausted soldiers needed. The colored population thinking their hour of jubilee had come, and freed from the restraint which forbids a slave to be abroad on the street at night, wandered about the city until a late hour.

On the fifteenth the following special order was issued :

"HEAD-QUARTERS, DEPARTMENT OF NORTH CAROLINA,
NEWBERN, March 15th, 1862.

Special Orders No. 51.

* * * * * *

4th. Brigadier-General J. G. Foster is hereby appointed military governor of Newbern and its suburbs, and will be obeyed and respected accordingly.

Brigadier-General J. G. Foster, military governor of Newbern will direct that the churches be opened at a suitable hour tomorrow in order that the chaplains of the different regiments may hold divine services in them. The bells will be rung as usual.

* * * * * *

By command of Brigadier-General
A. E. BURNSIDE.

LEWIS RICHMOND, Assistant Adjutant General."

General Burnside also, wisely enough, ordered every liquor cask in the city and camp to be staved.

The part which the gunboats performed in this victory was not small. Commander Rowan in charge of the fleet proved himself most efficient.

The river was full of obstructions, the shore was bristling with batteries; but he conquered every difficulty. Led by the flag ship Delaware the fleet sailed away to win a golden fame. Fort Dixie, mounting four guns, was the first battery to contest their advance, but it was soon silenced by Union shot and shell, and the triumphant battle-flags were planted upon its ramparts. Here the gunners caught sight of some Rebel cavalry in the woods behind the fort and sent over a warm salute of shells which dispersed them. The next battery encountered was Fort Thompson, mounting fifteen guns. This also was effectually silenced by our well directed shot, its garrison scattered, and once more the National standard waved defiantly over the captured redans. The men, wild with enthusiasm, rent the air with their cheers.

Night came on after this conquest, and hostilities were suspended until the next day. The morning of Saturday, the fourteenth, dawned murky with a dense fog. Soon, however, it lifted and the battle of the fleet was once more in progress.

Fort Brown, the next battery encountered, mounted two immense columbiads and protected the obstructions in the channels. In the right hand channel, twenty-four vessels interlacing each other had been sunk, while the left hand channel contained heavy upright timbers iron-pointed, designed to impale whatever craft might pass that way, at which point also were placed a number of destructive torpedoes.

These obstructions, covered by Fort Brown, were next in order, but Commander Rowan, nothing daunted, ordered the boats to follow his lead, and they succeeded in passing the impaling timbers and entangling masts, without serious injury. Singularly enough also, a shot from one of the gun-boats entering the embrasure of the fort, struck one of the columbiads directly upon the muzzle, dashing it from its carriage. The gunners fled in panic and consternation. The fort was immediately captured, the National banner raised, and the whole fleet passed on to the capture of the next battery, Fort Ellis, mounting nine guns. Here the dispersed Rebels had gathered for a last desperate effort and for a time the carnage went on fiercely enough. But a shell from the gunboats exploded the magazine of the fort, and when the smoke lifted, none but the dead and the dying were there. The next battery, Fort Lane, was abandoned without firing a shot, and the brilliant passage was completed triumphantly, the fleet anchoring before the city just as the land troops entered it.

In this grand advance of the gunboat fleet to Newbern, the navy lost not a single man.

One or two individual instances of the coolness and daring with which our men passed through this maelstrom of war and death may be related.

Lieutenant Fearing, of Burnside's staff, seated on his horse, was standing in conversation with a looker-on. A thirty-two pound shot whizzed between his horse's legs, causing scarcely a halt in the conversation, the Lieutenant merely bending over to see that his horse was all right and making no allusion to the danger.

At another time during the battle, when a handful of men made a heroic dash through an embrasure and two Rebel regiments charged down upon them, Captain J. D. Frazer from a severe wound in the right arm was compelled to drop his sword. But with his left hand he seized the fallen weapon, continued the fight, and endeavored to extricate himself from the surrounding enemy. Stumbling, he fell and was taken prisoner, a guard of three being placed over him. A few moments after, when the Fourth Rhode Island made their brilliant and successful charge, rescued at their hands, Captain Frazer in turn captured the three Rebel guards placed over him and escorted them to the Union ranks.

In this victory our loss was eighty killed and two hundred and ninety wounded.

Six forts, thirty-four heavy guns, six steamboats, and two million dollars worth of public property were captured. The Rebel loss in killed and wounded was about the same as ours. The National sharp-shooters kept up such an accurate fire that the Confederate infantry after loading behind the ramparts, raised their guns over their heads and fired almost at random, thus throwing many of their bullets away. The capture of Newbern made the final reduction of Beaufort and Fort Macon sure, and also made Burnside commander of the Army of the Potomac.

CHAPTER X.

WINCHESTER.

Topography of the Battle-Ground.—General Banks' Occupation of Winchester.—Stonewall Jackson's Attack.—Disposition of Forces.—The Battle.—Unwavering Firmness of Union Troops.—Heroic Defence of the National Colors by the Fifth Ohio.—"'T is sweet for One's Country to Die."—The Enemy put to Rout.—Stonewall Jackson in Retreat.—A Night of Sleep After a Day of Battle.—Kernstown.—Sheridan's Ride.

IN one of the most beautiful and fertile portions of Virginia, lying between the Blue Ridge and North Mountains and extending from the head waters of the Shenandoah River near Staunton to its confluence with the blue Potomac, is situated the far-famed Valley of the Shenandoah. From Strasburg a spur of the mountain chain called the Massanutten range divides the valley southward for a distance of fifty miles and abruptly ends near Harrisburg.

Strasburg commands the head of the western division which this range creates, and Front Royal the eastern, while Winchester, distant from Strasburg about twenty miles, holds the key, in a military sense, to the entire Valley. This ancient town, known in colonial times as Fort Loudon, is less than thirty miles from the Potomac River, and is a center, out of which well-made turnpikes diverge towards Romney, Sheppardstown, Martinsburg, Charlestown, and

Berryville, and also towards Centreville through Battletown.

On March twelfth, 1862, General Banks occupied Winchester with his advance force, Stonewall Jackson having abandoned the place on the same day. Jackson marched towards Staunton in order to cover the operations of the Southern foe in that vicinity, and also to protect the road leading from this part of the Valley to Gordonsville, the main force of the Confederates having retreated to that point. On the seventeenth of March, General Shields left Winchester with his command to pursue the enemy towards Strasburg, but returned on the twentieth, having been overtaken by the enemy near Middletown, between whom and the Union troops a sharply contested skirmish took place. The division of General Williams—one half of Banks's command—moved towards Battletown at the same time that the reconnoitering party under Shields returned to Winchester.

Supposing the whole army of Banks was marching to re-inforce McClellan, Stonewall Jackson determined to attack our forces at Winchester, to prevent if possible the expected movement. Accordingly, by forced marches from Mount Jackson, forty-five miles below Winchester, he reached Strasburg and from thence advanced to the little village of Kernstown, within three miles of Winchester. This was on Saturday the twenty-second, and at half past two on the afternoon of that day the Rebel advance appeared in front of the Union pickets.

Jackson had with him four regiments of infantry, assisted by Ashby's cavalry, which was discovered to be steadily advancing in the woods on both sides of the Strasburg turnpike, where the Eleventh Indiana was also picketed. The Union troops then fell back, pursued by the Rebel cavalry, and occasionally facing about to fire upon the enemy. General Shields, in command of the division, ordered four companies of infantry and a battery of artillery to the support of the Fourteenth Indiana until his force could be brought forward and formed in line of battle. While directing the battery, Shields received a wound in the arm from a splinter of a shell, but remained on the field until dark, when the troops began to arrive. Both armies bivouacked for the night, the enemy not seeming anxious to press the engagement. To General Shields, awaiting the return of Williams' troops to reënforce him, this suspension of hostilities was not unwelcome. But Williams did not arrive on the battlefield until after the action had commenced, on the next day.

At eight o'clock on the morning of the twenty-third, the enemy opened the conflict with four guns, receiving a reply of six guns from the Union troops, after which reënforcements for both batteries came up. The fire from the enemy's guns was so well directed and so effective that the Union general commanding determined to take the battery by storm; for which purpose the infantry columns of the First and Second brigades were massed for an attack upon the enemy's left. The brigade of Kimball was on the right, that of Tyler in the center and Sullivan on the left, with General Kimball in command of the entire force—General Shields being disabled on account of the wound received the day before. The enemy's center was a little to the left of the turnpike at Kernstown village, his left wing extending a mile and three-quarters west of the road, and his right wing one mile to the east of it. A mud road branches from the turnpike at this point and runs to the right over Cedar creek. Here the enemy's left center was placed, beyond which was a grove of trees, and farther yet a ridge of hills crowned by a stone wall, breast high. General Tyler moved his column on the mud road until within two hundred yards of the stone wall, when he received a murderous fire. But bravely and without wavering the Union troops rushed forward until within fifteen yards of the stone wall barricade, when the order to fire was obeyed with such vigor that the enemy fell back across the fields in consternation, unmasking in their retreat two six-pound guns. The cannister from these guns made great gaps in the Union lines but did not check the brave advance of our heroic men, though death faced them. One gun was captured with its caisson, but almost immediately two more brass pieces were unmasked by the enemy and were so destructive that our troops, forced to give way, upset the captured gun and left it. At this point in the conflict, the Fifth Ohio and Eighty-fourth Pennsylvania formed in line of battle and charged with the bayonet. It was a terrific encounter, and in its maelstrom of blood and death, the Fifth Ohio Regiment five times within the space of a few minutes lost its color-bearer. When the first standard-bearer sank to the soil, a sacrifice to the enemy's bullets, another brave soldier rushed forward, caught up the starry banner of liberty and unfurled its folds triumphantly to the breeze. Scarcely had his hand grasped the staff of the old flag when he, too, fell in the sacred cause. A third and a fourth and a fifth one shared the same fate, heroically rushing to this ill-fated post of death. And thus at such terrible cost of life the old flag was kept floating victoriously. But now, the struggling troops so desperately engaged were to have help from their comrades in arms. The Fourteenth and One Hundred and Tenth Indiana Regiments advanced at the quick to support them, and the enemy fell back leaving the captured gun behind. Now, however, at seven o'clock in the afternoon, the firing gradually lessened and the enemy retreated,—our pursuing cavalry capturing about two hundred prisoners.

That night the Union troops slept upon the field of their victory and in the morning went in pursuit of the enemy. But the routed Rebels would not fight, and retired on being attacked by our troops. The Union forces in consequence, rejoined the command of Banks, who arrived from Harper's Ferry at nine o'clock on the morning of the twenty-fourth.

Thus ended the battle of Winchester, made doubly famous by the defeat of Stonewall Jackson and as the historic ground from which afterwards, in 1864, Phil Sheridan, on his black charger, performed that glorious ride to Cedar Creek, afterwards immortalized by T. Buchanan Read, by which he reversed the tide of battle and made 'dark defeat' become a 'glorious victory,'

* * * * * * * "because
The sight of the master compelled it to pause."

The Union loss in this battle, to which Southern chroniclers give the name of Kernstown, was one hundred and thirty-two killed, five hundred and forty wounded, and forty-six missing. The loss of the enemy was estimated to be nine hundred, of whom two hundred and thirty-six were prisoners. Two guns and four caissons were also captured.

The enemy had been reënforced at ten o'clock Sunday morning by General Garnett, and claimed a force of six thousand, half of which only was engaged. The command of General Shields numbered eight thousand.

CHAPTER XI.

FALMOUTH HEIGHTS.

General McDowell in Command of the Army of Virginia.—Advance to Bristoe and Falmouth.—Harris Light Leading the Advance.—Sudden Fire on the Van-guard.—Furious Charge upon the Rebel Cavalry.—Death of Lieutenant Decker.—His Comrades Avenge His Death.—The Enemy Scattered Like Chaff Before the Whirlwind.—Outposts, Stores and Provisions Captured.—A Loyal Southern Citizen Greets the Old Flag.—Plan for a Night Attack on Falmouth.—Brilliant Capture of the Place by Kilpatrick.

WHEN the Army of the Potomac was transferred to the Peninsula in the Spring of 1862, the troops left in front of Washington were denominated the Army of Virginia. General McDowell commanding this force advanced to Bristoe in the early part of April, and on the seventeenth of that month, detaching General Auger with a brigade of Infantry and two regiments of Cavalry, directed him to proceed to Falmouth, a small village on the Rappahannock, opposite the City of Fredericksburg, with instructions to occupy the latter place if possible.

The author's regiment, the Harris Light Cavalry, had the advance and was followed by the Fourteenth Brooklyn. As our Infantry comrades became footsore and fatigued, we exchanged positions with them for mutual relief until at last one-half of the two regiments were bearing each others' burdens. This incident paved the way for a strong friendship between the Harris Light and Fourteenth Brooklyn. I cannot call to mind in the course of my military experience, a more novel sight than that of those gallant Brooklyn boys mounted upon our horses, while we marched by their side carrying their muskets; they amusing us with their knowledge of horsemanship and we essaying to show them that we were not wholly ignorant of the evolutions of infantry.

Seventeen miles were quietly traveled when a sudden fire on our advance-guard brought every cavalry man to his horse and infantry man to his musket. Everything assumed the signs of a fight. Kilpatrick, who was in command of the regiment, ordered his band to the rear. This precaution of the commander was no sooner taken than the van-guard in command of Lieutenant George Decker made a furious charge upon Field's Cavalry which was doing outpost duty ten miles from Falmouth.

On the very first assult Lieutenant Decker fell from his horse, pierced through the heart with a fatal bullet. The fall of this gallant young officer was much lamented by his associates of the Harris Light. His death, however, shocking as it was to the command, only seemed to nerve the men for bold revenge. Like chaff before the whirlwind the outpost was quickly scattered, and the whole regiment entered upon its first charge with a will,—a charge which continued for several miles with wild excitement. Picket reliefs and reserves were swept away like forest trees before the avalanche, and we fell upon their encampment before time had been afforded them for escape.

Here we captured several men and horses with large quantities of stores, and then rested our tired steeds and fed them with Confederate forage. The men enjoyed the captured rations. It was nearly night, and as the sun disappeared the infantry force came up to our newly-possessed territory.

The cavalry was ordered to "stand to horse" and a strong picket was thrown out to prevent any surprise attack or flanking movement of the enemy. In the early part of the evening one of our pickets was surprised by the friendly approach of a citizen of Falmouth who had come, as he said, to "hail once more the 'old star-spangled banner' and to greet his loyal brethren of the North."

Such a patriotic and fearless individual among the white population of that section of country was a great rarity and his protestations of friendship were at first received with some suspicion. He was, however, brought to General Auger's headquarters, where he gave satisfactory proof of his kind intentions, and then gave the General a full description of the position and strength of the enemy.

A plan for a night attack was thereupon laid and committed to Bayard and Kilpatrick.

Our instructions were conveyed to us in a whisper. A beautiful moonlight fell upon the scene which was as still as death; and with a proud determination the two young cavalry chieftains moved forward to the night's fray. Bayard was to attack on the main road in front, but not until Kilpatrick had commenced operations on their right flank by a detour through a neglected and narrow wood-path. As the Heights

FALMOUTH HEIGHTS.

were considered well nigh impregnable it was necessary to resort to some stratagem, for which Kilpatrick showed a becoming aptness.

Having approached to within hearing distance of the Rebel pickets, but before we were challenged, Kilpatrick shouted with his clear voice, which sounded like a trumpet on the still night air:

"Bring up your artillery in the centre and infantry on the left!"

"Well, but, Colonel," replied an honest though rather obtuse captain, "we haven't got any inf—."

"Silence in the ranks!" commanded the leader. "Artillery in the centre, infantry on the left!"

The pickets caught and spread the alarm, and thus greatly facilitated our hazardous enterprise.

"Charge!" was the order which then thrilled the ranks, and echoed through the dark dismal woods, and the column swept up the rugged Heights in the midst of blazing cannon and rattling musketry. So steep was the ascent that not a few saddles slipped off the horses, precipitating their riders into a creek which flowed lazily at the base of the hill, while others fell dead and dying struck by the missiles of destruction which at times filled the air. But our first field was won; and the enemy driven at the point of the sabre, fled unceremoniously down the Heights, through Falmouth, and over the bridge which spanned the Rappahannock, burning the beautiful structure behind them to prevent pursuit.

CHAPTER XII.

PITTSBURG LANDING.

The Log Cabin Church.—Buell's March from Nashville.—The Union Camp Surprised.—The Rude Awakening.—Sleep Exchanged for Death.—Rally of the Boys in Blue.—Slaughter from the Woods.—Stand on the Corinth Road.—The Brave Resistance.—The Wave of Rebellion Hurled Back.—Six Hours of Magnificent Fighting.—A Glorious Record.—Wallace Falls.—The Impregnable Line.—Tyler and Lexington Gunboats.—Death of Confederate Johnston.—Buell Reaches the Landing.—Last Day's Fight.—Capture of Field Peices.—Confederates in Retreat.—Splendid Victory.—Harvest of Death.

A small log cabin named Shiloh Church, on the western bank of the Tennessee river, about twenty miles north of Corinth, Mississippi, divides with Pittsburg Landing the honor of transmitting its name to the bloody engagement fought here, April sixth, 1862.

Early in March this movement up the Tennessee was projected, and Major-General C. F. Smith, with his command, occupied Savannah on the eleventh. Savannah is ten miles above Pittsburg Landing and consequently about thirty miles from Corinth. For strategic reasons General Smith removed his troops to Pittsburg Landing—a movement which General Grant approved, on his arrival there the latter part of March. It was designed to make the Tennessee River a base of operations and cut off communication between West Tennessee and the Eastern and Southern States. General Buell at Nashville with the Army of the Ohio, was directed to co-operate with Grant in the expected movement. This being suspected by the Rebels, they determined to attack Grant at Pittsburg Landing before he could be re-inforced by Buell. Beauregard held a strong force at Corinth to which were added the two divisions under General Polk from Columbus. and the corps of General Bragg from Pensacola.

General Albert Sidney Johnston, chief in command at Corinth, on April third issued an address to his army, and an order, dividing it into three corps,—the first under General Polk, the second under Bragg and the third under Hardee; while General Crittenden was assigned to a reserve consisting of two brigades.

Of this force, numbering about fifty thousand men, General Johnston was chief and Beauregard second in command. On April fifth, the army of West Tennessee, under General Grant at Pittsburg Landing, comprised five divisions—Major-General McClernand, Brigadier-General W. H. L. Wallace, Major-General Lewis Wallace, Brigadier-General Hurlbut and Brigadier-General W. T. Sherman commanding respectively.

The division of General Lew Wallace was six miles below Pittsburg Landing at a place known as Crump's Landing, while the rest of the Union forces remained in the vicinity of the Shiloh log church.

Twenty miles away, Buell's forces were slowly approaching, the condition of the roads greatly impeding their progress. In hourly expectation of their arrival, the army on the west bank of the Tennessee awaited them. Occupying the ground between Owl Creek and Lick Creek—two streams which run at right angles to the Tennessee, three miles apart—the Union command was arranged as follows: Sherman's division held the extreme right, resting on Owl Creek, about three miles from the Landing, McClernand's division was next, the sub-division of McClernand's command under Prentiss, came next on the left, resting on Lick Creek, three miles from the Tennessee, while the division of W. H. L. Wallace acted as a support to Sherman and McClernand, and Hurlbut supported the left wing under Prentiss. In addition to this force, several gun-boats, among which were the Tyler and Lexington, were anchored off the Landing ready to assist with their broadsides of shot and shell, whenever the tide of battle called them into action.

On the morning of the third, Johnston's troops were marching from Corinth towards the Tennessee, but did not reach the neighborhood of the Federal position until the evening of the fifth. The Confederate force was formed in three parallel lines wih an interval of eight hundred yards between the first and second line, the corps of Polk forming the third line in columns of brigades. Breckenridge held the reserves, and batteries were placed in the rear of each brigade. General Hardee commanded the first line which extended from Owl Creek on the left, to Lick Creek on the right. Bragg was in command of the second line.

At six o'clock on the morning of the sixth, the Confederate advance suddenly drove in the pickets of Prentiss' corps. The Union camp, not yet awakened from sleep, was surprised by the enemy who rushed upon them firing as they came and charging with the bayonet. Then ensued a scene of panic and heart-rending confusion. Union soldiers rushed from their tents, weaponless, hatless and coatless, towards the river, and many were shot dead on the way; others quietly exchanged the rosy sleep of life for the pallid repose of death, pierced with a fatal bullet before their eyes unclosed to behold the dawn. Others, it is said, surrendered only to be shot on the spot. Officers wounded and left for dead in their tents, were found two days afterwards, yet alive to tell the sickening tale, though suffering untold agonies. The sub-division of Prentiss and Hildebrand's brigade of Sherman's division were thus driven by the enemy, but the remainder of Sherman's division sprang to their arms and formed in line barely in time to receive the advancing legions of the Confederates and partially check their terrible onset. This movement enabled them to retire to a ridge in their rear—the key-point of the Landing—where by their firmness they repelled every attempt of the enemy to turn their flank. By this time the whole army was aroused to the peril of the attack, and McClernand soon formed his right to sustain Sherman. The corps of Prentiss was partially rallied in an open space surrounded by scrub oaks, from which the Confederates concealed there, slaughtered them without mercy. General Prentiss with two entire regiments were taken prisoners and the sub-division was disorganized. The division of W. H. L. Wallace now pressed forward to support Stuart of Sherman's division, but lost its way and was repulsed.

McClernand was compelled to withdraw his brigades in support of Sherman, in order to protect his left against a furious charge by the enemy. Two new regiments, the Fifteenth and Sixteenth Iowa, were brought into action, but the heavy firing proved too much for these raw troops and they gave way in confusion. Our batteries were placed in position along the Corinth road, and the division changed front so as to face on that highway. They defended it handsomely until ten o'clock, but at that time the enemy rushed through the gap between the lines of McClernand and Sherman, with the evident intention of turning McClernand's right. Dresser's Battery of rifled guns dealt them terrible slaughter as they passed, but their great numbers and the constant arrival of fresh troops overwhelmed McClernand's division until at last our forces began to fall slowly back, fighting bravely with well ordered resistance as they retired. An occasional rally and repulse of the enemy varied the order of their retreat. Our batteries were broken and several guns lost, and the disorganized brigades and divisions fell to the rear. In some instances patched-up regiments were brought to the front.

The left and center of our line on the Corinth road had been shattered, and at twelve o'clock none but the forces of Hurlbut, Wallace, and Sherman stood between our army and destruction.

Major General Lew Wallace was to flank the enemy in case of an attack, by marching across from Crump's Landing, but, directed by a circuitous route, he did not arrive on the battle-field until the fight for the day was ended.

The commands of Hurlbut and Wallace meanwhile sustained with perfect firmness the mad onsets of the enemy. Their overwhelming numbers, like a vast, living wave, swept against the solid columns of our troops only to fall back with repulse and slaughter. It was the sea of Rebellion dashing against the rocks of Union and Liberty. Thrice did the fresh troops of the enemy hurl themselves against our jaded and exhausted boys only to be thrice sent back in dismay and death.

The wave broke at our feet but did not engulf us. The skill of the enemy was something to be admired. Again and again a rush on our lines failed, but as quickly as the enemy's forces were hurled back, their broken divisions were taken to the rear and new attacking lines formed of fresh troops. For six hours was this unequal contest waged. For six hours did those noble men face the foe with heroic resistance.

Into those six hours was crowded a record of magnificent fighting, than which there could be none braver or more glorious.

Oh, patriots true! with brows now crowned with the victor's laurels, we thank you for revealing to us such sublime heights of human nature!

At last, retreat was imperative, and the two divisions of W. H. L. Wallace and Hurlbut fell back to within half a mile of the Landing. At this fatal moment the brave Wallace fell, and was borne from this field of glory and of death. It was now four o'clock in the afternoon, and exhausted by ten hours of almost continuous fighting, there was a lull in the storm of battle.

General Grant made good use of this opportunity. A new line was formed on the right by Sherman, which was prolonged to the left by re-formed brigades and regiments from the remaining divisions of the army, while Colonel Webster, Grant's Chief of Artillery, arranged the remaining batteries in a semicircle on the left, in order to pour a concentrated fire upon the enemy, massing in this direction. The *Tyler* and *Lexington* gunboats moved up to the mouth of Lick Creek and brought their guns within range of the enemy, a half mile away.

The intelligence that Nelson's division, constituting the advance of Buell, had reached the eastern bank of the Tennesee and would soon cross to their assistance, greatly cheered our exhausted troops. " Suddenly, at about five o'clock the enemy burst upon the Union left only to be swept down by steady volleys of musketry and the withering fire of the batteries. To add to their consternation the huge guns of the *Tyler* and *Lexington* ploughed into their ranks.

"Again and again did the Rebels attempt to break through the circle of fire within which the Union army stood at bay. The position seemed impregnable. Disappointed and disheartened they at length retired at nightfall, and the battle for the day was over." Sometime before this, General Grant had issued orders to his division commanders to prepare to assume the offensive at an early hour in the morning.

During the battle of that day, the Confederate General Albert Sidney Johnston was killed, his death resulting from a small wound under the knee, which severed an artery. He was in his saddle, when one of his aids, observing his blood stained uniform inquired if he was wounded. "Only a scratch," the General replied, but the next moment he reeled in his seat and fell dying into the arms of his officers.

His boot was filled with blood and the life current still ebbed rapidly away from the mortal hurt. Johnston's exhausted troops slept that night on their arms, and Beauregard, now in command, established his headquarters at Shiloh church, hoping some delay would prevent the arrival of Buell, who, he knew, was on the march for the scene of battle. Our gunboats bombarded the Rebel forces during the night, compelling them to retire a short distance from their position. In the midst of a drenching rain-storm which set in during the night, General Buell arrived. He had reached Savannah on the evening of the fifth, General Nelson leading the advance. Firing being heard from the direction of the Landing on the morning of the sixth, Buell ordered the division in the rear to leave their trains and hurry forward.

Nelson's command was marched to the Tennessee opposite Pittsburg Landing, their guns were ordered to be carried by steamboat, and late on the sixth, Buell himself arrived on the eastern bank of the Tennessee.

During that night, through the rain and darkness, Nelson's division crossed the river and occupied the left of the Union line. The commands of General T. L. Crittenden and McCook quickly followed, and were posted on the left-center and center, the veterans of the sixth occupying the right-center and right. General Lew Wallace having arrived with his command on the night of the sixth, held the extreme right.

The battle of the seventh was opened by Wallace. Some Rebel batteries directly in his front were shelled, and under cover of this fire the right wing advanced some distance. Wallace at one time was obliged to send to Sherman for aid, but at last the rebels were pushed back and obliged to retire from the hotly contested ground.

On the left, Nelson's division advanced so rapidly as to expose its right flank and was forced to retire until Boyle's Brigade of Crittenden's division re-inforced him. With this addition to his force, Nelson once more advanced, driving the enemy, capturing his batteries and taking possession of an eminence in the extreme front. Between eight and nine o'clock, he encountered a well-supported battery of the enemy. Smith's brigade—between Crittenden's left and Nelson's flank—dashed forward and for a short time the battle was hot and close and the discharge of musketry furious; but the enemy fled and our boys captured three field pieces—a twelve pound howitzer and two brass six-pounders. Around these guns the roar of battle surged with terrific force. Then came a solid line of Rebel infantry sweeping up to the captured battery. The commands of Nelson and Crittenden caught its full force and partially fell back, but taking a fresh stand, faced the enemy and held their ground. The batteries of Mendenhall and Bartlett now began shelling the Confederate ranks, which obliged the enemy to fall back.

"A gallant charge secured the contested battery while the Rebels retreated towards the left. Smith and Boyle, holding the infantry well in hand, Mendenhall again got their range and poured in shot and shell on the new position. The enemy's line now commenced a retrograde movement, which both Nelson and Crittenden vigorously pushed. The brigade of Wood arrived soon after and joined in the pursuit, and the left was safe."

The center, meantime, under McCook, had driven the enemy to the woods after a sharp fight.

About two o'clock in the afternoon, upon the arrival of Buell's fresh troops, the Confederates commenced a general retreat. A stand was made by them at the distance of eight hundred yards and their artillery was opened upon us; but Crittenden drove them and captured a battery. On the succeeding day General Sherman pursued the retreating columns of the enemy, capturing a Rebel cavalry camp and a quantity of ammunition; but owing to almost impassable roads, our pursuit soon terminated. Clothing, accoutrements and small arms marked the course of the flying rebels.

Beauregard placed his loss at one thousand, seven hundred and twenty-eight killed, eight thousand and twelve wounded, and nine hundred and fifty-nine missing. The Union loss was one thousand six hundred and fourteen killed, seven thousand seven hundred and twenty-one wounded, and three thousand nine hundred and sixty-three missing.

On the ninth, Beauregard sent a flag to General Grant asking permission to bury their dead, but Grant replied that the dead of both armies were already buried. This Golgotha received the woful number of three thousand three hundred and forty-two.

Two years after the battle, in refutation of hostile criticism, General Sherman published a voluntary statement vindicating Grant's management of the battle of the sixth. General Grant in turn, speaks in the highest terms of Sherman's services on that day, stating that it was to his individual efforts he was indebted for the success of that battle.

Thus another field of renown was added to the list, so rapidly increased during those years, where valor won deathless laurels, and principle was reckoned weightier than life.

Peacefully the Tennessee flows between its banks onward to the ocean, nor tells aught of the bloody struggle on its shore. Quietly the golden grain ripens in the sun, and the red furrow of war is supplanted by the plowshares of peace. To the child born within the shadow of this battle-field, who listens wonderingly to a recital of the deeds of this day, the heroes of Shiloh will, mayhap, appear like the dim figures of a dream, shadowy and unreal, but the results they helped to bring about are the tissue of a people's life, the dust he treads is the sacred soil from which sprang the flowers of freedom, and the institutions for which these men died, make his roof safe over his head.

CHAPTER XIII.

WILLIAMSBURG.

Battle of Williamsburg.—Scene of the Battle.—Historic Monuments.—College of William and Mary.—Washington and Patrick Henry.—Amusing Inscriptions on Tombstones.—The Battle Opens.—Attack of General Hooker.—Approaches to Fort McGruder.—Bravery of Kearney.—Gallantry of General Heintzelman.—Defeat and Retreat of the Enemy.

WILLIAMSBURG, the scene of one of the most sanguinary struggles of the Peninsular campaign, was for many years the seat of government as well as the most important town in the colonial history of Virginia. Captain John Smith laid the foundation of Jamestown in the year 1607; and this was for more than eighty years the center of influence and authority in the colony. But in 1697 the principal officers of the government removed to Williamsburg, which is four miles from Jamestown.

Of Jamestown, once and for ever famous as a landmark in the early annals of American history, nothing now remains but the tower of an ancient church and its broken walls which cast their shadows over the graves of many of the most distinguished pioneers of the Old Dominion. Williamsburg was chosen as the capital of the colony on account of the greater healthfulness of the climate. Some of the most interesting monuments of the State are to be found here; among them the College of William and Mary. This institution was founded by King William and his Queen Mary, and endowed by them with a thousand acres of land, with duties on fur and skins, and one penny per pound on all tobacco exported from Maryland and Virginia. The fame of this college is augmented by the fact that many of the most distinguished of Virginia's sons, including Washington, Jefferson, Patrick Henry, and Madison, received their educational training within its walls. The college itself and several antiquated monuments which stand adjacent, together with residences of the olden style give to Williamsburg a decided English aspect. On a beautiful square fronting the college may be seen the statue of Lord Botetourts, one of the colonial governors; and though considerably mutilated, may still be regarded an excellent specimen of sculpture. He appears in the flowing robe of his time, with the appendage of a short sword hanging at his side. The inscription cut in bold quaint letters on the pedestal of the monument reads:

"The Right Honorable Norborne Berkley Baron de Botetourts, His Majesty's late Lieutenant and Governor-General of the Colony and Dominion of Virginia. Deeply impressed with the warmest sense of gratitude for his excellences, prudent and wise administration, and that the remembrance of those many public and social virtues, which so eminently adorned his illustrious character, might be transmitted to posterity, the General Assembly of Virginia on the twentieth day of July, Anno Domini, 1771, resolved, with one united voice, to erect this statue to his Lordship's memory. Let wisdom and justice preside in any country and the people must and will be happy."

The old capitol in which Patrick Henry started in his brilliant career as the great and unrivalled orator of Virginia, has crumbled to the dust, and nothing save a few scattered bricks is left to mark the spot whereon it stood. It was in the halls of this same building that Washington was complimented by the speaker of the House of Burgesses after the close of his distinguished career in the French and Indian war. The hero was lauded for his valor and for the honor which he had conferred upon his native State. Stammering and bewildered the young colonel stood in the presence of the venerable aristocracy and was greatly relieved by the timely command of the speaker, "Sit down Colonel Washington; your modesty is equal to your valour and that surpasses the power of any language that I possess."

In the year 1736 the first newspaper published in Virginia was issued at Williamsburg. It was a sheet twelve inches long by six inches wide, and its dawn was regarded as an important event in the journalism of the day. The publication of this primitive sheet was continued until swallowed up in the Revolution, which it helped to inaugurate by espousing the cause of the patriots.

I regret to learn from history that public schools and printing presses were looked upon with suspicion and jealously by the early authorities of Virginia. Sir William Berkley, at one time honored with the title and clothed with the dignity of Governor, by His Majesty King George III., thanked God that there were no more free schools or printing presses within the limits of his rule and hoped that these should not be known for a hundred years to come, and in accordance with his real or pretended fancies, put down the first printing press established in Virginia in 1682. Prominent among the interesting monuments of the past, is the old English Church and its adjoining graveyard where rests the bones of many of the governors, judges and military heroes who are distinguished in the early history of the colony. The inscriptions on most of the tombstones are peculiar to the times in which they had their origin, and to the present generation seem ludicrous and amusing. Rev. J. J. Marks, D.D., who participated in the Peninsular Campaign and who visited Williamsburg the day after the battle, transcribes the following inscription from a slab which among others arrested his attention on account of its quaint, eccentric style.

"Near this monument lies the body of the Honorable David Parke, of ye county of Essex, Esq., who was of the magistrates of the county eleven years, and sometime Secretary of the dominion of Virginia. He dyed ye 6th of March, Anno Domini 1679. His other felicityes weare crowned by his happy marriage with Rebecca, the daughter of George Evelyn, of the co. of Surry, Esq. She dyed ye 2nd day of January, Anno 1672, at Long Diton, co. Surrey, and left behind her a most hopeful progeny."

Thus it may be seen that to the intelligent soldier and the student of history, the field of Williamsburg is one of more than ordinary interest. Having glanced at the scene of conflict which gives name to the battle, let us take a look at the forces which are marshaled for the contest.

The bloodless and fruitless siege of Yorktown has terminated; and the Rebels, whether from motives of interest or necessity, have decided to seek a new base of operations nearer their capital. The plains of Williamsburg seem to be the chosen field and Fort McGruder the back-bone of their new line of defense.

At two o'clock in the afternoon of Monday, May the fifth, General McClellan, commanding the Army of the Potomac, found the enemy in position for battle at Lee's Mill, two miles east of Williamsburg. After the usual preliminaries of skirmishing, General Joseph Hooker, leading the advance, was instructed to make an attack; and now opened one of the most sanguinary battles of the Peninsular Campaign. The advantage of position was clearly in favor of the enemy, whose fortifications completely covered the almost impassable approaches to the field. The Federal troops were compelled to march over a narrow strip of land, on either side of which were creeks and swamps, in order to reach the open plains in front of Williamsburg. Fort McGruder, a fortification of considerable magnitude and occupied by the enemy, commanded this road. Nothing but the most invincible and undaunted bravery on the part of officers and men, enabled General Hooker with his division of but eight thousand to fight and hold in check an army of twenty thousand, which was hurled against him repeatedly at this point. Column after column was thrown against his right, left and center, but as the crag beats back the blast, so this intrepid soldier reformed his shattered ranks and pressed forward and still forward until dark defeat became a glorious victory. Hooker on this occasion exhibited that nerve and unwavering courage which has since made his name immortal and given him the highest position in the American army. For hours this general fought the combined forces of McGruder, Hill and Longstreet, and held his own until Kearney and Heintzelman were ordered forward to his support.

A great want of ability and penetration on the part of McClellan seems to have characterized the opening of this engagement; and the army and country will wonder, until the future has explained, why Hooker was allowed to struggle alone in the early part of the battle.

Coming to the relief of Hooker, the chivalrous Kearney, never outdone in deeds of bravery, here performed one of those daring feats which made him the idol of his division, and which, under the eye of the great Napoleon, would have been rewarded with the "Cross of the Legion of Honor." With the purpose of disclosing to his command the concealed position of the enemy, he called the officers of his staff together, dashed out into the open field and rode leisurely along the entire line. Five thousand guns belched forth their death-dealing missiles, bullets fell around them like hail, two of his aids and three orderlies fell dead at his side, and before he reached the end of his perilous ride, he found himself almost alone. By this daring exploit he was enabled to accomplish his object of discovering the position and strength of the enemy; then riding back to his division, he shouted, "You see my boys where to fire!" Kearney now held his own until General Hancock came up and by a flank movement forced the enemy to retire to his fortifications.

On the evening of the fifth, the Rebels withdrew from their works and continued their retreat towards Richmond, and on the following morning General McClellan at the head of his victorious army marched triumphantly through Williamsburg in pursuit of the retreating foe.

CHAPTER XIV.

SEVEN PINES.

The Preliminaries of Battle.—Cannonading and Picket-firing.—Vigorous Attack of the Confederates.—Undaunted Bravery of the Unionists.—General Casey Unjustly Censured.—Testimony of the Enemy.—Incidents of the Battle-field.—Sufferings of the Wounded. —The First Night after Battle.

THE battle of Seven Pines opened somewhat disastrously to the Union Army. Cannonading and picket-firing had been kept up so continuously that it was difficult to know when a battle was in progress. Suddenly, while our troops were at dinner, the enemy made a vigorous attack upon our picket lines, which unfortunately were not more than eighty rods in advance of our camps.

The retreating pickets were vigorously pursued into camp, and in an instant the artillery and musketry of the Rebels brought our forces to a realization of the fact that no idle thunder or blank cartridges aroused them from their coffee. From every quarter, long lines of the enemy rushed out of the forest into the open field, and with a wild yell peculiar to the Southern soldier, charged the advanced battalions of General Casey's division. Several regiments jumped into line and stood their ground until half of their number strewed the plain. All the artillery horses were killed and the captured guns were turned upon them. General Casey now fell back a few hundred yards, and reforming his little division, again defied the onset of the enemy. And here for three hours less than six thousand men fought and held in check a force of twenty thousand; for the command of General Casey at the opening of the engagement did not exceed eight thousand men, and two thousand of their number were placed *hors de combat* in the first attack; thus crippled, the division had to sustain for so long a period this unequal contest, which would have defeated and demoralized less brave and determined soldiers.

It was thought for some time in military circles, that General Casey's defense was not so resolute as it should have been; but to his credit be it said, that the enemy, who is not expected to be over generous in the bestowal of praise upon a foe, spoke in the highest terms of his bravery, and said that his troops fought as well as they had ever known fresh and undisciplined regiments to fight, and that they met from them a far more vigorous resistance than they had anticipated. They said that the position of General Casey was one of the greatest peril. Thrown in advance of Hooker and Kearney three miles, if they threw against him a large force it was almost impossible to reinforce him in time to prevent defeat. That they had expected to cut his division to pieces, and before reinforcements could possibly arrive drive back the shattered regiments to bear with them consternation and panic.

But so far from this being realized, the unyielding firmness of this division prevented their cutting through our left wing, capturing a part and demoralizing the whole; for it held out against them until reinforcements came up. It was a gratification to hear this vindication of General Casey, and to see him relieved of those charges which, under the circumstances, were so unjust and painful.

The first night after a battle is always filled with indescribable horrors. Men in their death struggles begging for a cup of water; shivering under the knife of the surgeon as he amputates their mangled limbs; or praying, perhaps, that they may be spared to see their native hills once more, and the loved ones at home.

Rev. J. J. Marks, from whom we have previously quoted and who was with the Union Army at Seven Pines, thus describes the events which followed the battle. "During the entire night the wounded were brought in until they covered the grounds around the house of Mr. Savage, and filled all the out-houses, barns, and sheds.

"Lying alongside of our wounded men, were many Confederate soldiers and officers; and to the honor of our men be it said, I heard no words of anger or reproach, but the Rebels were uniformly treated as kindly as the Union soldiers.

"All night the surgeons were occupied in amputations, and, under the circumstances, they found it impossible to attend to many whose condition required food and stimulants.

"Wounded men suffer greatly from cold and shiver as in winter, or with an ague. It was therefore essential to lift them from the damp ground and cover them as far as possible.

"In the course of the evening twenty or thirty soldiers from different regiments, who had borne in upon their shoulders their wounded comrades, permitted me to organize them into a corps of nurses. Colonel M'Kelvy, than whom no man was more active for the relief of our men, furnished twenty bales of hay, a thousand blankets, and permitted me to draw on the Commissary Department for coffee, sugar, and crackers to an indefinite amount. The nurse-soldiers soon spread down this hay and many a shivering wounded man when lifted from the damp earth and placed upon the soft grass bed with a blanket spread over him, poured out his gratitude in a thousand blessings. When this was done we followed with hot coffee, and found our way to every suffering man. Everywhere we were compelled to place our feet in streams of blood; one spectacle of anguish and agony only succeeded another. The mind was overwhelmed and benumbed by such scenes of accumulated misery. Where there was so much to be done, and where we could do so little, the temptation was to hurry away from such painful spectacles, and remember them only as the visions of a frightful dream. Great must be the cause which demands such a sacrifice. Here and there over the grounds were seen through that night a circle of lanterns moving around the tables of amputators. Every few moments there was a shriek of some poor fellow under the knife, and one after another the sufferers were brought forward and laid down before the surgeons on stretchers, each waiting his turn.

"And then again one with face as white as marble,

and every line telling that he had passed through a suffering, the utmost which human nature could endure, was borne away and laid down for some kind-hearted man to pour into his lips a few drops of brandy, to lift up his head and give him the assurance of life and sympathy. There a brother knelt and wept over a dying brother, and his voice, broken with sobs, begged me to come and pray that his brother might be able to see Jesus and depart in peace. There a father held up in his arms a dying son and was receiving his last message to mother, sister, and brother; here a group of sympathizing soldiers stood around a dying companion who was loudly bewailing his early death and that he should never see again the loved associates of his youth. There, four or five were holding in their strong arms one whose brain having been pierced with a ball, and deprived of reason, was strong in the frantic energy of madness; here a beckoning hand urged me to come and at the sufferer's request sit down by his side and tell him what he must do to be saved. There was whispered a story of disobedience, of crime, that now stung like a serpent and bit like an adder. Another begged me to come early in the morning and write a line to father or wife. Others entreated that they should not be compelled to submit to the knife of the operator, but that their limbs might be spared them for they felt sure that under the surgeon's hand they should die. Others begged that some board might bear their names and be placed at the head of their graves.

"If I turned from these scenes on the open ground and entered into any of the houses, spots of blood stained the steps and the stairs. In the halls were lying alongside of each other many of the wounded and dead. The rooms were crowded with sufferers broken and shattered in every conceivable way by the enginery of death.

"From the mouth of one was running a stream of blood; another was upheld in the arms of a friend and gasping for breath, and the deep and unnaturally bright eye told that all the energies of life were summoned to the struggle.

"One lying on the floor, told by his loud snore, of the injury done to the brain, and that he in all probability would never open his eyes; and another begged for help that he might change his position and relieve the suffering of his shattered thigh.

'Night of nights! who can tell thy tales of woe?'

"At one place where a wounded soldier was panting his last, I was summoned. He begged me to pray for him, and taking from his finger a gold ring, he asked me to send it to his wife who had given it to him on the day of their marriage, and now he wished it to be restored to her. In a few moments the last battle was fought and the soldier was asleep. On examining the ring I found underneath the wrappings of a thread the initials 'J. S. to C. B.' This had been done to preserve the letters, and was the careful act of human love, anxious to preserve a sacred memento. In another group of sufferers I found a little boy, apparently not more than twelve years of age; the long hair thrown back from the beautiful forehead, enabled me to see by the lantern light a very child-like face.

His right leg had been amputated above his knee, and he was lying motionless and apparently breathless, and as white as snow. I bent over him and put my fingers on his wrist, and discovered to my surprise the faint trembling of a pulse. I immediately said to my attendant:

"'Why, the child is alive!'

"'Yes, sir,' said he, opening his eyes, 'I am alive; will you not send me to my mother?'

"'And where is your mother?' said I, 'my child?'

"'In Sumpterville, South Carolina,' he replied.

"'Oh! yes, my son, we will certainly send you to your mother.'

"'Well, well,' said he, 'that is kind; I will go to sleep now.'"

CHAPTER XV.

FAIR OAKS.

Positions Occupied by the Contending Forces.—General Hooker Commences the Action.—Advance of Sickles, Grover, and Robinson.—General Kearney and Colonel Hicks Protect the Flanks.—Both Armies Enveloped in a Cloud of Smoke.—The Engagement Becomes General.—Defeat of the Rebels.—They Fly to Their Entrenchments.—McClellan Orders a Cessation of Hostilities.—Renewal of the Battle.—Rout and Final Defeat of the Enemy.

THE battle of Fair Oaks was the first of a grand and never-to-be-forgotten series of engagements known as "The Seven Days' Battles." On the twenty-fifth of June, 1862, McClellan instructed General Heintzelman, then in command of the left wing of his army, to advance his entire front towards the enemy. For many days previous to this movement, the army had anticipated the order to advance, as everything seemed in readiness for a renewed demontration against Richmond.

It was determined as a first step in the programme to attack and drive the enemy from his rifle pits and earthworks and establish our lines where his then were. The accomplishment of this design was committed to General Hooker, a brave and sagacious officer who had already been tried in several of the most sanguinary battles of the Peninsular Campaign.

In front of Hooker's lines was a thick undergrowth of scrub-oaks, vines, and ragged bushes skirting a multitude of ponds and marshes. This swampy wilderness was from four to six hundred yards wide, and beyond stretched an open field of eighty rods in width. In this clearing were located the rifle-pits, earthworks and redoubts of the enemy.

The assaulting column was comprised of the brigades of Sickles, Grover, and Robinson.

General Kearney was directed to protect the left flank, and Colonel Hicks with the Nineteenth Massachusetts Infantry was commanded to advance to and cover the right.

All necessary appointments having been made, the three brigades, led by General Hooker, advanced cautiously but firmly into the forest, and after having proceeded about two hundred yards, encountered and pushed back the Rebel pickets to their main reserves. This demonstration was quickly followed by a spirited skirmish which soon resulted in rapid and incessant firing along the entire line. In a few moments the forest was a scene of furious contest and the ominous quiet was succeeded by the terrible din and clash of arms and the roar of cannon and musketry.

Both armies were, for a time, enveloped in a cloud of smoke, which rising up and twisting itself among the trees, hung over the contending forces as a pall of darkness: and then streams of fire like angry lightnings shot athwart the sky; and anon, a courier would dash out from the gloom, covered with blood and dust, bearing dispatches or hastening for orders.

In less than half an hour after driving in the pickets,

the divisions of Hooker and Kearney were involved in the liveliest action. The arrival of fresh troops on both sides was an evidence that a decisive battle was courted by the contestants.

The Federal troops pushed steadily forward routing the Confederates, and driving them from the forest into the open field beyond, over which they fled and sought protection in their intrenchments.

Our men now raised a shout of triumph which was caught up by regiment after regiment and borne through the army.

General Grover was about ordering an assault against the Rebels in their defences when he received an order from General McClellan to halt his brigade. From an erroneous impression concerning the actual condition of the forces engaged he ordered General Hooker to retire from the field of victory, and return to the position occupied before the battle; but when McClellan subsequently came upon the field, he ordered our troops to advance and re-occupy the woods and fields they had taken, and before night the Confederates were driven out of their rifle-pits and from the fields, and we had gained a victory which cost us nearly a thousand of our best men in killed and wounded.

The Rebels smarting under the punishment they had received in the afternoon, came out in force at six o'clock in the evening and re-opened the battle by attacking General Robinson's brigade.

This last onset was the closing scene in the battle of Fair Oaks, and was a bitter, earnest struggle for the fruits of conflict. The Confederates made a very determined charge led by a very brave regiment of Georgians, but they were met by men equally brave and determined, and receiving a check at the points of our bayonets were speedily repulsed and driven back leaving four hundred of their number dead on the field. The Federal troops were under arms the entire night following this engagement, with instructions to be prepared to advance at a moment's notice. Every now and then there was an attack upon some portion of our lines, the Confederates seemingly determined to regain by surprise or strategy what they had lost during the day; but it was subsequently ascertained that these apparently futile assaults were only feints intended to occupy our attention and to prevent McClellan sending reinforcements to the right wing of his army.

When McClellan on the twenty-fifth ordered an advance upon the Confederate works, our army was full of hope, believing that we were then taking the initiatory step in a series of actions which would in a few days place us in possession of Richmond. We were successful at Fair Oaks and confident that the next day would enable us to overcome half of the obstacles that disputed our march to the Rebel capitol. At an early hour on the morning of Thursday, the twenty-sixth, the roar of battle was heard along the Chickahominy.

This was the hotly contested battle of Mechanicsville, the second of the Seven Days' Battles which was successively followed with varying fortune, by Gains' Mills, Savage Station, White Oak Swamp, Glendale, and Malvern Hill.

CHAPTER XVI.

MALVERN HILL.

Battle of Malvern Hill.—The Final Engagement of the Peninsular Campaign.—Scene of the Battle.—Influence of our Gunboats.—Attack of the Rebels led by General Magruder.—Destructive Fire from Federal Cannon.—The Rebels Repulsed.—They Reform and Charge Again.—Another Tempest of Fire from our Batteries Sweeps them from the Field.—Their Guns are Silenced, the Horses Killed and Regiments Cut Down.—McClellan Orders a Retreat to Harrison's Landing.—Indignation of the Army.—General Kearney Protests Against the Order for Retreat.—General Martindale Sheds Tears of Shame.

MALVERN HILL, the scene of the final engagement of the Peninsular campaign, is an elevation of nearly two hundred feet and fronts on James river to the south, which flows lazily along at a distance of between two and three miles. To the north it faces an open field of from a half to two-thirds of a mile in length and one-third in width. To the north and east is a gentle, undulating slope, but to the south and west it is quite rugged and difficult of ascent.

On this elevated plain stands an old-fashioned but decidedly substantial country-seat, known as the Crew House, surrounded by a large number of out-houses which are embosomed in a multitude of vines and trees.

A bright, magnificent, enchanting prospect opened to the eyes of the Federal troops as they took position on Malvern Hill. From the darkness and gloom of the Chickahominy swamps and from fields trodden into barrenness, they were brought to gaze upon a country which had not as yet felt the devastating tread of armies.

The story of this battle has been so eloquently told by an eye-witness, that I cannot refrain from quoting it here. He says that during the night previous to the battle, rifle pits were dug under the guns, in the slope. The troops in these pits were covered with straw and freshly-reaped grain, and the glasses of the officers of the Confederate army could not see that before they could take these batteries, they would have to encounter ten thousand bayonets.

The strength of our position was increased by the presence of five gun-boats, ready at a moment's notice to open in action. The moral influence of these on our army was very manifest.

During the morning the enemy, now under the command of General Magruder, assisted by Jackson, Longstreet, Hill, and Huger, advanced from different points shelling the woods as they slowly felt their way, and at length, about noon, their skirmishers discovered our position. The field in our front was about three-fourths of a mile long and half a mile wide, and beyond it a deep, dark, pine forest. On the edge of this field at different points General Magruder threw out batteries and regiments, for what purpose could not be known; and no sooner were they disclosed than they brought on them a rain of death. In a moment the regiments were swept away like chaff before a storm.

The horses were killed at the guns, the carriages were tossed into a thousand fragments, the caissons were exploded, and the gunners who still lived, escaped into the shelter of the woods.

About four o'clock in the afternoon General Magruder ordered an advance along the entire left wing of his line ; and there were brought out into the field several divisions and batteries. Prominent among these were the brigades of Toombs, Cobb, Wright, and Armisted, among the finest troops in the Southern army. They were sustained by about twenty pieces of artillery thrown out into the plain. The first column advanced with steady step towards our batteries ; but long before it reached the middle of the open ground, the troops were met by such an iron tempest, that the few who survived fell to the ground, and abandoning their guns commenced crawling back on their faces towards the forest.

A second column with a courage which on the part of their officers was madness, but was at the moment the admiration of our army, ran out into the open field and pressed towards our death-dealing cannon.

These again were mowed down. They rallied, feebly shouted defiance, pressed into the cloud of smoke, and another tempest of fire lighted up the scene for a moment and that column was gone. Here and there a straggler emerged from the smoke and ran across the field to his friends ; he was but one, while the hundreds were lying mangled and dead on the plain.

A third column was thrown out from the cover of

the forest; fresh batteries were brought into play, and when the smoke had slightly lifted up from the field, the terrific conflict was renewed; again the guns of the Confederates were silenced, the horses killed, the caissons on fire, and the regiments cut down; re-forming, now prostrate, and then springing forward, until their thinned and ragged lines, as they came within musket range, presented so pitiable a spectacle that our men fired with little purpose to kill.

About half-past five o'clock in the afternoon, a powerful body of troops from General Magruder's center were advanced into the field; their orders were to press forward over every obstacle.

There is every reason to believe that these troops had been rendered insensible to fear by whiskey drugged with gunpowder; and undeterred by the fate of those who had perished in previous attacks, with shouts and yells they pressed on towards our men. Many pieces of our cannon opened upon them and grape and shell swept through their lines; treading on the dead, pressing down the living who had fallen to the ground, they with unwavering step still advanced; emboldened by their example, other regiments ran out with wild cheers from the forest; on and on over the field of carnage they advanced; every discharge of our guns made great gaps in their lines, but instantly closing up, they pressed forward: another sheet of flame would spread out over the field and the roar and thunder followed, moving the ground as if trembling in the convulsion of an earthquake.

MALVERN HILL.

When the smoke cleared away a little, the broken columns were seen still with fiery madness pressing on. Already they had begun to ascend the slope, and had succeeded in coming so near that our artillery could no longer so damagingly sweep the ground.

With all the frenzy of maniacs they still ran towards us ; the efforts of the artillery were re-doubled ; the men at our guns turned pale and stood aghast ; another moment and the day might be lost ;—just then up sprang our concealed men in the rifle-pits, and a long stream of fire darted forth from a thousand muskets, and springing forward with fixed bayonet, they met the foe who quailed, wavered and then renewed the conflict, but it was in vain ; with the insanity of men who sought death, they still continued the struggle, and a long line of their dead at the base of this hill, bore witness to the severity and destructiveness of the contest. The whole scene at this time was one of terror and appalling splendor.

The batteries on the heights continued to pour a constant and withering fire into the forests where the forces of the enemy were concealed, and simultaneously the thunder of a hundred great guns shook the hill and caused the waters of the river to tremble. The firing of the gunboats added very much to the overpowering grandeur of the hour. The shells discharged from the monster guns of these vessels rushed through the air with a frightful shriek that was heard above the roar of battle ; then when they entered the forests, great trees were shivered into a thousand fragments, the branches were torn from others and tossed into the heavens, or thrown far into the deep shades, and when they burst, it was with an explosion that shook the earth for miles. The terror inspired by these shells was such as to deprive the rebels of all courage and they fled into the deeper recesses of the forest.

The contest in front of the rifle-pits was but short, for, unable to bear up against the impetuous attack of our men, the enemy endeavored to remove their broken columns from the field. As they fled they were pursued three-fourths of a mile by the Union troops and the entire Rebel army was struck with a panic; and if at this moment we could have brought ten thousand reserves into the field, we might have marched back again and re-taken all we had lost, and without any difficulty reached Richmond;—this statement will be amply confirmed in subsequent chapters.

On the fleeing columns of the enemy, our batteries and gun-boats continued to fire until ten o'clock at night, throwing the shells into the forests; for hours not a gun replied and not even a courier dared to show himself in the open field.

The battle was over, but the cannonading still continued, and shells and balls of every kind tore through the woods in a ceaseless whirlwind of fury. In the meantime, thousands of the Confederates fled in the wildest disorder from the scene, and hid themselves in swamps and hollows:—soldiers without guns, horsemen without caps and swords came to the hospitals on the battle-field of Glendale and reported that their regiments and brigades were swept away and that they alone were "escaped to tell the tale".

It is one of the strangest things in this week of disaster that General McClellan ordered a retreat to Harrison's Landing, six miles down the James river, after we had gained so decided a victory. When this order was received by the impatient and eager army, consternation and amazement overwhelmed our patriotic and ardent hosts. Some refused to obey the command. General Martindale shed tears of shame.

The brave and chivalrous Kearney said in the presence of many officers; "I, Philip Kearney, an old soldier, enter my solemn protest against this order for retreat,—we ought, instead of retreating, to follow up the enemy and take Richmond. And in full view of all the responsibility of such a declaration, I say to you all, such an order can only be prompted by cowardice or treason."

And with all, hopelessness and despair succeeded the flush of triumph. In silence and gloom our victorious army commenced retiring from an enemy utterly broken, scattered, and panic-stricken.

And when there was not a foe within miles of us, we left our wounded behind to perish, and any one witnessing the wild eagerness of our retreat, would have supposed that we were in the greatest peril from a vigilant and triumphant enemy. During the nights of the first and second of July we were visited by one of the heaviest of rain-storms: this continued for twenty-four hours without intermission, until the entire Peninsula was covered with water, and rivers rushed where there had been only little streams. In this storm, on the morning of Wednesday, the army fell down to Berkely or Harrison's Landing. This was done on account of the superiority of the landing,

James river at this point being broad and deep. The position was of such a character that the army could be shielded from any force the enemy could bring against us. We could have taken many of his abandoned guns from the field, but satisfied ourselves with carrying off all our own with incredible difficulty, over worse than Crimean roads. We retired to Harrison's Landing without the enemy making any demonstration in our rear: and weary and exhausted by struggles and battles which have probably no parallel in human history, our troops found rest. And of the Grand Army of the Potomac, fifty-eight thousand remained, and sixty thousand were in the hospitals, lying wounded on the field, or killed in battle.

Our loss in the battle of Malvern Hill was slight compared with that of other days. But the loss of the enemy on this single field was fully equal in killed and wounded to our losses in the seven days.

CHAPTER XVII.

CEDAR MOUNTAIN.

The Battle-ground.—Jackson *En route* for Culpepper.—Occupancy of Cedar Mountain.—Three Miles of Batteries.—Banks Receives the Attack.—A Rain of Fire.—Charge on Enemy's Battery.—Overwhelmed by Superior Numbers.—Ricketts to the Front.—Enemy Compelled to Fall Back.—Artillery Battle at Night.—Interment of Fallen Braves.—Losses.—The Enemy Retires.—Cedar Mountain Occupied by Union Troops.

THE first stopping-point south of Brandy Station on the Orange and Alexandria railroad in Virginia, is Culpepper Court House. Midway between this point and the banks of the Rapidan, rises Cedar Mountain, a cone-shaped elevation with wooded sides and grassy slopes which gave its name to the engagement fought here, August ninth, 1862.

For nearly a month the forces of the enemy under Stonewall Jackson had been watching the line of the Rapidan, and when General Pope marched towards Culpepper Court House, the enemy made haste to push his forces in that direction, to cut off, if possible, the Union advance before the main body of the Federal army could come up. The Confederates did not reach Culpepper Court House, but at day-break on the ninth held Cedar Mountain and were intrenched behind its wooded heights.

They also occupied a range of heights and ravines westward of the mountain.

One mile away, on an elevated plateau extending to the eastward for the distance of a mile and westward an equal distance, General Banks drew up his army in battle array to receive the attack of the Confederates. At three o'clock in the afternoon, the pickets on our right were driven in and a battery directly in our front opened on us at long range. Then there came pouring in upon our troops a red rain of fire from batteries unmasking on the hill-side and arranged in a semicircle for a distance of three miles.

For two hours did this storm of destruction sweep our ranks. Cross fires and flank fires were received at every point. The enemy outnumbered us in men and in guns besides having the advantage of position. But up to five o'clock our batteries replied to theirs shot for shot.

Then it was that the enemy opened an enfilading fire on our right and General Banks gave orders to reserve fire and charge the Confederate guns.

Crawford's Brigade of Williams' Division made the charge and the Forty-sixth Pennsylvania regiment led the van. But a withering fire proceeding from a thicket of scrub oaks just back of the Confederate battery, mowed down the Union ranks with great slaughter.

The commands of Augur and Williams were brought to the support of the advance, but the overwhelming numbers of the enemy, his advantage of position and the great gaps in our lines compelled General Banks to fall gradually back, meeting as he did so the supports of Pope which were in close proximity.

General Pope at once ordered Ricketts to the front where his battery was used with such effect on the Confederates who attempted to follow up Banks, that they retired in confusion to their old position, sustaining considerable loss in the encounter.

A sharp artillery battle was kept up between the contestants until midnight, the battle-ground of the day previous being occupied by neither army, but swept by the guns of both. The hours of the tenth of August—the day after the battle—were occupied by our soldiers in giving burial to their fallen comrades. Dust was consigned to dust on the field where they fell, and another strike for country was recorded, at what precious cost of life!

During the night of the eleventh, Stonewall Jackson re-crossed the Rapidan and retired in the direction of Orange Court-House. The Union loss in this drawn battle was about eighteen hundred in killed, wounded, and missing, besides about one thousand stragglers who went back beyond Culpepper Court House and never entirely rejoined their commands.

General Prince was taken prisoner, and Generals Augur, Geary, and Carroll were severely wounded. General Banks, colliding with a runaway horse, was thrown from his own and injured.

The enemy's loss was nearly the same as ours, and Generals Winder and Trimble were killed. A heavy cavalry force under Buford and Bayard went in pursuit of the enemy and captured many stragglers. The Union head-quarters were now placed at Cedar Mountain and our forces advanced to the Rapidan.

General Pope, believing that the enemy's forces in his front were unnecessarily strong for reconnoitering purposes only, called in all his available troops. He was joined on the eleventh by King from Fredericksburg and on the fourteenth by General Reno with eight thousand men. The programme for the succeeding ten or twelve days was varied by the camp, the march, and the skirmish-line.

CHAPTER XVIII.

BRANDY STATION.

First Battle.—Lee Resumes Hostilities.—Stuart's Cavalry Attack.—Gallant Repulse by Kilpatrick.—Second Battle.—Skirmish at Kelly's Ford.—Splendid Charge of the Union Army.—Complete Rout of the Enemy.—Heroic Feats on the Field.—Charge of the First Maine.—Fall of Colonel Davis.—Third Battle.—The Enemy Swept from the Plains.—Prisoners and Materials of War Captured.—Fourth Battle.—Critical Situation of Kilpatrick.—Bravery of Custer and Davies.—The Exultant Battle-Cry.—Fresh Laurels for the Union Troops.—Scene on the Battle-field.—The Writer's Part in the Four Contests.

THE words Brandy Station will ever excite a multitude of thrilling memories in the minds of all cavalry-men who saw service in Virginia; for this was the grand cavalry battle-ground of the war.

On these historic plains our Bayard, Stoneman, and Pleasanton have successively led their gallant troopers against the commands of Stuart, Lee, and Hampton. The twentieth of August, 1862, the ninth of June, twelfth of September, and eleventh of October, 1863, are days which cannot soon be forgotten by the "Boys in Blue" who crossed sabres with the Confederates at Brandy Station.

Converging and diverging roads at this point quite naturally brought the cavalry of the contending armies together whenever we advanced to or retired from the Rapidan. Being both the advance and rear guard of the opposing forces, our horsemen always found themselves face to face with the foe on this field; in fact most of our cavalry men were so confident of a fight here that as soon as we discovered that we were approaching the Station we prepared for action by tightening our saddle-girths and inspecting our arms.

First Brandy Station.

Upon the withdrawal of the Army of the Potomac from the Peninsula, General Lee, contemplating the invasion of Maryland and Pennsylvania, started his army northward with the view, no doubt, of driving Pope from Northern Virginia and carrying the Confederate standard into the loyal states. The battle of Cedar Mountain temporarily checked his forward movement and compelled him to retire to the south bank of the Rapidan. The re-appearance of Rebel skirmishers at the various fords of this river on the morning of August eighteenth, 1862, was an evidence to our pickets that the enemy was about to resume hostilities.

General Pope at once ordered his artillery and infantry to retire beyond the Rappahannock, while General Bayard commanding the cavalry was charged with covering the rear of the retiring army. We disputed the advance of the Rebels so stubbornly that they found no opportunity to interfere with the retreat of the main column. The morning of the twentieth found the "Harris Light," Tenth New York, First Pennsylvania, First Maine, First Rhode Island, and First New Jersey Cavalry bivouacked at Brandy Station.

The engagement opened at six o'clock by an attack of Stuart's cavalry upon the Harris Light, acting as rear-guard of Bayard's Brigade.

This preliminary onset was speedily repulsed by the Harris Light, which regiment kept the enemy in check until General Bayard had gained sufficient time to enable him to form his command at a more favorable point, two miles north of the Station on the direct road to the Rappahannock. Here the Harris Light, led by Colonel Kilpatrick and Major Davies, again charged the advance regiments of the Confederate column, thus opening the series of memorable conflicts at Brandy Station and adding fresh laurels to its already famous record. A deep cut in a hill through which the Orange and Alexandria Railroad passes, checked our pursuit, else we should have captured many prisoners. The First New Jersey and First Pennsylvania coming to our relief enabled us to reform our broken squadrons, and as Pope had instructed General Bayard not to bring on a general engagement the cavalry now crossed the Rappahannock and awaited the orders of the general-in-chief.

SECOND BRANDY STATION.

The battle of Chancellorsville did not materially change the positions of the contending armies, but General Lee, emboldened by his success in compelling his new adversary to retrace his steps across the Rappahannock, began at once to put himself in a condition to take the offensive. This activity in the Rebel camp soon determined General Hooker to make a reconnoisance in force, and he accordingly instructed General Pleasanton, now in command of the cavalry corps, to proceed to Culpepper, break up Stuart's encampment at that point and ascertain, if possible, the whereabouts and probable destination of the Confederate Chief.

At eight o'clock in the afternoon of June eighth, the Cavalry Corps moved from its temporary headquarters at Warrenton Junction towards the Rappahannock. We moved in two columns, one taking the road to Beverly and the other to Kelly's Ford.

Early on the morning of the ninth we arrived at the river, where it was evident we were not expected in force, for we found nothing but a strong picket guard to contest our advance.

A brief though brisk skirmish took place at Kelly's Ford between the Harris Light Cavalry, acting as vanguard of the column under Kilpatrick, and the Confederate pickets. The latter were quickly driven back, and the division began to cross over. On reaching the south bank of the stream, the column was reformed and we advanced several miles at a trot and gallop, the men meantime cutting from their saddles overcoats, blankets, forage, and in short everything which was found to be an obstruction to speed.

The column at Beverly Ford, commanded by General Gregg, had been engaged since early in the morning, and the roaring of light arms and the booming of cannon clearly indicated to us that hot work was being done by our comrades below. It had been hoped that the column would be able to strike the enemy in flank at Brandy Station, in the early part of the day, giving us an opportunity to rake them furiously in front. Hence we were somewhat retarded in our movements, waiting or expecting the combinations and juxtapositions which had been planned. But failing in this, at length we advanced towards the Station, where at ten o'clock we engaged a regiment of Stuart's cavalry. As soon as we reached the field which they had evidently selected for the fight, we charged them in a splendid manner, routing them completely, and capturing many prisoners. Light artillery was used briskly on both sides. By twelve o'clock, Pleasanton's entire force had effected a union, after much severe fighting on the left, and the engagement became general.

The infantry fought side by side with the cavalry. There was some grand manœuvering on that historic field, and feats were performed worthy of heroes. One incident should be particularized. At a critical moment, when the formidable and ever-increasing hosts of the enemy were driving our forces from a desirable position we sought to gain, and when it seemed as though disaster to our arms would be fatal, Kilpatrick's battle-flag was seen advancing followed by the tried squadrons of the Harris Light, the Tenth New York, and the First Maine. In echelons of squadrons our brigade was quickly formed, and we advanced like a storm-cloud upon the Rebel cavalry which filled the field before us. The Tenth New York received the first shock of the Rebel charge, but was hurled back, though not in confusion. The Harris Light met with no better success; and, notwithstanding its prestige and power, we were repulsed under the very eye of our chief, whose excitement at the scene was well-nigh uncontrollable. His flashing eye now turned to the First Maine, a regiment composed mostly of heavy, sturdy men who had not been engaged as yet during the day, and, riding to the head of the column, he shouted, "Men of Maine, you must save the day! Follow me!" With one simultaneous war-cry these giants of the North moved forward in one solid mass upon the flank of the Rebel columns. The shock was overwhelming; and the opposing lines crumbled like a "bowing wall" before this wild rush of prancing horses, gleaming sabres, and rattling balls.

On rode Kilpatrick with the men of Maine, and, on meeting the two regiments of his brigade, which had been repulsed and were returning from the front, the General's voice rang out like clarion notes above the din of battle, "Back, the Harris Light! Back, the Tenth New York! Re-form your squadrons and charge!" With magical alacrity the order was obeyed, and the two regiments which had been so humbled by their first reverse, now rushed into the fight with a spirit and success which redeemed them from censure, and accounted them worthy of their gallant leader. The commanding position was won; a battery lost in a previous charge was re-captured, and an effectual blow was given to the enemy which greatly facilitated the movements which followed. But the Rebel cavalry was greatly emboldened and strengthened by reënforcements of infantry which were brought in railroad cars from Culpepper. We, however, continued to press them closely until six o'clock in the afternoon, when, by a grand charge of

BRANDY STATION.

our entire force, we gained an important position, which ended the contest.

Heavy columns of Rebel infantry could now be distinctly seen advancing over the plains from the direction of Culpepper, to the rescue of their fairly-beaten cavalry. But it was too late for them, for we had won a splendid victory, and had gained all the information of Rebel movements which we desired to obtain. Under cover of the night we re-crossed the Rappahannock in safety.

The whole command had lost about five hundred-men, and we brought over with us one hundred prisoners. In the early part of the engagement, fell Colonel Davis, of the Eighth New York Cavalry, who was instantly killed. His loss was a subject of general lamentation. He had distinguished himself for great sagacity, wonderful powers of endurance, and unsurpassed bravery. He it was who led the cavalry safely from Harper's Ferry, just before Miles' surren der of the place, and who, on his way to Pennsylvania, captured Longstreet's ammunition train.

Among our wounded was Colonel Percy Wyndham. The enemy's killed included Colonel Saul Williams, of the Second North Carolina, and Lieutenant-Colonel Frank Hampton, of the South Carolina Cavalry. They acknowledged a loss of six hundred men.

Two important ends were reached by this advance; namely, first, a cavalry raid contemplated by Stuart, who had massed his forces near Culpepper, was utterly frustrated; and second, General Pleasanton ascertained conclusively, that General Lee was marching his army northward, with the evident design of invading the Northern States. Indeed, it was a suspicion of such a movement that led General Hooker to order the reconnoissance.

The day following this glorious fight, in which the men of the North had proved themselves to be more than a match for the boasted Southern chivalry, and had gained a name which placed Pleasanton's command at the head of the world's cavalry forces, Pleasanton was made a Major-General, and Kilpatrick a Brigadier. Their stars were well deserved and proudly won.

THIRD BRANDY STATION.

On the eleventh of September, 1863, General Meade ordered the cavalry to be withdrawn from the various picket posts along the Rappahannock, and instructed to be in readiness to take the advance in a forward movement against the enemy. At an early hour on the following morning the entire cavalry corps, acting as vanguard to the Army of the Potomac, was advancing towards the Rappahannock.

In order that the enemy might not be prematurely warned of our designs, the several commands were ordered to make as little noise as possible. Consequently, the bugle-calls were dispensed with, and the officers conveyed their orders from rank to rank in a whisper.

The three division commanders, Buford, Gregg, and Kilpatrick, were instructed to cross the river as follows:—Gregg at Sulphur Springs, Buford at Rappahannock Bridge, and Kilpatrick at Kelly's Ford.

At six o'clock in the morning, the Harris Light plunged into the river at Kelly's Ford, leading the advance as usual, when an engagement was expected at Brandy Station;—in fact, the officers and men of the Harris Light had become so familiar with this field by former experiences here that it was unquestionably policy on the part of the commander to assign to our regiment the work of measuring the ground and testing the strength of the enemy.

A strong detachment of Stuart's cavalry, consisting of pickets and reserves, opposed our crossing with dogged pertinacity, but finally, yielding to our superior numbers and to the deadly accuracy of our carbines, gave way. We then moved in the direction of Brandy Station. The farther we advanced the stronger grew the ever-accumulating force of the enemy, who disputed every inch of ground with great stubbornness. On arriving near the Station we found the enemy in strong force, with artillery posted on the surrounding hills. We saw clearly that a third cavalry fight was destined to be fought on this historic field, and we began to make preparations for the onset. It was the writer's privilege to command and lead the advance squadron against the Confederates in this fight, and I shall not soon forget the circumstance of forming my command after the first onset, for but a moment after the formation, and while sitting on my horse in front of the line, a solid shot from the Rebel artillery came crushing through our ranks, killing three men and four horses. The concussion of the ball nearly drew me from my horse, and when I turned in my saddle to mark the result, saw that not more than the width of a sabre had saved me from sharing the fate of the poor men who had been struck by the deadly missile.

We had not been fighting long before the other divisions joined us. At their approach, great enthusiasm among our boys prevailed. Before our combined force the enemy was swept from those plains like chaff before the whirlwind. They fled in the direction of Culpepper, a naturally strong and now fortified position, where we knew we must soon encounter the Rebel chivalry *en masse* upon their chosen field.

From Brandy Station, General Pleasanton directed Kilpatrick to make a detour via Stevensburg, in order to operate as a flanking column upon the enemy at the proper time. With the First and Second Divisions, Pleasanton pushed straight on to Culpepper, driving the enemy before him without much resistance until within about a mile of the town. Here our advance was effectually checked. A fearful duel now took place with varying fortune. For some time the enemy baffled all our efforts to dislodge him from his strong position, and our men began to look wishfully for the flankers, when lo! Kilpatrick's flags were seen advancing from the direction of Stevensburg, and his artillery was soon thundering on the Confederate flank and rear. Under this unexpected and well-directed fire, that portion of the enemy which had kept our main column at bay, fell back in confusion into the town; and before they had time to re-form their broken lines, the Harris Light, Fifth New York, First Vermont, and First Michigan, led by General Custer, dashed upon the "Johnnies" in the streets, throwing the boast of the chivalry into a prefect rout. Many prisoners were captured, more or less material of war, and three Blakely guns. The Rebels retreated hastily in the direction of Pony Mountain and Rapidan Bridge, whither they were closely pursued by our victorious squadrons. The day following this brilliant advance, Pleasanton occupied all the fords of the Rapidan, extending his pickets on our right as far forward as the Robertson and Hazel Rivers.

Fourth Brandy Station.

A little after sunrise on the tenth of October, 1863, the Confederates in heavy force came down upon our pickets along the Robertson River, driving us back in haste and occupying the fords. The flank movement of General Lee was fully understood. He had crossed the Rapidan, advanced to Madison Court House, and was lapping around our right wing threatening it with destruction. Quick work on our part was now necessary. Swift messengers from officers high in command, brought orders to retire with promptness, but in good order if possible.

Sharp skirmishing took place at the river, and the successive crack of carbines afforded the music of our march to James City, where the conflict deepened into a battle, which raged with fury and slaughter. The enemy, conscious of having outgeneraled us in this instance, and having at least a temporary advantage, was bold and defiant. He was met, however, with corresponding vigor. Those contesting legions, which had so often measured sabres in the fearful charge and hand-to-hand encounter, again appealed to the God of battle, and wrestled with Herculean strength for the mastery. Night came on at length to hush the strife, and the weary men and horses sought repose from the bloody fray.

With the first pencilings of the morning light of October eleventh, we took up our line of march towards the Rappahannock. Skirmishing continued nearly every step of the way. On the Sperryville pike to Culpepper, we were closely pursued and heavily pressed. At Culpepper the corps separated. Gregg, who had come by way of Cedar Mountain, passed out on the road to Sulphur Springs. Buford moved in the direction of Stevensburg, leaving Kilpatrick alone on the main thoroughfare along the railroad line. Kilpatrick, accompanied by Pleasanton, had scarcely left Culpepper, when Hampton's legions made a furious attack upon his rear-guard, with the hope of breaking through upon the main column to scatter it, or of so retarding its progress that a flanking column might fall upon him ere he could reach the safe shore of the Rappahannock.

Our infantry, which yesterday occupied this ground, had retired, leaving the cavalry to struggle out of the toils of the enemy as best it could.

Gallantly repelling every attack of the enemy, our command moved on, without expending much of its time and material, until opposite the residence of Hon. John Minor Botts, where a few regiments suddenly wheeled about, and, facing the pursuing foe, charged upon them with pistols and sabres, giving them a severe check and an unexpected repulse.

On arriving at Brandy Station, Kilpatrick found himself in a most critical situation, with an accumulation of formidable difficulties on hand, which threatened his annihilation.

Buford, who had been sharply pursued by Fitzhugh

Lee's division over the plains of Stevensburg, had retired more rapidly than Kilpatrick, and, unaware of his comrade's danger, had suffered Lee to plant his batteries on the high hills which commanded Kilpatrick's right, while the rebel troopers, in three heavy lines of battle, held the only route by which Kilpatrick could retreat. Lee's sharp shooters also occupied the woods in the immediate vicinity of Kilpatrick's columns, where they were making themselves a source of danger and great annoyance. To increase the danger of the situation, Stuart, by hard marching, had swung around to Kilpatrick's left, and had taken possession of a range of hills, planted batteries, and was preparing to charge down upon the surrounded division below.

This was a situation to try the stoutest hearts. Nothing daunted, however, by this terrific array of the enemy, Kilpatrick displayed that decision and daring which have ever characterized him as a great cavalry leader, and proved himself worthy of the brave men who composed his command. His preparation for the grand charge was soon completed.

Forming his division into three lines of battle, he assigned the right to Davies, the left to Custer, and placing himself with Pleasanton in the center advanced with unwavering determination to the contest. Having approached to within a few yards of the enemy's lines in his front, he ordered his band to strike up a national air, to whose spirit-stirring strains was joined the blast of scores of bugles, ringing forth the charge.

With his usual daring, Davies was foremost in the

fray, leading his command for the fourth time on this memorable field. To his men he addressed these stirring words: "Soldiers of the First Brigade! I know you have not forgotten the example of your brave comrades, who, in past engagements *here*, were not afraid to die in defence of the 'old flag'."

Custer, the daring, terrible demon that he was in battle, pulled off his cap and handed it to his orderly, then dashed madly forward in the charge, while his yellow locks floated like pennants on the breeze. Pennington and Elder handled their batteries with great agility and success, at times opening huge gaps in the serried ranks of the enemy.

Fired to an almost divine potency, and with a majestic madness, this band of heroic troopers shook the air with their battle-cry, and dashed forward to meet the hitherto exultant foe.

Ambulances, forges, and cannon, with pack horses and mules, non-combatants, and others, all joined to swell the mighty tide. Brave hearts grew braver, and faltering ones waxed warmer and stronger, until pride of country had touched this raging sea of thought and emotion, kindling an unconquerable principle, which emphatically affirmed every man a hero unto death. So swiftly swept forward this tide of animated power that the Rebel lines broke in wild dismay before the uplifted and firmly-grasped sabres of these unflinching veterans, who, feeling that life and country were at stake, risked them both upon the fearful issue.

Kilpatrick thus escaped disaster, defeated his pursuers, captured several pieces of the enemy's artillery, and presented to the beholders one of the grandest scenes ever witnessed in the New World.

" By Heaven! it was a splendid sight to see, for one who had no friend or brother there."

No one who looked upon that wonderful panorama, can ever forget it. On the great field were riderless horses and dying men; clouds of dust from solid shot and bursting shell occasionally obscured the sky; broken caissons and upturned ambulances obstructed the way, while long lines of cavalry were pressing forward in the charge, with their drawn sabres glistening in the bright sunlight. Far beyond the scene of tumult were the quiet dark green forests which skirt the banks of the Rappahannock. The poet Haverd, in his "Scauderberg", has well described the scene;

> Hark! the death-denouncing trumpet sounds
> The fatal charge, and shouts proclaim the onset.
> Destruction rushes dreadful to the field
> And bathes itself in blood: havoc let loose
> Now undistinguished, rages all around:
> While Ruin, seated on her dreary throne,
> Sees the plain strewed with subjects truly hers,
> Breathless and cold."

The Rebel cavalry, undoubtedly ashamed of their own conduct and defeat, reorganized their broken ranks, and again advanced upon Kilpatrick and Buford whose divisions had united to repel the attack.

For at least two long hours of slaughter these opposing squadrons dashed upon one another over this historic field. Charges and counter-charges followed in quick succession, and at times the "grey" and the "blue" were so confusedly commingled together, that it was difficult to conjecture how they could regain their appropriate places. Quite a number of prisoners were made on both sides. It was a scene of wild commotion and blood. This carnival continued until late at night, when the exhausted and beaten foe sank back upon safer grounds to rest, while our victorious braves, crowned with undying laurels, gathered up their wounded and dead companions, and unmolested, crossed the Rappahannock.

In reflecting upon the successive engagements at Brandy Station, the author feels a natural and, I trust, a commendable pride when he remembers that in each instance he shared the varied fortunes of his regiment on this field.

In the first action, on the twentieth of August, 1862, I was a corporal in the front rank of the first squadron that charged the Confederate cavalry under Stuart. My horse was wounded in the neck in this charge and the pommel of my saddle and canteen were struck with bullets.

On the ninth of June, 1863, being at that time a sergeant, I was chief of the first platoon of the first battalion that crossed the Rappahannock at Kelly's Ford and with my platoon acted as advance guard to the column. Accompanied by Lieutenant Estes of Kilpatrick's staff, we pushed the Rebel pickets and skirmishers back to the Station where we joined the regiment in time for the grand charge of Kilpatrick's brigade.

The twelfth of September, a Lieutenant commanding my company, I was again with the first battalion that crossed the Rappahannock and was sitting on my horse in front of the regiment after its formation for a charge when the first shot fired by the Confederate artillery struck our ranks as described in my account of the Third Brandy Station.

On the eleventh of October following, my command having been increased to a squadron, I was with the battalion commanded by Captain Grinton, and being cut off from the corps by the sudden junction of the columns of Stuart and Lee, were compelled to cut our way through. My command being broken and scattered in this fight, I acted as a volunteer aid to General Davies and in the course of the engagement my horse was shot under me. I received a sabre stroke on the shoulder, two bullets through my hat, and found after the affair was over, that my sabre scabbard had been split by a bullet or fragment of a shell. In the evening of this day General Davies sent Captain Pokeepsie of his staff to thank me for the personal services I had rendered him at Brandy Station, and to say that I should have the next promotion in the Harris Light Cavalry.

CHAPTER XIX.

MANASSAS, OR SECOND BULL RUN.

The Opening Scene.—Sigel in the Foreground.—Sharp Skirmish on the Twenty-eighth.—Fitz-John Porter's Delay.—Attack on the Twenty-ninth.—Bayonet Charge of Grover's Brigade.—Thoroughfare Gap Left Open.—The Enemy Re-enforced.—Victory on the Twenty-ninth.—Where Was Porter?—Pope's Despatch.—Battle of the Thirtieth.—Exhausted Troops.—Out of Rations.—Pope Discouraged.—Our Forces at Centreville.—Personal Experience.—A Shell from the Enemy and What it Did.—An Unknown Hero.—"Tear off Your Chevrons."—Successful Stand.—Charge of the Harris Light Cavalry.

ON the twenty-ninth of August, 1862, the storm of battle again broke over the Plains of Manassas and surged furiously along the borders of Bull Run Creek and down the Warrenton pike. The figure of General Franz Sigel stands out in bold relief against the background of battle, the first actor appearing on the scene in this drama of war and death.

The time is daybreak, and the rosy light of early dawn, so peaceful and so pure, flushes the sky in painful contrast to the scene of strife and bloodshed below.

At noon on the day previous, General Pope had ordered Reno, Kearny, and Hooker to follow Jackson who, through the miscarriage of well-laid plans, had been allowed to escape in the direction of Centerville. McDowell's command, then on the way to Manassas, was ordered to march to Centerville, while Porter was directed to come forward to Manassas Junction. The orders were promptly executed by the various commands excepting that of Fitz John Porter, who unaccountably on loyal principles, remained inactive during the ensuing contest. Kearny drove the enemy out of Centreville and in their retreat along the Warrenton road they encountered the division of King, McDowell's advance, marching eastward to intercept them.

A sharp fight took place, terminating to the advantage of neither, and at night the contestants bivouacked near the battle field.

On the night of the twenty-eighth, Pope's forces were so disposed that twenty-five thousand men under McDowell, Sigel, and Reynolds, were ready to attack Jackson from the south and west, and the corps of Reno, Heintzelman, and Porter, consisting of an equal number of troops, were to complete the attack from the east. Lee was pushing forward his forces to support Jackson at Thoroughfare Gap, and it was necessary for the Union army to use all possible celerity of movement in order to make the attack before the main body of the Confederate army under Lee, could come up. But this combination failed like many another, and during the night King's division fell back towards Manassas Junction, at which place Porter's corps had recently arrived, and the road to Gainsville and Thoroughfare Gap was thus left open to Jackson. A new arrangement of troops became therefore necessary.

Soon after Sigel's attack at daylight on the twenty-ninth, Heintzelman's two divisions came up and Jackson fell back to the neighborhood of Sudley Springs, with his right just south of the Warrenton turnpike.

Kettell, in his history of the "Great Rebellion," describes this part of the battle as follows:—

"Upon arriving on the field at noon, Pope, seeing that Jackson was hard pushed by that portion of the Union army which had come into action, sent urgent orders to McDowell and Porter to advance rapidly on the left, and turn the Confederate right flank. According to the calculation of General Pope, they ought to reach their new positions towards the close of the afternoon, and pending their arrival the tired troops of Sigel, Heintzelman, and Reno were allowed a few hours' rest. Soon after two o'clock P. M., news arrived that McDowell would be on the field in a couple of hours, and at half past four peremptory orders were sent to Porter to turn the enemy's rear. Supposing that these orders would be fulfilled, Pope, soon after five P. M., directed Heintzelman and Reno to re-commence the attack. It was made with great energy, Grover's Brigade of Hooker's Division distinguishing itself by a determined bayonet charge which broke through two of Jackson's lines. The latter again fell back, leaving the battle-field and his dead and wounded in the hands of the Federal troops, and at sunset, McDowell's troops came into action along the Warrenton turnpike.

By this time, however, the troops of Lee had begun to arrive on the field, their progress through Thoroughfare Gap having been ineffectually opposed by

Ricket's Division of McDowell's Corps, left there for the purpose of delaying their march. The Rebel advance under Longstreet offered such a determined resistance to the Union left wing, that the night of the twenty-ninth fell on a drawn battle on that portion of the field—the National arms having been decidedly triumphant on the right."

But where, during all this time was Fitz John Porter and his command? Why did he remain passive within sight and sound of the battle, at Manassas Junction, disregarding the repeated and imperative orders of Pope? Why did he sit placidly in his tent and look out upon the hurrying troops of Longstreet hastening to aid Jackson, and yet make no move to check their advance, in accordance with his instructions? He *said* that the enemy was encountered in flank in the direction of Gainsville, and that he was compelled to fall back towards Manassas. Pope, however, disbelieved this excuse. "I believed then as I am very sure now", said the General in his official report, "that it was easily practicable for him to have turned the right flank of Jackson, and to have fallen upon his rear; that if he had done so, we should have gained a decided victory over the army under Jackson, before he could have been joined by any of the forces of Longstreet, and that the army of General Lee would have been so crippled and checked by the destruction of this large force, as to have been no longer in condition to prosecute further operations of an agressive character." But despite the lethargy of Porter and the success of Longstreet in effecting a union with Jackson, the advantage of the day's fight was so plainly with our forces that after the firing had ceased Pope sent the following despatch to Washington:—

"HEAD-QUARTERS, FIELD OF BATTLE,
GROVETTON, NEAR GAINSVILLE, Aug. 30th, 1862.

"*To Major General Halleck, General in Chief, Washington, D. C.*

"We fought a terrible battle here yesterday with the combined forces of the enemy, which lasted with continuous fury from daylight until after dark, by which time the enemy was driven from the field which we now occupy.

Our troops are too much exhausted to push matters, but shall do so in the course of the morning, as soon as Fitz John Porter's corps come up from Manassas.

"The enemy is still in our front, but badly used up.

"We have lost not less than eight thousand men, killed and wounded, and from the appearance of the field, the enemy have lost at least two to our one. He stood strictly on the defensive and every assault was made by ourselves.

"The battle was fought on the identical battle field of Bull Run, which greatly increased the enthusiasm of our men.

"Our troops have behaved splendidly.

"The news just reaches me from the front that the enemy is retreating towards the mountains. I go forward at once to see.

"We have made great captures, but I am not able yet to form an idea of their extent.

"JOHN POPE,
"MAJOR-GENERAL COMMANDING."

Our losses in this day's battle were not less than six or eight thousand, and those of the enemy were, no doubt, considerably greater.

From the night of the twenty-ninth up to ten o'clock of the thirtieth, the movements of the enemy all indicated retreat. Their left wing receded towards Gainsville, from which direction the forces under Lee swept through Thoroughfare Gap in hourly increasing numbers. Thus the Confederate army was strengthened by large reinforcements, while the Union troops suffered proportional depletion from the almost continuous labors of the previous ten days. Cavalry and artillery horses had remained saddled and in harness almost without interruption during those ten days, and for two days had been without forage. In addition to this, the troops were actually suffering for rations. Tell egram after telegram had been despatched by General Pope for forage, rations, and ammunition. The available force in readiness on the eventful morning of the thirtieth were only forty thousand, while the enemy confronted us with an army twice as large. Pope had been assured that the corps of Franklin and Sumner should be hurried forward immediately; but they did not arrive. Hour after hour passed by and yet no help came for the worn out army of Virginia.

At last the following dispatch was received on the morning of the thirtieth :—

AUGUST 29th, 1862—8 P. M.

To Commanding Officer at Centreville:

I have been instructed by General McClellan to inform you that he will have all the available wagons at Alexandria loaded with rations for your troops, and all of the cars, also, as soon as you will send in a cavalry escort to Alexandria as a guard to the train.

Respectfully,

W. B. FRANKLIN,

Major-General Commanding Sixth Corps.

"Such a letter," said General Pope, "when we were fighting the enemy, and Alexandria was swarming with troops, needs no comment.

"Bad as was the condition of our cavalry, I was in no situation to spare troops from the front, nor could they have gone to Alexandria and returned within the time by which we must have had provisions or fallen back in the direction of Washington. Nor do I yet see what service cavalry could have rendered, in guarding railroad trains."

But if General Pope was discouraged by this complication of disaster gradually inclosing him in its meshes, he did not sit down and fold his hands in idleness.

Resolutely he went about re-arranging the tangled ends of this sad business. He determined to make the best fight possible with his limited means, and endeavor to cripple Lee before the entire southern army could arrive on the field.

As rapidly therefore on the thirtieth as he could bring his forces into action he advanced to the attack, and between twelve and two o'clock both wings of the Union army were in line of battle. As fast as the troops of Lee arrived on the field they were massed for an attack on the Union left, and Pope therefore strengthened that part of his line. Porter having come up at last, in consequence of peremptory orders, the Union left was held by McDowell, Porter, and Sigel who, despite the swarming masses of the enemy hurled against them, made a determined stand. In front of Heitzelman and Reno on the center and right, the Confederates were in such force that it was impossible to re-enforce the Union left until late in the afternoon, when Reno's command went to their assistance. The left had by this time fallen back a half mile and darkness now came between the contending armies like a black-robed nun petitioning peace.

The right wing of the Union army had not lost an inch of ground during the day. Nevertheless this army was worsted in its most unequal contest.

Before the tide of battle ebbed for the day, General Pope learned that Franklin's corps was near Centreville, followed at an interval of four miles by the corps of Sumner.

But his men were too much exhausted to so soon renew the battle, and he accordingly fell back across Bull Run to the heights of Centreville where an effective stand could be made against the enemy. Therefore, between the hours of eight and twelve, the Union army slowly retired to its new position.

The Confederates did not attempt pursuit. On the morning of the thirty-first, the Union army was concentrated about Centreville, with out-lying bodies on the road to Chantilly and Fairfax Court-House.

That portion of this battle-drama whose scenes occurred under my own observation and in which I was an actor, I recall with distinctness.

Forms forever vanished resume once more their material outlines and the action of that day again comes up with all the vividness of reality. At such times the fire seems yet to glow in the ashes of these long dead events, and shadowy heroes figure with added light on the field of their renown.

On the eventful thirtieth, our artillery occupied the crest of a hill a short distance beyond Bull Run creek, the cavalry regiments under Bayard being stationed next and the infantry drawn up in a line behind the cavalry.

A short time before the battle opened, I was sent to a distant part of the field to deliver an order. An ominous stillness pervaded the ranks. The pickets as I passed them were silent, with faces firmly set towards the front, and the shadow of coming battle hovered portentiously, like a cloud with veiled lightnings, over the Union lines.

It was the calm which precedes a storm, and the thunder-bolts of war fell fast and heavy when the storm at length broke over our heads. I had just taken my place in the cavalry ranks when a shell from the enemy's guns whizzed over our heads with a long and spiteful shriek. One of the horses attached to a caisson was in the path of the fiery missile and the next instant the animal's head was severed entirely from his neck. The deathly silence was now broken, and more shot and shell followed in quick succession, ploughing through the startled air and falling with destructive force among the Union troops. This iron hail from the guns of the enemy was composed in part of old pieces of chain and broken iron rails as well as the shot and shell ordinarily used. Our artillery soon replied, but from some unexplained cause the Union troops in this portion of our line broke and fled in panic before a shot had been fired from the muskets of the enemy. This battle, like the first Bull Run, had been well planned, and every effort which good generalship and good judgment could dictate in order to insure success, had been made by Generals Pope and McDowell.

At this crisis of affairs, the cavalry under Bayard and Kilpatrick were ordered to the rear to stem, if possible, the tide of retreat, but the effort was well nigh fruitless. Regiment after regiment surged by in one continuous and almost resistless wave. A cheer was heard to go up from the Confederate ranks as Stuart's cavalry charged us, and though we returned the charge it did not stop the panic which had taken possession of our troops.

One of its causes was undoubtedly the supposition that the enemy was executing a flank movement on our left. In forty-five minutes from the beginning of the battle, this part of our army was in full retreat; but the determined stand made by Heintzelman and also one or two heroic attempts to stop the backward surging wave, saved our forces from utter rout and possible capture.

As soon as the Union batteries were captured by the enemy, they were turned upon us, in addition to their own guns, and afterwards, on came Stuart in a headlong charge, with one of those hideous yells peculiar to the Southern chivalry. With thousands of others who were rapidly retiring, I had re-crossed Bull Run creek when my attention was arrested by a mounted officer who sprang out from the mass of flying men and waving his sword above his head called on every one, irrespective of regiment, to rally around him and face the foe. He wore no golden leaf, no silver star; he was appealing to officers higher in command than himself, who, mixed with the crowd, were hurrying by. His manner, tense with excitement, was strung up to the pitch of heroism, and his presence was like an inspiration as he stood outside the mass, a mark for the bullets of the enemy.

I halted, filled with admiration for so noble an example of valor, and then rode slowly towards him. Seeing me, he galloped forward to meet me and asked my aid in making a stand against the enemy.

"Sergeant," said he, "you are just in time. As you are mounted, you can be of great service in rallying these men for a stand on this ground."

"Lieutenant," I replied, "they will not listen to the wearer of these chevrons."

"Tear off your chevrons," said this unknown hero, —"the infantry will not know you from a field officer—and get as many men to turn their muskets to the front as you can."

"Lieutenant," I replied, "I will do all I can to help you," and the insignia of non-commissioned rank was immediately stripped from my sleeves.

I put myself under his command and fought with him until he gave the order to retire. While he was talking with me he was at the same time calling on the men to make a stand, telling them they could easily hold the position. He seemed to take in the situation at a glance.

The enemy having advanced to the first crest of hills, were throwing their infantry forward with full force, and with the three thousand or more men who rallied around this heroic officer, a stand was made on the rising ground north of Bull Run from which the advance of the enemy was opposed. We held this position for half an hour, which gave considerable time for re-organization.

While riding along the line, helping my unknown superior as best I could, my horse was shot under me, —the first experience of this kind which had befallen me.

Just as the disaster was occurring which culminated in retreat, General McDowell on his white horse, galloped up to the guns behind which Heintzelman was blazing destruction on the Confederates. Alighting from his horse he sighted the guns and gave a personal superintendence to this part of the action. An artillery captain, standing by his battery while his horses were shot down, his pieces in part disabled, and the infantry deserting him, shed tears in consequence.

"You need not feel badly over this affair," said the General, "General McDowell is responsible for this misfortune. Stand by your guns as long as you can. If the General is blamed, *your* bravery will be praised."

Was there a touch of irony in this remark which met in advance the grumblings and questionings of the future? Was it the sarcasm of a man who, having done his utmost, could not yet prevent disaster and who knew that an unthinking public sometimes measured loyalty by success?

Later in the day our regiment—the "Harris Light Cavalry"—lost a squadron. Most of them were killed.

In the deepening twilight we charged the enemy just as they were forming for a similar attack on us. They were compelled to halt, and Pope was thus enabled to discover their position and arrange for the next day's defense.

On the night of the thirtieth, the enemy occupied the battle field, and buried the dead of both armies. Thus once more, Bull Run ran red with patriot blood and witnessed the retreat of the Union battalions. By what strange fatality General Pope was allowed to struggle on alone against an army twice the size of the Federal force, cannot be satisfactorily explained. One is almost tempted to believe, with astrologists, that baleful stars sometimes preside with malign influence over the destinies of battles, as they are said to do over individuals and nations.

CHAPTER XX.

CHANTILLY.

Union Troops on the Defensive.—Historic Chantilly.—Pope at Fairfax Court-House.—Stonewall Jackson's Attack.—The Battle of the Sky.—Furious Charges.—The Enemy Repulsed.—Death of Stevens and Kearny.—The March to Washington.—Pope Resigns.—Porter Cashiered.—Tribute to Kearny.

THE Union army under General Pope was allowed little respite from its almost continuous fighting during the late summer and early autumn days of 1862.

After the tide of war· had surged back from the field of Bull Run, leaving its course strewn with fallen heroes, and the last days of August had gone out in blood, the battle-line was again formed at Chantilly. Chantilly is northwest from Fairfax Court-House and Centreville, and is not more than ten miles south of the station of Thornton on the Loudon and Hampshire Railway. On the thirty-first of August, 1862, the brave Army of Virginia rested behind its intrenchments at Centreville, while a strong force was stationed at Chantilly under Hooker, Reno, and McDowell. On September first the united strength of the Armies of the Potomac and Virginia, was reported by the commanding officers at less than sixty thousand.

General Pope, believing this force too small for offensive operations, determined to remain on the defensive and await further developments from the enemy.

As the Confederates were making demonstrations for the purpose of turning the Union right, and were also advancing northward, General Pope fell slowly back to Fairfax Court-House, ordering the force at Chantilly to remain on the defensive at that point.

Just as the sun was setting on the first of September, and while a furious thunder-storm was in progress, Stonewall Jackson, the great flanker, made a sudden descent on the Union forces at Chantilly—the corps of A. P. Hill and Ewell making the attack. The battle of the storm and the battle of the plain raged in concert, and the thunder-crash above drowned the roar of artillery below.

Gallantly our boys under Reno advanced to the attack and impetuously drove back the foe. At all points the enemy met with repulse. Brigadier General Isaac J. Stevens, while leading a charge with the second division under Reno, was shot dead at the head of his troops.

His command, thrown into confusion, uncovered the first division of Reno, which was also demoralized and broken.

At this crisis of affairs General Kearny, leading one of Heintzelman's divisions, advanced to the rescue and with a terrific charge drove the Confederates from the field. The defeated ranks of the enemy recoiled and fled before this onset of the Union troops; but it cost the country the life of one of its bravest officers; for when the smoke lifted and the storm ceased raging, victory unfurled her flag over the lifeless form of Philip Kearny. His spirit had gone outward, like that of Napoleon at Helena, amid a war of elements;—and the thunder rolled his requiem.

It was dark when the battle ended, and on the next morning General Pope's whole command was massed behind Difficult Creek, between Flint Hill and Alexandria turnpike. At noon of that day, in accordance with orders from General Halleck, they marched to Washington, at which place they arrived in good order on the evening of the third. Here General Pope, at his own request, was relieved of his command and at the same time preferred charges of insubordination and negligence against General Porter, on which the latter officer was court-marshaled and cashiered.

No more intrepid or accomplished officers, no hearts more loyal to our sacred cause, ever died on glory's field than Major-General Philip Kearny and Brigadier-General Stevens.

I cannot forego the insertion here of the following beautiful tribute to the memory of our Kearny. It always excites in me the noblest emotions, and will, I think, afford as much pleasure to my readers as it has to myself:

"Our country bleeds
With blows her own hands strike. He starts, he heeds
Her cries for succor. In a foreign land
He dwells; his bowers with luxury's pinions fanned,
His cup with roses crowned. He dashes down
The cup, he leaves the bowers; he flies to aid
His native land. Out leaps his patriot blade!
Quick to the van he darts. Again the frown

Of strife bends blackening; once again his ear
War's furious trump with stern delight drinks in;
Again the Battle-Bolt in red career!
Again the flood, the frenzy, and the din!

At tottering Williamsburg his granite front
Bears without shock the battle's fiercest brunt.
So have we seen the crag beat back the blast,
So has the shore the surges backward cast.
Behind his rock the shattered ranks reform;
Forward, still forward, until dark defeat
Burns to bright victory!

* * * * * * * *

Fame commands
The song; we yield it gladly; but the glow
Fades as we sing. The dire, the fatal blow
Fell, fell at last. Full, full in deadliest front
Leading his legions, leading as his wont,
The bullet wafts him to his mortal goal!
And not alone War's thunders saw him die;
Amid the glare, the rushing, and the roll,
Glared, crashed, the grand dread battle of the sky;
There on two pinions,—War's and Storm's,—he soared,
Flight how majestic! up! His dirge was roared,
Not warbled, and his pall was smoke and cloud;
Flowers of red shot, red lightnings strewed his bier,
And night, black night, the mourner.

* * * * * * * *

Now farewell,
O hero! In our Glory's Pantheon
Thy name will shine, a name immortal won
By deeds immortal! In our heart's deep heart
Thy statued fame, that never shall depart,
Shall tower, the loftier as Time fleets, and show
How Heaven can sometimes plant its Titans here below."

CHAPTER XXI.

ANTIETAM.

The Enemy Concentrating on Antietam Creek.—Stonewall Jackson Has the Left.—Battle at Daybreak.—The Contested Cornfield.—Hooker Wounded.—Furious Struggle.—Fate of the Thirty-Fourth New York.—War's Fierce Tug.—Franklin and Fresh Troops.—Four Times Lost and Won.—Burnside Takes the Bridge.—Union Troops Carry the Hill and are Driven Back.—McClellan Sends Aid.—A Moment when Events Hang in the Balance.—"The Bridge!—Always the Bridge!"—McClellan's Star in the Ascendant.

THE dawn of September seventeenth, 1862, witnessed the opening scene of one of the bloodiest battles of our civil war. For two days previous to that time the Confederate army, under Lee, had been concentrating on the low range of hills near Antietam Creek and in the immediate vicinity of the little town of Sharpsburg.

General Burnside on the fourteenth had carried Turner's Gap and General Franklin had occupied Crampton's Gap on the same day, thus obtaining possession of the mountain range and its gates into the valley; the corps of Sumner, Hooker, and Mansfield had been ordered to follow the Confederate army, retiring in the direction of Sharpsburg. The forces of the enemy, under cover of a mass of woods, were disposed in two lines six miles long, having Antietam creek in their front. Three bridges at short intervals crossed the creek in front of the battle line, leading respectively to Hagerstown, Shepardstown, and Williamsport.

Stonewall Jackson having arrived from Harper's Ferry on the sixteenth, held the left of the Confederate line, D. H. Hill's division had the center and Longstreet's Corps occupied the right.

About sixty guns had been placed in position to command the Antietam bridge by which the Union troops advanced.

Hooker was ordered to cross on the right and if possible flank the enemy's left, while Sumner, Franklin, and Mansfield were to sustain the attack of Hooker. Burnside, on the left, was to carry by storm the lower bridge of Antietam Creek, turn the Rebel flank, and cut off his retreat, while the principal work in the center was left to the batteries.

At daybreak on the seventeenth the bloody battle commenced. Rickett's batteries under Hooker opened fire on the enemy and Meade's infantry made the attack. The action very soon became severe and raged furiously, with destructive results. The battle-ground was a field of ploughed land with a cornfield at the rear bordered by a mass of woods.

At the end of half an hour the fire of the enemy decreased and Meade perceiving that the Confederate line wavered, rushed forward with his Pennsylvanians, the boys cheering as they ran. The enemy was pushed to the shelter of the woods before the overwhelming onslaught of the Pennsylvania troops, leaving the field strewn with large numbers of the dead and wounded.

As the conquering Union line swept up to the wood, a tempest of fire was poured upon their advancing ranks from fresh Confederate troops concealed in the forest. The line wavered a moment and closing up its broken ranks retired. The Rebels now rushed wildly out from their concealed position and with yells like demons re-gained the ground just lost by their comrades. Hooker sent a brigade to stem this adverse wave of war, but it was not enough. The brigade of Hartstuff then advanced at the double-quick and rapidly formed in battle line on a ridge in the cornfield—a position which they held until their General was wounded.

Rickett's division and part of Mansfield's corps had fallen back, the General commanding Mansfield's corps having been carried from the field mortally wounded. But Doubleday's guns enabled the left to stand firm and hold its ground. Crawford and Gordon, commanding Mansfield's remaining brigades, were now ordered to advance, and the entire line was concentrated upon a point of woods to the right of the cornfield, which, if taken, would give to the Union forces the key to the position.

Hooker, leading the advance, received at this crisis, a rifle-shot in his foot.

For four hours the battle had raged with bloody fury, and now, at nine o'clock, General Sumner arrived and took command. Hooker's right and the two brigades of Mansfield were still fresh, and Sedgwick's division moved forward in advance to support Crawford and Gordon. The enemy was also re-inforced and preparations to renew the struggle with greater intensity, were made. Richardson and French had the left while Sedgwick, moving in columns of division in the rear, deployed and advanced in line over the cornfield. Between his force and the nearest division the space was so broad and the danger of being flanked so imminent that he executed a manœuvre to prevent it by ordering the Thirty-fourth New York to move by the left flank—thus extending his front to its utmost limits. The movement was performed under a fire so scathing that the regiment gave way, half their officers were killed or wounded, their colors were shot to pieces, the color-sergeant killed and every one of their color-guard wounded. Only thirty-two out of all the brave men of the regiment who entered that baptism of fire for the sake of country, could ever afterwards be got together. Into the fierce flame of this conflict went the Fifteenth Massachusetts with seventeen officers and six hundred men. It came out with six officers and one hundred and thirty-four men. Sedgwick being wounded, General Howard assumed command and endeavored to restore order, but in vain. "General Sumner ordered the line to be re-formed under fire; but the test was too severe for volunteer troops. Sumner himself attempted to arrest the disorder but to little purpose. As it seemed impossible to hold the position, Sumner withdrew the division to the rear and once more the cornfield was abandoned to the enemy. At the same moment the enemy perceiving his advantage, came forward with fresh troops." One o'clock had arrived and the outlook was discouraging. The list of officers killed and wounded was positively alarming. Hooker's and Mansfield's troops were exhausted with the trying contest and Richardson was severely wounded while leading his men in the fray.

General Meagher was in the same plight, the ammunition for some of the guns had entirely given out, though the artillery in our front was yet keeping up its fire with vigor. Doubleday with his guns still held the right firmly. The officers of the various commands were confident of being able to hold their ground, but considered an advance impossible.

Fortunately the enemy's batteries seemed too much disabled to take the offensive and their troops too much exhausted for an attack.

The timely arrival of Franklin with fresh troops changed the complexion of affairs. Slocum advanced along the hill slopes, on the heights of which the enemy was posted, and Smith with his Maine and Vermont regiments went forward on the run, re-took the hotly-contested corn-field and charged the woods in gallant style, routing the foe in the space of ten minutes.

Four times had this ground been lost and won, but at last it remained in possession of the Union forces.

On the left, Burnside, after a sharp engagement took the stone bridge, and the enemy retiring to some hill-tops beyond, placed their batteries in position to command the Union troops.

At four o'clock Burnside received orders from McClellan to carry the batteries in his front at all hazards, while Franklin sent forward his artillery to aid Burnside in obtaining a position on the Sharpsburg road, in the rear of the enemy. General Burnside had sixteen thousand men to handle, in this movement. Rapidly and with determined front they pressed forward directly up the hill in range of the most dangerous batteries of the enemy. The guns of Franklin were placed in the field on the other side, at about the same time, and the battle opened from all sides with increased activity. The guns of Burnside held the enemy's batteries in check, and the infantry columns swept up the hill to meet the enemy on its crest. A thick cloud of dust enveloped the spot where the Rebel guns were planted and a furious struggle now ensued.

With a shout the Union troops rush forward and carry the hill. But on the ridge above them another Confederate battle-line comes in view. They move rapidly down upon our troops but are met firmly by the brigades of Burnside in heavy column. The enemy halts, intimidated; but at this critical moment A. P. Hill arrives on the ground from Harper's Ferry and with his fresh troops reënforces the Confederates. A newspaper correspondent describes this part of the scene with dramatic power.

"The enemy's left gives way and scatters over the field, the rest stand fast and fire. More infantry comes up. Burnside is outnumbered, flanked, compelled to yield the hill he took so bravely. His position is no longer one of attack; he defends himself with unfaltering firmness, but he sends to McClellan for help. McClellan's field-glass for the last half hour has seldom been turned away from the left. He sees clearly enough that Burnside is pressed—needs no messenger to tell him that. His face grows darker with anxious thought. Looking down into the valley where fifteen thousand troops are lying he turns a half-questioning look on Fitz-John Porter who stands by his side, gravely scanning the field. They are Porter's troops below, are fresh, and only impatient to share in this fight. But Porter slowly shakes his head, and one may believe that the same thought is passing through the minds of both Generals. 'They are the only reserves of the army; they cannot be spared.' McClellan re-mounts his horse, and with Porter and a dozen officers of his staff, rides away to the left in Burnside's direction.

"Sykes meets them on the road—a good soldier whose opinion is worth taking. The three Generals talk briefly together. It is easy to see that the moment has come when everything may turn on one order given or withheld, when the history of the battle is only to be written in the thoughts and purposes and words of the General. Burnside's messenger rides up. His message is: 'I want troops and guns; if you do not send them, I cannot hold my position half an hour.' McClellan's only answer for the moment is a glance at the western sky. Then he turns and speaks very slowly; 'Tell General Burnside this is the battle of the war. He must hold his ground till dark at any cost. I will send him Miller's battery. I can do nothing more. I have no infantry.' Then as the messenger was riding away he called him back. 'Tell him if he *cannot* hold his ground, then the bridge to the last man!—always the bridge! If the bridge is lost, all is lost.'"

General Morrell, however, was sent to the aid of

Burnside with five thousand men. But at this crisis of affairs the fire of the Confederates died away, the sun went down and darkness brought to a close the tumultous conflict of the day. Burnside held the bridge and Hooker, Sumner, and Franklin occupied all the vantage ground gained during the day. A renewal of the fight was anticipated for the morrow, but McClellan failed to give the expected order. On the eighteenth, the Union army rested.

On the morning of the nineteenth, when McClellan had determined to renew the attack he discovered that Lee had withdrawn across the Potomac and with his army once more occupied Virginia soil.

The battle of Antietam freed Maryland from Confederate troops and was considered a Union victory. It was, perhaps, a questionable victory but in contrast with the almost continuous reverses previous to that time, it looked positively bright. The colors of McClellan which had trailed in the dust at the disastrous ending of the Peninsular Campaign, were once more flying high in the popular view, and had he pressed home this reaction in his favor by straightforward action instead of wasting the opportunity in temporizing delays, he might have been re-instated as the army's beloved commander and again surrounded by his old atmosphere of enthusiastic admiration.

But the golden opportunity was allowed to slip by, unimproved. To many a Northern hearth-stone the battle of Antietam brought desolation and death, but on the book of National remembrance are inscribed the names of those who here fought and fell in liberty's cause, by whose death the Nation garnered a glorious harvest.

CHAPTER XXII.

CORINTH.

Topography of the Battle-ground.—The Enemy Marching upon Corinth.—Price and Van Dorn Unite their Forces.—Three Tiers of Earthworks.—Preliminary Battle of the Third.—Generalship of Rosecrans.—Battle of the Fourth.—Two Hours of Hot Work.—Forts Richardson and Robinett.—Price Driven Back.—Desperate Charge of Van Dorn.—A Forlorn Hope.—Colonel Rogers.—The Enemy Driven.—Confusion and Flight.—Heaps of Slain.—The Handkerchief Flags.—" For God's Sake Spare us !"—Pursuit of the Foe.—Captured Spoils.—West Tennessee Safe.

ABOUT seventy miles south-east of Memphis on the Mississippi river, near the Tennessee state line, lies the village of Corinth, renowned as the field where the Confederate Generals Price and Van Dorn at the head of forty thousand troops, met half that number in battle array and were hurled back in defeat and rout, their colors trailing in the dust.

Corinth is a strong strategic point, located in a branch of the Appalachian range of mountains, at the Junction of the " Memphis and Charleston," and " Mobile and Ohio " railroads, which communicate with the Atlantic seaboard on one side and the Gulf shore on the other.

General Rosecrans, in command of our forces at Corinth, had been advised of the contemplated attack of the Confederates and in anticipation of it began erecting a new line of earthworks. The combined

Rebel forces marching upon Corinth, September thirtieth, 1862, encountered the advance of Ogleby thrown forward by Rosecrans on the Chewalla road with the design of falling back and thus leading the enemy under the heavy guns of Corinth. Ogleby resisted the attack of the enemy's advance very firmly and McArthur and Davies were ordered forward to his support. On the third of October these brigades were pushed back by the increased force of the enemy with the loss of General Hackelman killed and Ogleby wounded.

General Rosecrans discovered that Price, Lovell, and Van Dorn had united their armies for an attack, with the design of cutting off his communications and crushing his small force before reënforcements could arrive.

Beauregard, during his occupancy of the place earlier in the war, had built extensive fortifications to resist the Union advance under Halleck, and when Halleck occupied Corinth he also had erected works, not so extensive as the original fortifications. General Rosecrans now constructed a third line, the others being too large for his small force. Four redoubts covered the approaches to Corinth, while batteries were placed in position, to sweep with their fire the entire space in front of our lines. General Hamilton held the extreme right of the Union army, and during the night of October third, a new five-gun battery had been placed on his left which commanded the Bolivar road. Davies occupied the center and McKean held the left, while three regiments under Colonel Oliver were sent forward on the Chewalla road from whence the Confederates were advancing. The preliminary battle took place on October third, beginning about seven and a half o'clock in the morning.

General Rosecrans, in order to develop the strength of the enemy, advanced his troops down the road as the Confederates came up and then retired behind his works, his batteries commanding their approach.

The Union troops were hotly assailed, and by one o'clock in the afternoon it became evident that the attack was no feint, as General Rosecrans had at first supposed, but that no less a prize than Corinth with all its stores, was the object in view. The Union troops were accordingly disposed so as to make the best resistance, the afternoon being consumed by these arrangements, varied with more or less fighting. Night compelled a cessation of hostilities, and under cover of the darkness a Rebel battery was placed in front of their line, only two hundred yards distant from Fort Robinett in our center.

The battle was re-opened at three o'clock on the morning of October fourth, by this battery. But our guns did not reply until day-break.

The village of Corinth was startled from sleep by exploding shells in streets and dwellings and a sudden stampede of teamsters, sutlers, and non-combatants ensued. Fort Williams on a commanding height with its twenty pound Parrot guns soon silenced the Rebel battery, whose guns were dragged away and captured. Very soon the action of the batteries became general, and the air was full of bursting shells. At about half past nine in the morning heavy masses of the enemy under Price, with gleaming bayonets, emerged from the woods east of the railroad and moved up the Bolivar road, towards the Union batteries. Steadily and with brave front the host advanced in column of divisions, Price holding the left and Van Dorn the right. As they swept onward in the face of the certain destruction awaiting them, the huge living mass expanded into long lines like two great arms extending to crush the bristling batteries in front. But now they are within range of the Federal guns and a great blaze of shot cuts and tears their ranks. But the gaps instantly close up and with desperate determination they sweep up the crest, returning the Union fire so vigorously that the division of Davies breaks in disorder. Pushing this momentary advantage, the Confederates rush through the opening thus made and capture the house which Rosecrans occupied as headquarters. Rosecrans, whose eye has never for a moment left the struggling mass below, sees with a start of dismay, the division of Davies break, and galloping headlong to the broken line, he rallies the troops in person. The dead and the dying in the enemy's ranks fall like leaves in autumn, thickly strewing the ground, but the living never falter. " Seemingly insensible to fear or infuriated by passion, they marched steadily to death with necks bent downward, and faces averted like men striving to protect themselves against a driving storm of hail."

In a moment after Davies' division gave way, the fire of the enemy was pouring into the public square of Corinth, and Hamilton's veterans fell back before their impetuous advance. With a wild yell they rushed on Fort Richardson only to be enveloped in a sheet of flame from the guns of the battery, and when the cloud of smoke lifted none save the dead and the dying were seen. But with the fury of demons and the madness of men in despair they re-form and charge the fort. Richardson falls at his battery and the Rebels are leaping over its ramparts, when suddenly the Fifty-sixth Illinois spring from a ravine near by and delivering a close volley of fire, charge the enemy impetuously and recover the lost ground. Hamilton also gives the order to charge, and his line sweeps forward, completing the Rebel repulse, and sending them in utter disorder to the woods. It is said that such a shout of victory went up then from the throats of the Union boys, as was never heard in Corinth before. Van Dorn on the Confederate left heard the shout and to him it sounded like the knell of doom. Van Dorn's advance had been much slower than that of Price owing to the difficulties encountered on the way—being obliged to march through ravines, thickets, and abattis. Their attack was designed to be simultaneous, but owing to these obstructions, Price breasted the full fury of the storm from our batteries, alone, and his defeat was accomplished before Van Dorn was in line.

Van Dorn having advanced in front of Fort Robinett, realized his difficult situation. A deadly enfilading fire had swept his ranks from Forts Robinett and Williams, but unmindful of the slaughter, he had pressed on until directly in his path stood Fort Robinett. Everything depended on his carrying the works. Van Dorn determined at once to make the attempt though unaided and alone. It was a desperate resolve and was executed with sublime bravery. Colonel Rogers at the head of his Texan and Mississippi troops moved forward on Fort Robinett. Immediately its Parrot guns flashed their iron anger in destructive discharges of shot which raked the ranks of the enemy. The guns of Fort Williams also opened fire upon them, and as they advanced to close range the carnage was awful. Their ranks were rent and torn, but instantly closing up they pressed on, urged by the clarion voice of Rogers, at their head, shouting, "forward." At last the ditch in front of the position was reached, and pausing for one moment on its brink, Rogers waved the Rebel flag in his left hand and holding a revolver in his right while he still shouted 'forward!' sprang over the ditch and rushing up the slope planted his banner on the ramparts of the Fort. The next moment he fell headlong into the ditch shot dead, followed by five brave Texans who never left his side and who shared his fate. Just behind the ridge the Ohio troops were lying flat on their faces, reserving their fire until the enemy came within short range, when they sprang up and delivered six sharp volleys with destructive effect. The front line of the enemy now fell back upon their supports who rushed forward with desperate determination into the hottest of the fight. The Sixty-third Ohio encountered them at this point and a hand to hand struggle ensued. Bayonets and clubbed muskets were used in the fearful contest, and the yells and curses and demoniac uproar were hideous. At length the enemy's line gave way, and they fled in terror and dismay before our troops, flinging aside their arms as they ran. Many of them tied their handkerchiefs upon sticks, shouting to "spare them for God's sake!" The abattis of Fort Robinett was full of them and over two hundred of them were taken within an area of a hundred yards. More than twice that number fell in the frightful assault upon Fort Robinett. Fifty-six of their dead were heaped together in front of that redoubt, belonging principally to the Second Texas and Fourth Mississippi. "They were buried in one pit: but their brave general sleeps alone: our own noble fellows testifying their respect by rounding his grave smoothly, and marking his resting place."

The Twenty-seventh Ohio and Eleventh Missouri went in pursuit of the flying foe, chasing them back to their cover of woods.

The battle had lasted two hours—beginning at nine in the morning and the pursuit commencing at eleven o'clock.

"A great shout went up all over Corinth. The battle was a shock. * * * The pursuit of the beaten foe was terrible. Sheets of flame blazed through the forest. Huge trunks were shattered by crashing shells. You may track the flying conflict for miles by scarified trees, broken branches, twisted gun-barrels and shattered stocks, blood-stained garments and mats of human hair, which lie on the ground where men died; hillocks which mark ditches where dead Rebels were covered, and smoothly rounded graves where slaughtered patriots were tenderly buried."

Over two thousand of our own soldiers had fallen, while six thousand of the enemy went to their death on that red field.

Two thousand two hundred and forty-eight prisoners were captured, also two pieces of artillery, fourteen stand of colors and over three thousand small arms. As Rosecrans, after the battle, rode along the line, he was greeted with thundering cheers. He began to be looked upon as invincible. Victory hovered over his banners wherever he went, and he was affectionately nick-named " Old Rosy."

The fields around Corinth were frightful with the débris of battle, and for weeks the place could be scented miles away.

On the morning after the battle, McPherson, having arrived at Corinth with a fresh brigade, went in pursuit of the retreating foe ; but though narrowly escaping destruction in the forks of the Hatchie, they succeeded at last in eluding the vigilance of our troops and getting away. The battle of Corinth placed West Tennessee securely in the hands of the Federal Government, and won for General Rosecrans fresh and undying laurels.

CHAPTER XXIII.

FREDERICKSBURG.

Burnside in Command of the Army of the Potomac.—The Advance to Fredericksburg.—Surrender of the City Refused.—Confederate and Union Cavalry Raids.—Capture of Rebel Picket-Posts.—Exodus of Citizens from Fredericksburg.—Delay In Laying Pontoons.—The Seventh Michigan Crossing the River under a Murderous Fire.—Death of a Massachusetts Chaplain.—General Gibbon Opens the Battle.—Desperate Fighting.—Terrific Charge of Meade's Division.—The Hillside Strewn with the Dead.—Death of Bayard.—Night after the Battle.—Heart-rending Scenes.—Termination of the Campaign of 1862.

GENERAL McCLELLAN'S failure to grasp the fruits of victory after the battle of Antietam, led to his removal and the appointment of General Ambrose E. Burnside to the command of the Army of the Potomac.

General Burnside accepted his new position with great reluctance and unfeigned self-distrust, and only as a matter of obedience to orders. This change of the commanding officer, deleterious and dangerous as it might be upon the *morale* of the army, was nevertheless considered necessary and expedient.

Having secured by strategy the principal gaps of Blue Ridge, which had been occupied by the enemy since their advance into the Valley, General Burnside began to make preparations to move his army to Fredericksburg, that point being in the direct line from Washington to Richmond. To mask, as long as possible, his real design, he threatened an attack upon Gordonsville, but General Lee, by the aid of his emissaries and raiders, soon ascertained his plans, and moving his army across the Blue Ridge, through the western passes, he took his position on the south bank of the Rappahannock, to prevent our crossing.

General Burnside halted at Warrenton, a beautiful village of Fauquier county, and here a few days were consumed in effecting the changes incident upon the advent of a new commander, and on the fourteenth, the Army of the Potomac was constituted into three grand divisions, to be commanded respectively by Generals Sumner, Franklin, and Hooker. The following day Warrenton was abandoned and the army swept on towards the Rappahannock.

Two days' march brought our advance to Falmouth, and on the twenty-first, General Patrick, our Provost-Marshal-General, was directed to repair to Fredericksburg under a flag of truce, and request the surrender of the city. The authorities replied that while its buildings and streets would no longer be used by Rebel sharp-shooters to annoy our forces across the river, its occupation by Yankee troops would be resisted to the last. Had the means of crossing the river been at hand, General Burnside would have made hostile demonstrations at once; but through some misunderstanding between himself and General Halleck, at Washington, the pontoons were not in readiness.

On the twenty-eighth of November a strong force of Rebel cavalry under General Wade Hampton, dashed across the river at some of the upper fords, raided up around Dumfries and the Occoquan, captured several prisoners and wagons and returned to their side of the river without loss. As a sort of off-set to this, on the twenty-ninth General Julius Stahl, who commanded a brigade of cavalry at Fairfax Court House, commenced an expedition of great daring and success, to the Shenandoah Valley. Having advanced to Snicker's Gap, in the Blue Ridge, a strong Rebel picket-post was captured by our vanguard. Pressing forward on the main thoroughfare, they soon reached the Shenandoah river, and were not a little annoyed by Rebel carbineers, hidden behind old buildings across the stream. Captain Abram H. Krom, commanding a detachment of the Fifth New York Cavalry, and leading the advance, dashed across the river, though deep and the current swift, closely followed by his men. On reaching the opposite bank a charge was ordered, and executed in so gallant a manner that several Rebels were made prisoners, and the remainder of the squad was driven away at a break-neck speed. Our men pursued them in a scrambling race for nearly three miles, when they came upon a rebel camp, which was attacked in a furious manner. Our boys made music enough for a brigade, though only a squadron was at hand.

The enemy attempted a defence but utterly failed. Re-inforcements coming to our aid, the Rebels were thoroughly beaten and driven away, leaving in our hands one captain, two lieutenants, thirty-two privates, one stand of colors, and several wagons and ambulances. Most of these were laden with booty taken by White's guerrillas, in a recent raid into Poolesville, Maryland. Sixty horses and fifty heads of cattle were also captured in this gallant charge.

With all their spoils the expedition returned, via Leesburg, arriving at their camps in safety. But all eyes were turned expectantly towards Fredericksburg, with its two vast armies preparing for a grand encounter.

Nearly all the citizens of the city had left their homes and fled southward.

While General Burnside waited for his pontoons, General Lee was fortifying the Heights in rear of the city, and concentrating his forces for the anticipated onset. This state of things was greatly regretted. The laying of pontoons was commenced on the night of the eleventh of December, but the work progressed so slowly that the task was not half completed when daylight made the sappers and miners a fair mark for the sharpshooters, who were hidden among the buildings which lined the opposite shore, and whose numbers had largely increased within a few days. Battery after battery was opened on Falmouth Heights, until not less than one hundred and fifty guns at good range, were belching fire and destruction upon the nearly tenantless city, and still the sharpshooters prevented the completion of the pontoons, and disputed our crossing. At this critical moment the Seventh Michigan regiment of infantry, immortalized its name. Failing, after some entreaty, to secure the assistance of the engineer corps to row them across, they undertook the perilous labor themselves, and amid the rattling of bullets, and the cheers and shouts of our own men, they reached the opposite shore with five of their number killed, and sixteen wounded, including Lieutenant Colonel Baxter. They immediately dashed through the streets of the city, and being quickly reënforced by other regiments, they soon cleared the rifle-pits and buildings adjacent to the stream, of all annoyance. Foremost among the noble men who performed this heroic work was the Rev. Arthur B. Fuller, chaplain of the Sixteenth Massachusetts infantry, who was killed by a rifle-shot.

Our pontoons were now laid in quietness to the city; and about three miles below, General Franklin laid his pontoons without opposition. Several bridges were thus constructed, and before night the main body of infantry and cavalry filed across the river, preparatory to a grand engagement. The morning of the thirteenth of December was dimmed by a heavy fog which covered friend and foe. But orders for an attack upon the formidable works of the enemy had been given, and even before the mist arose, General Gibbon opened fire with his heavy artillery, which was responded to, but without much effect owing to the fog, which however disappeared about eleven o'clock. The engagement now became general, and the fighting was of a character more desperate and determined than ever known before.

The line of Rebel fortifications was so far back from the river, that our artillery, posted on the Falmouth Heights, was out of range, and made more havoc in our advancing ranks than in the ranks of the enemy, until the fire was silenced by order of General Burnside. About one o'clock, one of the most brilliant movements of the day was performed by General George G. Meade's division, which by a terrific charge gained the crest of the hill, near the key of the position. But not being sufficiently supported, they were compelled to retire, bringing away several hundred prisoners with them.

Another masterpiece of gallantry was presented nearer the town, at Marye's Heights, where General Meagher's Irish Brigade repeatedly charged the Rebel works, until at least two-thirds of his stalwart men strewed the ground, killed and wounded. Brigade after brigade was ordered to take these Heights, and though their ranks were mown down like grass before the scythe, in the very mouth of Rebel guns the effort was again and again made. Midway up the Heights was a stone wall, behind which lay the hosts of the enemy, who delivered their fire with scarcely any exposure, sweeping down our columns as they approached. This hillside was completely strewn with our dead and disabled, and at length our assailing ranks retired, compelled to abandon their futile and murderous attempts. But in the language of General Sumner, "they did all that men could do." This could be applied to all the troops engaged.

Night at length threw her sable mantle over the bloody field, covering in her somber folds the stiffened corpses and mangled forms of not less than fifteen thousand dead and wounded, including the casualties of both armies.

Not one of all our dead fell more lamented than Major General George D. Bayard, who was struck by a shell in the early part of the engagement while stand ing in front of his cavalry brigade awaiting orders. He was but twenty-eight years of age, of prepossessing appearance and manners, with as brave a spirit as ever defended the flag of the Union, and a capacity of mind for military usefulness equal to any man in the service. Gradually he had arisen from one position of honor and responsibility to another, proving himself tried and true in each promotion, while his cavalry comrades especially were watching the developments of his growing power, with unabating enthusiasm. But " death loves a shining mark," and our hero, with his own blood, baptized the day which had been appointed for his nuptials. The recital of his early death brought tears to many eyes, and caused many a loving heart to bleed.

> " Death lies on him like an untimely frost
> Upon the sweetest flower of all the field."

The night following this bloody conflict was horrible in the extreme. Every available spot or building in the city was sought for a hospital, to which the wounded were brought on stretchers by their companions. Now and then there came a poor fellow who was able to walk, supporting with one hand its bloody mangled mate. At times two men might be seen approaching through the darkness, supporting between them their less fortunate comrade, whose bloody garments told that he had faced the foe. But many of our hospitals proved to be very unsafe refuges, into which Minie balls and broken shells would come rattling, and in some instances destroying the precious lives that had escaped—though not without suffering —the terrible and deadly shock of battle. Many of the wounded were taken across the river, and made perfectly safe and as comfortable as circumstances would permit. The Sanitary and Christian Commissions rendered very effective service, enshrining themselves in the memory of a grateful people. Their deeds of charity and mercy can never be forgotten. By their timely supplies and personal labors, many lives were saved, and thousands of the wounded were comforted.

The dawn of December fourteenth was hailed with gladness by many a gallant soldier who had suffered from the chill of the night, wounded and alone upon the bloody field. A little firing occurred during the day but no general engagement resulted. This was greatly feared, for had General Lee advanced upon us, it is difficult to see how our men, though somewhat covered by the fire of our batteries from Falmouth Heights, could have recrossed the stream without fearful loss. But both armies spent most of the holy day in the sacred task of caring for the wounded and burying their dead. Monday was also spent principally in the same employment, and in the night, so skillfully as to be unknown even to the Rebel pickets, our whole army was withdrawn to the north side of the river in perfect order and without loss. Our pontoons were then taken up.

General Burnside was not willing to remain totally idle, and after some time had elapsed he planned another grand movement, which with more or less opposition from his subordinates who did not confide in his judgment, he endeavored to execute. But he had just taken the first step in the programme when he was signaled to desist, by a telegram from the President, who had been informed that the temper of the army was not favorable to a general move under its present commander.

With the battle of Fredericksburg terminated the campaign of 1862, and the two great armies established their winter quarters facing each other along the line of the Rappahannock. Our camps extended several miles along the northern shore above and below Falmouth, and the enemy occupied the south bank above and below the Heights of Fredericksburg. Indeed, nearly the whole territory between the Rappahannock and the defences of Washington, a dark, forsaken wilderness region, with only here and there a plantation or a village, was soon converted into a vast camping ground, and became, for a time, the most populous section of Virginia.

CHAPTER XXIV.

MURFREESBORO OR STONE RIVER.

Rosecrans in Command of the Army of the Cumberland.—The Christmas Night War-Council.—The Muddy March Southward.—The Midnight Cavalcade.—"Push Them Hard."—Fog and Hard Marching.—In front of Murfreesboro.—The Rail Tent.—The Calm that Precedes the Battle-Storm.—Star Spangled Banner.—McCook Surprised.—Sheridan Stands Firm.—The Battle nearly Lost.—General Rosecrans Turns the Tide.—Desperate Valor.—Negley's Men Cut their Way Through the Confederate Ranks.—The Enemy Driven.—The Last Grand Charge.—Magnificent Victory.—Rosecrans' Star in the Ascendant.

GENERAL ROSECRANS, having succeeded General Buell in the command of the Army of the Cumberland, established his headquarters at Nashville, and for two months previous to January, 1863, had been occupied in re-organizing and recruiting his army, securing his communications and accumulating supplies.

On Christmas night, 1862, a council of war was held at General Rosecrans' headquarters, which did not break up until midnight. McCook was there, and Crittenden and Thomas. It was decided to commence the march to Murfreesboro in the morning. There Bragg's army was concentrated and there Rosecrans proposed to give him battle.

When at the middle of night, the corps commanders left their general's door, he grasped each one by the hand saying as he did so, "Spread out your skirmishers far and wide! Expose their nests! Keep fighting!"

At daylight on the morning of the twenty-sixth the advance was commenced. The army of Rosecrans, nearly fifty thousand strong, took up their line of march along the muddy roads and drenched fields, while the rain poured down in torrents and the valleys were thick with mist. But after two months of comparative inactivity, the army was full of excitement at the prospect of renewing the contest, and with brave hearts they marched on, seemingly unmindful of the rain.

McCook commanded the right, Crittenden the left, and Thomas held the center—the three grand divisions filling every road leading south or southwest from Nashville. It was not until some hours afterwards that Rosecrans and staff rode out from the city to join his command. The fog was so dense on the right that McCook was obliged to halt. The country as they advanced increased in roughness and was heavily wooded with thickets of oak and cedar.

Two miles beyond the picket lines our advance encountered large bodies of Confederate cavalry, supported by infantry and artillery. Sharp skirmishing ensued and the progress of the Union troops was rendered difficult and bloody. After the day's toilsome march through the mud and rain and over the broken country, the army, at night, bivouacked in the wet fields. "Through the darkness and storm, Rosecrans with his escort went dashing over the country, in search of McCook's headquarters. Their horses' hoofs struck fire among the rocks, and they swung along at such a slashing pace that one of his escort finally exclaimed: "General, this way of going like h—l over the rocks will knock up the horses." "That's true," he replied, "walk." Moving on more slowly through the impenetrable blackness, he called an orderly and said, "Go back and tell that young man he must not be profane." Reaching McCook's headquarters in the woods the two entered a wagon and sitting down on the bottom, with a candle between them stuck in the socket of a bayonet, the point of which was driven into the floor, they consulted together of the movements for the morrow. "*Push them hard*," were his last words as he arose to his feet. Emerging from the wagon between ten and eleven o'clock, he exclaimed, "We mount, now, gentlemen." The blast of a bugle suddenly rung through the forest, rousing up the staff, some of whom, tired with being ten hours in the saddle, were dozing in their blankets upon the rocks around. To the "Good night," of McCook, Rosecrans added, "God bless you!" and striking the spurs into his horse, dashed down the road, splashing the mud over himself and those who pressed hard after him. Losing his way on his return, he "charged impatiently" through the woods, in the vain effort to find the right road. Amid bugle calls and shouts, the escort got separated and confused, and lost their leader, who, with a part of his staff, wandered off alone, and at length, at one o'clock in the morning, reached his camp—having been in the saddle eighteen hours. The others did not arrive there till two hours later." On the next morning the landscape continued to be enveloped in mist and the marching columns pressed slowly on; but in the early afternoon the fog lifted and their progress was more sure. As they advanced, they drove the Confederate skirmishers before them. The next day being Sunday, the army rested, but before sunrise on Monday morning, the Union columns were again in motion, sweeping southward. Crittenden, with Palmer's division in the van, went forward on the main Murfreesboro road to Stone River. At about three o'clock in the afternoon, General Palmer signaled Rosecrans that Murfreesboro was in sight and that the enemy were retreating. Rosecrans at once ordered a division into the town. The brigade of Harker was sent across the river and drove a regiment of the enemy back upon their main supports, but some captured prisoners, reporting that the entire corps of Breckenridge occupied Murfreesboro, Crittenden withdrew Harker across the river without serious disaster. The Confederates were driven in so sharply on the Jefferson and Murfreesboro pikes that they had no time to destroy the bridges behind them, on which they crossed Stone River. The next day—December thirtieth—Rosecrans was up at three o'clock in the morning, and the Union columns were pushed through the cedar thickets towards the point where the enemy were drawn up in line of battle. At about seven o'clock Crittenden's advance received a sharp fire from the enemy.

It becoming apparent that some of the Confederate

cannoneers were making a target of Rosecrans' headquarters, the general changed his position to the crest of a slope a short distance away, and halting under some road-side trees, remained there, directing the disposition of his troops, for the rest of the day. A shed was constructed by placing a pole in a couple of crotched sticks and covering one side with rails and rubber blankets. Sheltered from the rain under this improvised roof, the staff here wrote their orders before a blazing camp fire. The boom of cannon from the front, the Union columns wheeling into position, the roll of musketry, and the galloping cavalry and flying orderlies all indicated with unerring certainty, a great battle at hand. Just at this time, in the gloom and rain, the band of the Fourth Cavalry struck up the "Star Spangled Banner" and the patriot strains awoke an answering chord in every heart that beat under the army blue.

By night the army was nearly all in position, stretching along an irregular north and south line for the distance of three miles and facing the enemy. Our left rested on Stone River, the extreme right under Willich, brigade commander, being placed at right angles to the main line in order to meet, if necessary, any flank movement of the enemy. The right wing, which had suffered to some degree from the determined efforts of the Confederates to repel their advance, was placed along an elevation of ground, covered with woods and fronting an open field. A valley of cedar and oak thickets occupied the space between the front of this ridge and the lines of the enemy.

The center was slightly in advance of the main

line, while the left, with its two extremities placed in opposite tracts of woods, had its center across a broad cotton-field. Thickets, fields, patches of forest-growth and half-burned clearings stretched behind.

Half a mile away lay the Confederate army, arranged in a line parallel to our own.

The right wing of our army was in three divisions, Johnson holding the right, Davis the center and Sheridan the left, which joined the center of Rosecrans' army.

The peaceful dawn of the thirty-first was broken by the roll of the drum and the bugle-call, ringing down the line. Very soon, Van Cleve's division was in motion. In the tent of General Rosecrans, the solemn ceremony of High Mass was being celebrated, after which the officers with their overcoats on, gathered around the fires in the wintry morning. Suddenly, Rosecrans heard the sound of distant firing from the direction of McCook's position. But in nowise disturbed he went on talking, supposing that all was going on as he expected. But there had been a serious mistake somewhere in calculations.

"Before seven o'clock in the morning, Hardee's corps burst from the thickets in McCook's front and on his right; Cleburne's four brigades charging vehemently its extreme right, Cheatham's and McCown's divisions striking it more directly in front, hurling back our skirmishers at once on our lines, and crumbling these into a fleeing mob within a few minutes. Of the two brigade commanders in Johnson's division, holding our extreme right, General Kirk was severely wounded at the first fire; while General Willich had his horse killed and was himself captured. So sudden and unexpected was the attack, that a portion of our battery horses had been unhitched from the guns and sent off to drink, a few minutes before. The guns, of course, were lost." McCook's attempt to re-form his broken ranks behind his first position was a failure. His right was utterly routed and chased back towards our center. If Sheridan's division had given way before the sudden onset of the enemy like the other two divisions under Johnson, Rosecrans' battle would have been a lost cause. But Sheridan stood fast. Every man was at his post and every artillery-man at his gun, awaiting the shock.

The hostile columns massed before the batteries, several regiments deep, and marched firmly upon our guns, though the cannon-shot tore open their ranks with fearful havoc. But the gaps closed up as quickly as made, and they marched up to within pistol-shot of Sill's brigade. At this point, another terrible volley of fire blazed in their very faces, and the entire line broke and fled. Sill, with his brigade, charged after them in pursuit, chasing them to the woods. But the enemy rallied again with fresh forces and moved against Sheridan's flank. Sheridan then moved up to Negley and joining that part of the center, placed his troops in such a position that they presented two slender fronts to the enemy. His artillery was located at the angle thus formed and in this manner they awaited the attack. Three times a desperate advance was made by the Confedérates and three times did Sheridan send them back repulsed. The enemy's artillery was pushed forward until the guns of the opposing batteries played on each other at rifle-shot range. The slaughter was deadly. At last the ammunition gave out, and owing to the capture of supply trains no more could be obtained. In this desperate strait and with the Confederates swarming on all sides, Sheridan was compelled to fall back, leaving nine guns on the field. There was no panic—no disorder; but slowly, with unbroken ranks and flying colors, did those brave men retire.

The center was now exposed by Sheridan's retreat, and the combined forces of the Rebels concentrated their attack upon that portion of our line. Rosecrans arrived on the field just as Sheridan was retiring. An aide dashed up to him with the news that the right had given way and the center was fighting alone.

"Tell General McCook I will help him," exclaimed Rosecrans, and almost immediately his troops were marching, on the double-quick, across the field.

An aide was dispatched to Van Cleve to send a brigade to the right, and the artillery and troops were hurried to the scene of battle.

Rosecrans dashed forward with his staff at a breakneck pace, and galloping through the thickest of the fight, down Harker's front, he gained an eminence near by, from which the position of his troops could be seen. Observing a hostile battery playing with deadly effect on Harker's brigade, he shouted to the Chief of Artillery, "Silence that battery!" and planting the guns himself, again galloped off through a whirlwind of shot. He met Sheridan with his retreating troops when that General said to him, "We have no cartridges and our guns are empty. Rosecrans directed where ammunition could be found, and very soon, Sheridan, with his decimated ranks, was once more facing the foe.

The right of the center under Negley, uncovered by Sheridan's retreat, was flanked, and the brave men were obliged to cut their way through to the rear. The left still occupied its position on the river, holding it with determination, and Hazen, commanding the left of Negley's division, stood like a rock, holding the key of the position, while the enemy charged his line furiously, but in vain.

Meantime Rosecrans rapidly formed a new line of battle. He dashed from one point to another on the field, giving orders and imbuing the men with his own enthusiasm. Six batteries were massed on an eminence which commanded the approach of the enemy. Their advancing columns came on with steady front and bristling steel.

The shot from our guns tore through their lines with awful havoc, and when they drew nearer, a wild and resistless charge was made on their reeling ranks. The staff officers, in imitation of their brave general, threw themselves enthusiastically into the thickest of the fight, waving their caps and leading the men forward.

The Confederate line halted and then gave way before the terrible onset of our troops, leaving the ground thick with their dead. But though driven back, their broken lines were re-formed with their reserves and again they advanced to the attack only to be again hurled back.

About four o'clock Bragg made his last attempt, and at this time it was chiefly directed against Palmer's division on the river. But Hazen with his immortal thirteen hundred, still held the ground to which they had clung with such marvelous tenacity during the day. Says Hazen in his report: * * * "About four o'clock the enemy again advanced upon my front, in two lines. The battle had hushed, and the dreadful splendor of this advance can only be conceived, as all description must fall vastly short. His right was even with my left, and his left was lost in the distance.

"But this proud array had lost its strength; the confidence of victory was wanting, and at the first volley it wheeled and disappeared."

At sunset the battle for the day was over and that night there was a meeting of generals at head-quarters. Despite the desperate fighting of the past twenty-four hours and the advantages gained, they knew that the enemy was not beaten and that the battle would probably be renewed on the morrow. The anxious question in debate was whether the fight should be continued next day. Rosecrans, mounting his horse, rode over the battle-ground, ascertained that there was ammunition enough on hand, examined the country and returning, said, "Gentlemen, we conquer or die right here."

The die was cast, and Rosecrans, making a few changes in the disposition of his troops, awaited with anxious heart the morning.

In the forenoon of the next day, Beattie was sent across the river with two brigades of Van Cleve's division, and occupied a hill commanding the upper ford.

At about three o'clock in the afternoon, the enemy advanced from the thickets in front of Breckenridge's position, and moved forward to the attack. They crossed the open cotton-fields in three heavy battle-lines, supported by three batteries. White puffs of smoke soon shot out from the hill-side; our single battery responded, and the roar of guns shook the shores of the stream. At first they came on with steady step and even front, and then, like a swollen torrent, flung themselves forward on that portion of Van Cleve's division which was across the river, and bore it back and over the stream to the main body. But Rosecrans was prepared for this movement—in fact, when it occurred, was about to execute his original plan and swing his left against Breckenridge. He hastily massed fifty-eight cannon on an eminence, where they could completely enfilade the successive columns as they advanced. Their opening roar was terrific, and the crash of the iron storm through the thick-set ranks was overwhelming. It was madness to face it, yet the Rebel columns closed up and pressed on; but as they came within close range of our musketry, the line suddenly seemed to shrivel up like a piece of parchment, in the fire that met it, yet, pushed on and cheered by the rear lines, the ranks endeavored to bear up against it and advance, but again halted; while officers, with waving caps and flashing swords, galloped along the lines and still urged them on. They had now got so near that the men could be seen to topple over separately, before the volleys.

A third and last time they staggered forward, the foremost ranks reaching even to the water's edge. But here they stopped—it was like charging down the red mouth of a volcano. Balancing a moment on the edge of battle, they broke and fled. With a wild and thrilling shout, our troops sprung to their feet, and charged with the bayonet—dashing like madmen through the stream. They chased the flying foe for a half mile, cheering as they charged, their cheers caught up by those on the other side of the river, and sent back with increased volume and power. Darkness ended the fight, and Crittenden's entire corps passed over, and with Davies occupied the ground so gallantly won.

The next night Bragg evacuated Murfreesboro, and the following morning Rosecrans celebrated High Mass in praise of the victory.

The Union loss in killed and wounded reached the startling estimate of nearly nine thousand men, or twenty per cent. of the force engaged. Fifty pieces of artillery were also lost; but though the cost was terrible, the *battle was won;* thanks to the grand generalship of Rosecrans, the desperate valor of Sheridan, the firmness of Hazen, the bravery of Thomas, Crittenden, and others, and the unflinching support rendered by the soldiers of the Army of the Cumberland. There is little doubt that at one time the battle was nearly lost to us, and but for the decisive action of Rosecrans, our arms would have met with reverse instead of being crowned with victory. That General rose at once to a dizzy height in the popular esteem, and his name became a talisman of victory.

CHAPTER XXV.

CHANCELLORSVILLE.

Successful Strategy of General Hooker.—Crossing the Rappahannock at Sunrise.—The Chancellorsville House.—Lee's Position Flanked. —The Battle Opened by Sykes.—Loss of Prestige and Position by the Union Troops.—Capture of Prisoners by General Birney.—Stonewall Jackson Appears Upon the Scene.—Our Divisions Overwhelmed by the Rebel Hordes.—A Frantic Stampede.—Heroism of Major Keenan, and his men.—Death of Stonewall Jackson.—A Fatal Hour.—Beating a Retreat.—Hooker's Words of Praise.—Lincoln Visits the Camp at Falmouth.

THE last days of April 1863, witnessed the stratagem and skill of General Hooker, in his advance upon the Confederate position on the south bank of the Rappahannock. A feint of crossing the river below Fredericksburg with his entire army completely deceived the enemy who immediately withdrew his forces from the upper fords and concentrated them opposite the feigned point of attack.

Three corps commanded respectively by Generals Howard, Slocum, and Meade, had been sent up the river but marched at a sufficent distance from the hostile southern banks to avoid all observation. Arriving at Kelly's Ford they began to cross though it was night, and the men were compelled to wade in water up to their armpits. The moon which shone brightly assisted them several hours, but went down before the last corps had crossed, when fording had to be suspended until morning. Pontoons were brought up and laid at sunrise, and then the remainder of the infantry and cavalry corps crossed briskly.

The columns advanced towards the Rapidan, and the commands of Howard and Slocum crossed this river at Germania Mills, while Meade's Corps crossed below at Ely's Ford, and then all marched on roads which converge at the Chancellorsville House, a large brick edifice, which was used as a mansion and tavern, situated in a small clearing of a few acres and which with its few appendages of out-buildings constituted the village known by that name.

Other forces, including General Pleasanton with nearly a brigade of cavalry who guarded the flanks of the advancing columns had crossed the river, and taken position near Chancellorsville.

By this wily movent General Lee's position on the Rappahannock had been entirely flanked ; and, flushed with incipient success, General Hooker followed his great captains, and in the evening, thirtieth of April, he established his headquarters in the historic brick mansion above described. So completely absorbed was our General with the brilliancy of his advance, that, in the moment of exultation, he forgot the danger of his situation and issued the following congratulatory order :

HEAD-QUARTERS, ARMY OF THE POTOMAC,
CAMP NEAR FALMOUTH, VIRGINIA, April 30th, 1863.

It is with heartfelt satisfaction that the commanding General announces to the army that the operations of the last three days have determined that our enemy must either ingloriously fly, or come out from behind his defences and give us battle on our own ground, where certain destruction awaits him. The operations of the Fifth, Eleventh, and Twelfth Corps have been a succession of splendid achievements.

By command of MAJOR-GENERAL HOOKER.

S. WILLIAMS, *Assistant Adjutant General.*

It would seem as if the General had overlooked the fact that his army had but eight days supplies at hand; that a treacherous river flowed between him and his depots; that he was surrounded by a labyrinth of forests, traversed in every direction by narrow roads and paths, all well known to the enemy, but unknown even to most of his guides; and that many of his guns of heaviest calibre, and most needed in a deadly strife, were on the other side the river.

General Lee had undoubtedly been outgeneraled by Hooker in this movement, but he appeared not to have been disconcerted. Leaving the Heights of Fredericksburg with a small force, he advanced towards Chancellorsville.

The first collision between the contending forces took place on the first of May. General Sickles with a division of regulars was despatched at nine o'clock in the morning on the Old Pike to Fredericksburg. He was followed by a part of the Second Corps. Sykes had not proceeded far before he encountered Lee advancing, and a sharp contest ensued, with heavy losses on both sides. The Rebels having the best ground, and being superior in numbers, compelled our men to fall back, which they did in tolerable order, bringing away everything but their dead and badly wounded. But the enemy followed our retreating column, though cautiously, and filled the woods with sharpshooters. They also planted their heavy batteries on hills which partially commanded the clearing around the Chancellorsville House. This gave them great advantage. They were also greatly elated with the success which had crowned the first onset. This was Hooker's first misfortune or mistake. The first blow in such an engagement is quite as important as the last. This first movement ought to have been more powerful, and ought to have given to our men a foretaste of victory. But we had lost prestige and position which undoubtedly weakened us not a little. The night following passed quietly away, except that the leaders were laying their plans for future operations.

About eight o'clock on the morning of the second, it was reported that a heavy column of the enemy was passing rapidly towards our right, whither the Eleventh Corps had been stationed. This movement was hidden by the forests, though the road over which the column passed was not far from our front. A rifled battery was opened upon this moving column, which, though out of sight, was thrown into disorder, at which time General Birney made a charge upon them with such force as to capture and bring away five hundred prisoners. By successive and successful advances, by sunset our men had broken this column and held the road upon which they had been marching to some scene of mischief. But the evil was not cured, as other roads more distant and better screened were followed by the wily foe.

Just before dark Stonewall Jackson, with about twenty-five thousand veterans, fell like a whirlwind upon the Eleventh Corps, which he had flanked so cautiously and yet so rapidly that our German comrades were taken by surprise while preparing their suppers, with arms stacked, and no time to recover. It is not at all wonderful that men surprised under these circumstances should become panic stricken and flee. Let not the censure rest upon the rout, but upon the carelessness that led to the surprise.

Whole divisions were now overwhelmed by the Rebel hordes, that swept forward amid blazing musketry and battle-shouts, which made the wilderness resound; and a frantic stampede commenced which not all the courage and effort of commanding generals, or the intrepidity of some regiments could check, and which threatened to rout the entire army. This unforeseen disaster changed the whole programme of the battle, and greatly disheartened our men.

However, the ground was not to be abandoned so ingloriously, and though our lines were broken, and the enemy had gained a great advantage, heroism was yet to manifest its grand spirit, and to achieve undying laurels. The sun had gone down refusing to look upon this Union defeat and slaughter, but the pale-faced moon gazed with her weird light upon the bloody scene, while the carnage still continued.

With the disaster of the Eleventh Corps, General Sickles, who was stationed in the front and center of our lines, and had been preparing to deal a heavy blow upon the enemy, was left in a critical position. His expectation of assistance from General Howard was not only cut off, but he was left with only two divisions and his artillery to meet the shock of the advancing hosts. General Pleasanton, with his small force of cavalry, being under Sickles' command, was ordered to charge the proud columns of the enemy, with the hope of checking them until our batteries could be suitably planted.

Pleasanton, addressing Major Keenan of the Eighth Pennsylvania Cavalry, said, "You must charge into those woods with your regiment, and hold the Rebels until I can get some of these guns into position. You must do it at whatever cost."

"I will," was the noble response of the true soldier, who, with only about five hundred men, was to encounter columns at least twenty-five thousand strong, led by Stonewall Jackson! The forlorn charge was made, but the martyr-leader, with the majority of his dauntless troopers, soon baptized the earth upon which he fell, with his life blood. But the precious sacrifice was not in vain. The Rebel advance was greatly checked, as when a trembling lamb is thrown into the jaws of a pursuing pack of ravenous wolves.

The two determined generals improved these dearly bought moments in planting their own batteries, and getting in readiness also several guns which had been abandoned by the Eleventh Corps in its flight. All these guns were double-shotted, and all due preparation was made for the expected stroke. It was a moment of trembling suspense. Our heroes waited not long, when the woods just in front of them began to swarm with the advancing legions of the foe, who opened a vigorous musketry fire, and charged towards our guns. Darkness was falling; but the field where the batteries were planted was so level that the gunners could do wonderful execution. And this they did. The Rebel charge had just commenced when our guns simultaneously opened with a withering fire, which cut down whole ranks of living flesh like grass. As one line of embattled hosts melted away, another rushed forward in its place to meet the same sad fate. Three successive and desperate charges were made, one of them to within a few yards of the guns, but each was repulsed with terrible slaughter. In many places the dead were literally in heaps. Our resistance proved successful.

A little later in the night, and right in front of these batteries, fell Stonewall Jackson, mortally wounded by our scathing fire, as was at first supposed, but more likely by the fire of his own infantry, as one of their writers alleges. Speaking of Jackson, he says, "Such was his ardor, at this critical moment, and his anxiety to penetrate the movements of the enemy, doubly screened as they were by the dense forest and gathering darkness, that he rode ahead of his skirmishers, and exposed himself to a close and dangerous fire from the enemy's sharpshooters, posted in the timber.

"So great was the danger which he thus ran, that one of his staff said: 'General, don't you think this is the wrong place for you?' He replied quickly: 'The danger is all over; the enemy is routed. Go back, and tell A. P. Hill to press right on.' Soon after giving this order General Jackson turned, and, accompanied by his staff and escort, rode back at a trot, on his well-known 'Old Sorrel,' toward his own men. Unhappily, in the darkness—it was now nine or ten o'clock at night—the little body of horsemen was mistaken for Federal cavalry charging, and the regiments on the right and left of the road fired a sudden volley into them with the most lamentable results. Captain Boswell, of General Jackson's staff, chief of artillery, was wounded; and two couriers were killed. General Jackson received one ball in his left arm, two inches below the shoulder joint, shattering the bone and severing the chief artery; a second passed through the same arm, between the elbow and wrist, making its exit through the palm of the hand; a third ball entered the palm of his right hand, about the middle, and, passing through, broke two of the bones.

"He fell from his horse, and was caught by Captain Wormly, to whom he said, 'All my wounds are by my own men.'"

The loss of this heroic chieftain, this swift flanker and intrepid leader, was undoubtedly the greatest yet felt by either army in the fall of a single man. Some report that, on hearing of the sad fall of his chief captain, General Lee exclaimed, "I would rather have lost twenty thousand men!"

Admitting that the Rebels gained in this battle a great victory, its advantages were dearly purchased by the loss of Thomas Jonathan Jackson. About midnight a fierce charge was made by General Sickles' forces, which proved successful, enabling our boys to recover much of the ground formerly occupied by the unfortunate Eleventh Corps, and they brought back with them some abandoned guns and other valuable articles from the *débris*, which the Rebels had not time or disposition to disturb.

General Hooker then ordered this exposed position to be abandoned, and by daylight our lines were falling back in good order towards Chancellorsville, but were closely pursued by the enemy, who filled the woods. Several determined charges were made upon our retreating columns, which, however, were repelled mostly by the fire of our artillery, which mowed down hundreds as they rushed recklessly almost to the cannon's mouth. But these batteries had been played and worked so incessantly for the last twelve hours, that ammunition began to fail, and General Sickles sent a message to Hooker that assistance must be granted him, or he would be compelled to yield his ground. The officer who brought the despatch, found General Hooker, in a senseless state, surrounded by his hopeless attendants, while general confusion had possession of the head-quarters. A few minutes previous to this a cannon-ball had struck the wall of the mansion upon which the general was incidentally leaning, the concussion felling him to the floor. For some time he was supposed to be dead, but soon giving signs of returning consciousness, General Couch, who was next in rank, refused to assume command, and hence about an hour of precious time was lost. This was a fatal hour. Had General Hooker been able to receive Sickles' message, and ordered a heavy force to his assistance, it is thought that a great disaster could have been prevented, and probably a victory might have been gained.

But the golden opportunity, which is seldom duplicated in a given crisis or a life-time, was lost; and the enemy, though somewhat disorganized and badly disheartened by our well-managed batteries, had time, during this lull, to recover strength. They then advanced again with such power as to compel our men to retire from Chancellorsville toward the Rappahannock, leaving the brick mansion a mass of ruins, made such by the fire of the enemy.

By noon General Hooker had recovered his consciousness sufficiently to order the movements of his troops. The fighting on his front was now nearly over, but his position was critical. General Sedgwick, who had been directed to cross the Rappahannock below Fredericksburg, with orders to advance thence against all obstacles until he could fall upon General Lee's rear, while the grand army engaged him in front, found it impossible to proceed as rapidly as was expected of him, and was finally repulsed with such slaughter and pursued with such vigor as to be compelled to recross the river, leaving at least five thousand of his men killed, wounded, and captured in the hands of the enemy.

No alternative seemed now left to the Army of the Potomac but to beat a retreat and recross the river. On the evening of the fifth, General Hooker held a council of war with his commanders, at which, however, nothing was decided upon; but in the night he took the responsibility of ordering all his forces to recross the Rappahannock, which they did in good order and without molestation; and thus ended the disastrous battle of Chancellorsville, with a loss of about eighteen thousand men on each side, and our remaining troops returned to bivouac on their old camping-ground on the north bank of the river near Falmouth.

This retrograde movement was undoubtedly considered to be necessary in consequence of the impending storm, which set in about four o'clock of the afternoon of the fifth, and rendered the march and night exceedingly disagreeable. The river was swollen so rapidly as to set adrift several of our pontoons, and the act of recrossing, though orderly, was by no means pleasant. The storm was cold and violent, and the roads soon became so bad as to remind the boys of Burnside's unfortunate advance in January. It is supposed by some that the rain explains satisfactorily the conduct of the enemy, who seemed to make no attempt whatever to follow our returning troops.

While yet the rain was drenching our weary boys, on the sixth, General Hooker issued a congratulatory order to them and the country, in which are to be found the following characteristic passages:

"The Major-General commanding tenders to this army his congratulations on its achievements of the last seven days. If it has not accomplished all that was expected, the reasons are well known to the army. It is sufficient to say they were of a character not to be foreseen nor prevented by human sagacity or resources.

"In withdrawing from the south bank of the Rappahannock before delivering a general battle to our adversaries, the army has given renewed evidence of its confidence in itself and its fidelity to the principles it represents. In fighting at a disadvantage, we would have been recreant to our trust, to ourselves, our cause, and our country. Profoundly loyal, and conscious of its strength, the Army of the Potomac will give or decline battle whenever its interest or honor may demand. It will also be the guardian of its own history and its own honor.

"By our celerity and secrecy of movement, our advance and passage of the rivers was undisputed, and, on our withdrawal, not a Rebel ventured to follow.

"The events of the last week may swell with pride the heart of every officer and soldier of this army. We have added new luster to its former renown. We have made long marches, crossed rivers, surprised the enemy in his intrenchments, and, wherever we have fought, have inflicted heavier blows than we have received. We have taken from the enemy five thousand prisoners and fifteen colors; captured and brought off seven pieces of artillery; placed *hors de combat* eighteen thousand of his chosen troops, destroyed his depots filled with a vast amount of stores; deranged his communications; captured prisoners within the fortifications of his capital, and filled his country with fear and consternation. We have no other regret than that caused by the loss of our brave companions; and in this we are consoled by the conviction that they have fallen in the holiest cause ever submitted to the arbitrament of battle."

This order, if not perfectly satisfactory to the country and to the authorities, was generally hailed with applause by the army, which recognized in its sagacious rendering of our difficulties and humiliations the meed of praise awarded where it was due.

The two great armies once more confronted each other from either bank of the river, as they had done during all the winter and spring months. On the seventh of May, President Lincoln visited the camp near Falmouth, conferred with his generalissimo on movements past and future, appeared pleased with the spirit and *morale* of the troops, and returned to Washington to continue his earnest toil for the nation's life and well-being.

During the month of May, quite a depletion of the rank and file of the army took place, by the mustering out of large numbers of three months' and two years' men. And such had been the depressing influence of Chancellorsville upon the country, that the places of these men were not very easily filled. To the sagacious leaders in political and military circles this state of things was not a little alarming. But to the Confederate leaders the times were affording opportunities for grand schemes, and for the execution of movements most startling.

CHAPTER XXVI.

ALDIE.

Hooker Entraps Lee.—Reconnoissance of Pleasanton.—Aldie in Sight.—The Grand Charge.—Harris Light in the Van.—Fitzhugh Lee's Desperate Efforts.—The Desired Opportunity.—Battle of the Haystacks.—The Harris Light Wins.—Colonel Cesnola.—The Sword Presentation.—Last Desperate Attempt of the Enemy.—Driven From the Field in Panic.—The Battle Won.

THE second cavalry battle at Brandy Station, fought June ninth, 1863, exposed the real movements of Lee and convinced Hooker beyond question that it was the intention of his opponent to cross the Potomac at some point near Harper's Ferry and again lead his army into Maryland and Pennsylvania. No effort was made to prevent or check this advance. General Hooker contented himself with moving slowly on and carefully watching the development of the Confederate plans, until his various corps reached Fairfax Court House. Here he made his head-quarters for several days, pushing his columns well out towards Aldie and Thoroughfare Gap.

This delay was purposely made, in order that Lee might have ample time to reach a point from which he could not retreat without a battle. The tardiness of the Confederate general in reaching the banks of the Potomac caused considerable uneasiness in the mind of Hooker. To solve this mystery, General Pleasanton was instructed to make a reconnoisance in force. At six o'clock on the morning of June seventeenth, 1863, the Cavalry corps, with Kilpatrick's division in the advance, moved from its temporary encampment near Centreville.

Taking the Warrenton Turnpike we soon crossed the memorable field of Bull Run, passed the famous Plains of Manassas, and at mid-day came in sight of the mountain heights surrounding the little village of Aldie. This place is situated in a gap of the Bull Run Mountains, and Kilpatrick had orders to pass southward through this gate, thence through the Blue Ridge at Ashby's Gap, and track the movements of Lee.

The force under Kilpatrick consisted of the Harris Light, Colonel Davies; Fourth New York, Colonel Cesnola: The First Massachusetts, First Rhode Island, Sixth Ohio Cavalry, Colonel Duffie; and a section of artillery under Lieutenant Randall. The Harris Light led the division. We marched in column of fours, and on that day my squadron was the advance guard. As I was at that time chief of the first platoon, my place was at the head of the long column which wound down the road.

As we came upon Aldie, the advance guard of the enemy under W. H. F. Lee was unexpectedly encountered. But Kilpatrick proved himself equal to the occasion and met the surprise gallantly. Dashing to the front, he made a rapid survey of the situation, and then came the command, in his clear, ringing tones, "Form platoons! Trot! March!" Down through the streets of the town we charged, and along the Middleburg Road leading over the low hill beyond. This fine position was gained so quickly and so successfully, that Fitzhugh Lee, taken by surprise, made no opposition to our brilliant advance; though immediately afterwards he rallied and fought desperately for two hours to gain the lost position, while the guns of his battery blazed destruction upon our lines. But Randall's guns blazed in return, tearing open the Confederate ranks with their shot and shell, and our boys handsomely repulsed their attack.

On the crest of the hill up which our platoons charged, there was a field of hay-stacks, not yet garnered, inclosed in a barricade of rails. Behind these the enemy occupied a strong position, and their sharpshooters had annoyed our lines to such an extent that they prevented our advance on the left.

It was well known to the officers of the Harris Light, that our regiment had not met Kilpatrick's expectations, on the field of Brandy Station, and on the morning of this battle we had asked our General "for an opportunity to retrieve our reputation." This chance came soon enough. Kilpatrick, ordering forward a battalion of the Harris Light, and giving the men a few words of encouragement, turned to Major McIrvin and pointing to the field of hay-stacks, said, "Major there is the opportunity you have asked for. Go take that position!" Away dashed this officer and his men. In a moment the enemy was reached, and the struggle began. The horses could not leap the barricade, but the men dismounted, scaled those formidable barriers, and with drawn sabres, rushed upon the hidden foe, who quickly asked for quarter.

"Another incident occurred worth mentioning. Colonel Cesnola, of the Fourth New York Cavalry, had that morning, through mistake, been placed under arrest, and his sword being taken from him was without arms. But in one of these wild charges, made early in the contest, his regiment hesitated. Forgetting that he was under arrest, and without command, he flew to the head of his regiment, reassured his men, and, without a weapon to give or ward a blow, led them to the charge. This gallant act was seen by his general, who, meeting him on his return, said: 'Colonel, you are a brave man; you are released from arrest;' and, taking his own sword from his side, handed it to the colonel, saying: Here is my sword; wear it in honor of this day!' In the next charge Colonel Cesnola fell, desperately wounded and was taken prisoner."

But the enemy, though repulsed and driven on every side, again rallied for a last desperate attempt. Massing a heavy force on our right, General Rosser led them in a wild charge upon our lines. The First Massachusetts, on the extreme right, received the shock of this terrible onset, and though compelled to fall back, they fought steadily and bravely until the rest of the right gave way. Then ensued a scene of confusion and flight that sickened the heart of their brave General. But Kilpatrick quickly rushed to the rescue and prevented the threatened disaster. Randall was ordered to double-shot the guns of his battery; the center and left were told to hold their ground, and placing himself at the head of the First Maine, he waited until the Confederate columns were within fifty yards of Randall's battery. "Forward!" was the order that then rung along the lines, aad with resistless fury they swept down on the advancing Rebel ranks, causing them to reel and break in confused and disordered flight. Kilpatrick's horse was killed under him, but determined to complete the victory, he mounted a fresh one and led his whole line in a last charge against the flying foe. For a short time Lee endeavored to withstand this fierce attack, but finding his effort useless, sounded a retreat which quickly became a rout. His troops were driven in confusion as far as Middleburg, and night alone saved the remnant of his command.

"This was by far the most bloody cavalry battle of the war. The Rebel chivalry had again been beaten, and Kilpatrick, who was the only general on the field, at once took a proud stand among the most famous of our Union cavalry generals. The fame of our cavalry was now much enhanced, and caused the greatest joy to the Nation."

Many a brave soul suffered death's sad eclipse at Aldie, whose hopes brimmed high on the morning of that eventful day; and many a one escaped the storm of bullets unscathed when to escape was marvelous. In looking back upon that desperate day, I have often wondered by what strange fatality I passed through its rain of fire unhurt, but the field which brought a harvest of death to so many others, marked an era in my own humble, military history which I recall with pride and pleasure; for from the battle of Aldie I date my first commission. The mantle of rank which fell from one whom death made a shining mark, on that ground, dropped upon my shoulders, and I was proud and grateful to wear it in my country's service. I feel a just pride also in having been a participant in the "battle of the haystacks", where the glorious squadrons of the Harris Light, swept into the mad conflict with the same resistless bravery that distinguished them on the field of Brandy Station.

Every soldier of the saddle who there fought under the grand leadership of Kilpatrick, may justly glory in the laurels won at Aldie.

CHAPTER XXVII.

UPPERVILLE.

Union Advance from Middleburg—Rebel Pickets Encountered.—The Fight Commenced.—Stone Fence Barricades.—A Succession of Brilliant Charges.—The Harris Light Drives the Enemy.—Splendid Cavalry Action.—Stand at Upperville.—The Enemy Again Driven.—Union Forces Triumphant.—General Pleasanton's Report.

THE running cavalry fight which began at Middleburg and ended at Upperville, on a hot day in June, 1863, was a marvel of splendid action, and is of especial interest to me as a participant in its succession of brilliant charges.

At eight o'clock on the morning of the twenty first of June, General Pleasanton, at the head of the Cavalry Corps, moved out of Middleburg towards Ashby's Gap in the Blue Ridge. We had not proceeded far before the Rebel outposts were encountered, and driving them before us, we came upon a large cavalry force under the leadership of Fitzhugh Lee. A running engagement then commenced which was kept up for a distance of six miles.

The country between Middleburg and Upperville is a succession of ridges and hollows, and our artillery was rushed forward and planted on one eminence after another as we advanced, from which positions we shelled the opposing guns of the enemy.

Along this uneven ground, stone fences occurred with unpleasant frequency, the Confederates taking shelter behind them and firing to great advantage upon our advancing troops. But our brave boys of the saddle galloped forward, charging the Rebels behind their stone barricades and sending them flying before the Union sabres.

In the vicinity of Rector's Cross Roads the surface of the country is very rough and the roads are narrow and rocky. Near this point the enemy had planted a section of artillery on a hill in advance of us, and Kilpatrick sent the Fourth New York to take the position; but that regiment halting in a ravine out of range of the enemy's fire, Kilpatrick rode down the line calling for the Harris Light to come forward. Our regiment was ordered to charge the battery on the flank and clear the road of obstruction. The Harris Light galloped forward in column of fours down the ravine and up the hill beyond, in the very face of the enemy's guns, forming in platoon under fire and charging the foe in splendid style. Utterly routed, they wheeled with their batteries and fled. At Upperville our advance was met with great desperation, the enemy charging us handsomely, but with no great damage. When our forces had been properly arranged and the right time had come, Kilpatrick was ordered to charge the town. With drawn sabres —weapons in which the General always had great confidence, and generally won success—and with yells which made the mountains and plains resound, we rushed upon the foe. The fray was terrible. Several times did the Rebels break, but being reënforced, or falling back upon some better position, again endeavored to baffle our efforts. But they were not equal to the task, and we drove them through the village of Paris, and finally through Ashby's Gap, upon their infantry columns in the Shenandoah Valley. In these charges and chase we captured two pieces of artillery, four caissons, several stand of small arms, and a large number of prisoners.

At Rector's Cross Roads, when Kilpatrick ordered the Harris Light to charge the enemy's battery on a hill in advance of us, as we galloped down the intervening gully where the Fourth New York had halted, sheltered by the rise of ground, and while we were forming in column of platoons under the enemy's fire, a fatal bullet pierced my horse and he fell dead under me. Fortunately I was not dragged down in his fall, and as I struck the ground, a riderless horse in an Indiana company near by came up. One of the sergeants of this company had been shot dead at the same time that my animal had fallen, and mounting his horse I rode forward with the regiment as they charged the enemy's position.

Our scouts, during this engagement, had managed to gain an entrance into the Valley, where they ascertained that the Rebel army, in heavy columns, was advancing towards the Upper Potomac.

This fight was of sufficient importance to call forth from the commanding general the following official document.

HEADQUARTERS CAVALRY CORPS,
Camp near Upperville, June 21, 1863.

Brigadier-General S. Williams:

GENERAL: I moved with my command this morning to Middleburg, and attacked the cavalry force of the Rebels under Stuart, and steadily drove him all day, inflicting a heavy loss at every step.

I drove him through Upperville into Ashby's Gap.

We took two pieces of artillery, one being a Blakely gun, and three caissons, besides blowing up one; also, upwards of sixty prisoners, and more are coming; a lieutenant-colonel and major, and five other officers, besides a wounded colonel and a large number of wounded Rebels left in the town of Upperville.

They left their dead and wounded upon the field; of the former, I saw upward of twenty.

We also took a large number of carbines, pistols, and sabres. In fact, it was a most disastrous day to the Rebel cavalry.

Our loss has been very small both in men and horses.

I never saw the troops behave better, or under more difficult circumstances.

Very heavy charges were made, and the sabre used freely but always with great advantage to us.

A. PLEASANTON,
Brigadier-General.

CHAPTER XXVIII.

GETTYSBURG.

Meade in Command of the Army of the Potomac.—The Camp on Marsh Run.—The Advance to Gettysburg.—Charge of Buford's Cavalry on the Rebel Van-guard.—The Enemy Driven Back.—Fall of General Reynolds.—Capture of General Archer and Eight Hundred Prisoners.—Victory Followed by Defeat.—The Eleventh Corps Break and Fly.—Strengthening the Union Position.—Occupancy of Culp's Hill and Round Top.—Sickle's Command Shattered.—Activity of Kilpatrick's Cavalry.—The Enemy Falls Back to Benner's Hill.—The Last Effort.—Terrible Slaughter of Troops.—The Desperate Final Charge.—The Tempest of Fire.—Death of Farnsworth.—Capture of Prisoners.—Glorious Victory.

ON Tuesday evening, June thirtieth, 1863, General Reynolds commanding the First, Third, and Eleventh Corps of the Army of the Potomac, was encamped on Marsh Run near the village of Emmitsburg, Maryland. By direction of General Meade, General Reynolds with his First and Third Corps moved early in the morning to Gettysburg, and soon after sent orders to General Howard to follow with the Eleventh. Howard received the order of Reynolds at eight o'clock and immediately directed General Barlow's division to follow the First Corps by the most direct route, while the divisions of General Steinwehr and Shurz were instructed to proceed by the road leading through Horner's Mills. Having thus disposed of his command, General Howard pushed on in advance of the troops, accompanied by his staff.

General John Buford, commanding the Third Cavalry Division, had moved directly from Meade's headquarters at Frederick City to Gettysburg on the previous day, and went into camp on the Chambersburg Pike, about two miles west of the village. At half past nine o'clock on Wednesday morning the vanguard of the Rebel army under General Heth of A. P. Hill's Corps, appeared in front of Buford's Cavalry. The dauntless troopers charged vigorously the advancing columns of the enemy and drove them back upon their reserves where we were checked and in turn driven back before overwhelming numbers. General Wadsworth coming up from Emmitsburg, hearing the familiar sound of battle, went into a double-quick and hastening through Gettysburg, struck the Confederate advance just in time to seize and occupy the range of hills that overlook the place from the northwest, in the direction of Chambersburg.

While Wadsworth was placing his division in position, General Reynolds rode forward, unattended, to reconnoitre, when he discovered a heavy force of the enemy in a grove not far distant. Raising his field-glass to his eyes, he sought to survey the force and its position, when a whistling ball from a sharpshooter's musket struck him in the neck. He fell on his face and baptized with his life-blood the soil which had given him birth. His untimely fall, especially at this crisis and almost in sight of his childhood's home, was generally lamented. His lifeless form was borne away to the rear just as the Rebels in heavy force advanced upon not more than one-third their number.

General Abner Doubleday had to assume command of our forces under this galling fire, having arrived with a portion of the First Corps, the remainder of which and the Eleventh Corps, not being able to join them until two hours of fearful destruction had gone on. Our feeble advance was compelled to fall quickly back upon Seminary Hill, just west of the village, and were pursued very closely, so that one portion of our line, seeing its opportunity, swung around rapidly, enveloping the Rebel advance and capturing General Archer the leader, and about eight hundred prisoners.

General Howard heard the cannonading, and riding rapidly up the Emmitsburg road, sent messengers in search of General Reynolds, for instructions, not knowing that he had been killed. While waiting the return of his aids, he went to the top of the college to take a survey of the surrounding country. His aid, Major Biddle, soon came back with the sad intelligence that General Reynolds had fallen, and that the command devolved on himself.

General Howard now assumed command of all the troops engaged, giving the command of his own corps to General Carl Shurz. Our men, now emboldened by the arrival of fresh supports, and having secured a fine, commanding position, renewed the fight with spirit and wonderful success. Victory continued to perch upon the banners of the Union at every point along the lines, until one o'clock in the afternoon, when our right wing was furiously assailed by General Ewell's Corps which had been marching from York, directed by the thunder of battle.

Thus flanked and outnumbered by the gathering

hosts, the Eleventh Corps, which was most exposed to the enfilading fire of the newly arrived columns, began to waver, then to break, and soon fled in perfect rout. The First Corps was thus compelled to follow, or be annihilated. The two retreating columns met and mingled in more or less confusion in the streets of the town, where they greatly obstructed each other, though the First Corps retained its organization quite unbroken. In passing through the town the Eleventh Corps was especially exposed to the fire of the enemy, who pressed his advantage and captured thousands of prisoners. Our wounded, who up to this time had been quartered in Gettysburg, fell into the enemy's hands, and scarcely one half of our brave boys, who had so recently and proudly passed through the streets to the battle lines, had the privilege of returning, but either lay dead or dying on the hard-fought field, or were captives with a cruel foe. The number of killed and wounded showed how desperately they had fought, and the large number captured was evidence of the overwhelming numbers with which they had contended.

General Buford with his troopers, covered our retreat, showing as bold a front as possible to the enemy, who, it was supposed, would follow fiercely, as they were in strong force and several hours of daylight yet remained. But doubtless fearing that a trap might be laid for them if they advanced too far, they contented themselves with only a portion of the borough, their main force occupying the hills which form a grand amphitheatre on the north and west.

Our decimated forces repulsed by overwhelming odds took possession of Cemetery Hill, south of the town, and being reënforced by General Sickles' Corps, they began to intrench themselves with earthworks and rifle pits, to extend their lines to right and left, and to select the best positions for our batteries. This work was continued quite late into the evening, the broad moonlight greatly facilitating the operations.

General Meade, who had selected his ground for the impending battle along the banks of Pipe Creek, and who at one o'clock P. M. was at Taneytown when the news of the fight, and the death of the brave Reynolds at Gettysburg, reached him, despatched General Hancock to the scene of conflict to take command, and to ascertain whether Gettysburg afforded better ground than that which had been selected. Hancock arrived at Cemetery Hill just as our broken lines were hastily and confusedly retreating from the village; our advance, however, had already taken this commanding position and was making some preparation for resistance. The newly arrived general began at once to order the forces which had been engaged and others which were occasionally arriving. He ordered the occupancy of Culp's Hill on our extreme right, and extended the lines to our left well up the high ground in the vicinity of Round Top, a rocky eminence about two miles from Gettysburg, and nearly equidistant from the Emmitsburg and Taneytown roads. The line having been made as secure as possible, Hancock wrote to Meade that the position was excellent. His despatch had scarcely gone, when he was relieved by General Slocum, a ranking officer, and so, leaving the field, Hancock hastened to report in person to his chief the condition of things at Gettysburg. On arriving, Meade informed him that he had decided to fight at Gettysburg, and had sent orders to the various commands to that effect; then together they rode to Gettysburg, arriving about eleven o'clock at night.

All night long our forces were concentrating before this historic village, where they were all found on the morning of the second of July, except the Sixth Corps, General Sedgwick's, which did not arrive until two o'clock in the afternoon, after marching nearly all the previous night.

Second Day.

Until three o'clock all was quiet along the battle lines, except an occasional shot from a picket or sharpshooter. There had been considerable manœuvering however. On our left General Sickles, in his eagerness for a fight, had advanced his corps across the Emmitsburg road, and on a wood-crowned ridge in the immediate vicinity of the main portion of the Rebel army. General Meade, in his inspection of the lines, remonstrated against the perilous position which Sickles had taken the liberty to gain. Sickles, however, intimated that, if desired, he would withdraw to the ridge which Meade had justly indicated as the proper place where our forces would be better protected, and would be able to cover Round Top, a point which it was considered essential to retain. General Meade thereupon expressed his fear to Sickles that the enemy would not permit him quietly to retire from the trap in which he had placed his foot; and the last words had scarcely fallen from his lips, when the Rebel batteries were opened with fearful accuracy and at a short range, and the infantry came on with their fierce charging yell. General Longstreet was in command.

With such long and strong lines of infantry in his front, which lapped over his flanks on either side, and a fearful enfilading fire from the heavy batteries on Seminary Hill, Sickles and his brave men were torn, shattered, overwhelmed, and with terrible loss and in great confusion fell back to the ridge from which he ought not to have advanced. In the struggle, the Rebels made a desperate attempt to reach and possess Round Top, which they came near doing, before General Sykes, who had been ordered to advance and hold it, had gained the elevation. But their failure to possess this coveted prize proved a great disaster; for before they could withdraw their charging columns across the plain between Round Top and the ridge where Sickles stood at the beginning of the fray, they were attacked by General Hancock with a heavy force, and driven almost like chaff before the wind. Their loss was terrible. At the close of this encounter our lines stood precisely where General Meade desired they should be before the fight commenced, with Round Top fully in our possession and now strongly fortified with heavy artillery and good infantry support.

On our right General Ewell had succeeded in pushing back some portions of our lines under Slocum, who occupied Culp's Hill, and some of our fortified lines and rifle-pits were occupied by the Rebels. Night came on to close the dreadful day. Thus far the battle had been mostly in the advantage of the

Rebels. They held the ground where Reynolds had fallen, also Seminary Ridge, and the elevation whence the Eleventh Corps had been driven. They also occupied the ridge on which Sickles had commenced to fight. Sickles himself was *hors de combat*, with a shattered leg which had to be amputated, and not far from twenty thousand of our men had been killed, wounded, and captured! The Rebels had also lost heavily in killed and wounded: but having gained several important positions were deluded with the idea that they had gained a victory.

General Lee, in his official report, says: "After a severe struggle, Longstreet succeeded in getting possession of and holding the desired ground. Ewell also carried some of the strong positions which he assailed; and the result was such as to lead to the belief that he would ultimately be able to dislodge the enemy. The battle ceased at dark. These partial successes determined me to continue the assault next day."

During these days of deadly strife and of unprecedented slaughter, our cavalry was by no means idle. On the morning of the first, Kilpatrick advanced his victorious squadrons to the vicinity of Abbottstown, where they struck a force of Rebel cavalry, which they scattered, capturing several prisoners, and then rested. To the ears of the alert cavalry chieftain came the sound of battle at Gettysburg, accompanied with the intelligence, from prisoners mostly, that Stuart's main force was bent on doing mischief on the right of our infantry lines, which were not far from the night's bivouac.

He appeared instinctively to know where he was most needed; so in the absence of orders, early the next morning he advanced to Hunterstown. At this point were the extreme wings of the infantry lines, and as Kilpatrick expected, he encountered the Rebel cavalry, commanded by his old antagonists, Stuart, Lee, and Hampton. The early part of the day was spent mostly in reconnoitering; but all the latter part of the day was occupied in hard, bold, and bloody work. Charges and counter-charges were made; the carbine, pistol, and saber were used by turns, and the artillery thundered long after the infantry around Gettysburg had sunk to rest, well-nigh exhausted with the bloody carnage of the weary day. But Stuart, who had hoped to break in upon our flank and rear, and to pounce upon our trains, was not only foiled in his endeavor by the gallant Kilpatrick, but also driven back upon his infantry supports, and badly beaten.

In the night, Kilpatrick, after leaving a sufficient force to prevent Stuart from doing any special damage on our right, swung around with the remainder of his division to the left of our line, near Round Top, and was there prepared for any work which might be assigned him.

Third Day.

Friday, July third, the sun rose bright and warm upon the blackened forms of the dead, which were strewn over the bloody earth; upon the wounded who had not been cared for, and upon long glistening lines of armed men ready to renew the conflict. Each antagonist, rousing every slumbering element of power, seemed to be resolved upon victory or death.

The fight commenced early, by an attack of General Slocum's men, who, determined to re-gain the rifle-pits they had lost the evening before, descended like an avalanche upon the foe. The attack met with a prompt response from General Ewell. But after several hours of desperate fighting, victory perched upon the Union banners, and with great loss and slaughter the Rebels were driven out of the breastworks, and fell back upon their main lines near Benner's Hill.

This successful move on the part of our boys in blue was followed by an ominous lull, or quiet, which continued about three hours. Meanwhile the silence was fitfully broken by an occasional spit of fire, while every preparation was being made for a last, supreme effort, which, it was expected, would decide the mighty contest. The scales were being poised for the last time, and upon the one side or the other was soon to be recorded a glorious victory or a disastrous defeat. Hearts either trembled or waxed strong in the awful presence of this responsibility.

At length one o'clock arrived ; a signal-gun was fired, and then at least one hundred and twenty-five guns from Hill and Longstreet concentrated and crossed their fires upon Cemetery Hill, the centre and key of our position. Just behind this crest, though much exposed, were General Meade's headquarters. For nearly two hours this hill was ploughed and torn by solid shot and bursting shell, while about one hundred guns on our side, mainly from this crest and

Round Top, made sharp response. The earth and the air shook for miles around with the terrific concussion, which came no longer in volleys, but in a continual roar. So long and fearful a cannonade was never before witnessed on this continent. As the range was short and the aim accurate, the destruction was terrible. But the advantage was decidedly in favor of the Rebels, whose guns were superior in number to ours, and of heavier caliber, and had been concentrated for the attack. A spectator of the Union army thus describes the scene :

" The storm broke upon us so suddenly, that soldiers and officers—who leaped, as it began, from their tents, or from lazy siestas on the grass—were stricken in their rising with mortal wounds, and died, some with cigars between their teeth, some with pieces of food in their fingers, and one at least—a pale young German, from Pennsylvania—with a miniature of his sister in his hands. Horses fell, shrieking such awful cries as Cooper told of, and writhing themselves about in hopeless agony. The boards of fences scattered by explosion, flew in splinters through the air. The earth, torn up in clouds, blinded the eyes of hurrying men ; and through the branches of trees and among the grave-stones of the cemetery a shower of destruction crashed ceaselessly. As, with hundreds of others, I groped through this tempest of death for the shelter of the bluff, an old man, a private in a company belonging to the Twenty-fourth Michigan, was struck, scarcely ten feet away, by a cannon-ball, which tore through him, extorting such a low, intense cry of mortal pain as I pray God I may never again hear. The hill, which seemed alone devoted to this rain of death, was clear in nearly all its unsheltered places, within five minutes after the fire began."

A correspondent from the Confederate army who witnessed the battle, says: "I have never yet heard such tremendous artillery-firing. The enemy must have had over one hundred guns, which, in addition to our one hundred and fifteen, made the air hideous with most discordant noise. The very earth shook beneath our feet, and the hills and rocks seemed to reel like a drunken man. For one hour and a half this most terrific fire was continued, during which time the shrieking of shell, the crash of falling timbers, the fragments of rocks flying through the air, shattered from the cliffs by solid shot, the heavy mutterings from the valley between the opposing armies, the splash of bursting shrapnell, and the fierce neighing of wounded artillery-horses, made a picture terribly grand and sublime, but which my pen utterly fails to describe."

Gradually the fire on our side began to slacken, and General Meade, learning that our guns were becoming hot, gave orders to cease firing and to let the guns cool, though the Rebel balls were making fearful havoc among our gunners, while our infantry sought poor shelter behind every projection, anxiously awaiting the expected charge. At length the enemy, supposing that our guns were silenced, deemed that the moment for an irresistible attack had come. Accordingly, as a lion emerges from his lair, he sallied forth, when strong lines of infantry, nearly three miles in length, with double lines of skirmishers in front, and heavy reserves in rear, advanced with desperation to the final effort. They moved with steady, measured tread over the plain below, and began the ascent of the hills occupied by our forces, concentrating somewhat upon General Hancock, though stretching across our entire front.

Says a correspondent of the *Richmond Enquirer:* "Just as Pickett was getting well under the enemy's fire, our batteries ceased firing. This was a fearful moment for Pickett and his brave command. Why do not our guns re-open their fire? is the inquiry that rises upon every lip. Still, our batteries are silent as death!" And this undoubtedly decided the issue—was God's handwriting on the wall. The Rebel guns had been thundering so long and ceaselessly that they were now unfit for use, and ceased firing from very necessity.

"Agate," the correspondent of *The Cincinnati Gazette*, gives the following graphic description of the struggle:

"The great, desperate, final charge came at four. The Rebels seemed to have gathered up all their strength and desperation for one fierce, convulsive effort, that should sweep over and wash out our obstinate resistance. They swept up as before; the flower of their army to the front, victory staked upon the issue. In some places they literally lifted up and pushed back our lines; but, that terrible position of ours!—wherever they entered it, enfilading fires from half a score of crests swept away their columns like merest chaff. Broken and hurled back, they easily fell into our hands; and, on the center and left, the last half hour brought more prisoners than all the rest.

"So it was along the whole line; but it was on the Second Corps that the flower of the Rebel army was concentrated; it was there that the heaviest shock beat upon, and shook, and even sometimes crumbled, our lines.

"We had some shallow rifle-pits, with barricades of rails from the fences. The Rebel line, stretching away miles to the left, in magnificent array, but strongest here—Pickett's splendid division of Longstreet's corps in front, the best of A. P. Hill's veterans in support—came steadily, and as it seemed resistlessly, sweeping up. Our skirmishers retired slowly from the Emmitsburg road, holding their ground tenaciously to the last. The rebels reserved their fire till they reached this same Emmitsburg road, then opened with a terrific crash. From a hundred iron throats, meantime, their artillery had been thundering on our barricades.

"Hancock was wounded; Gibbon succeeded to the command—an approved soldier, and ready for the crisis. As the tempest of fire approached its height, he walked along the line, and renewed his orders to the men to reserve their fire. The Rebels—three lines deep—came steadily up. They were in point-blank range.

"At last the order came! From thrice six thousand guns there came a sheet of smoky flame, a crash, a rush of leaden death. The line literally melted away; but there came the second, resistless still. It had been our supreme effort; on the moment we were not equal to another.

"Up to the rifle-pits, across them, over the barricades—the momentum of their charge, the mere machine-strength of their combined action, swept them on. Our thin line could fight, but it had not weight enough to oppose to this momentum. It was pushed behind the guns. Right on came the Rebels. They were upon our guns—were bayoneting the gunners—were waving their flags over our pieces.

"But they had penetrated to the fatal point. A storm of grape and canister tore its way from man to man, and marked its track with dead bodies straight down their line! They had exposed themselves to the enfilading fire of the guns on the western slope of Cemetery Hill; that exposure sealed their fate.

"The line reeled back—disjointed already—in an instant in fragments. Our men were just behind the guns. They leaped forward upon the disordered mass; but there was little need of fighting now. A regiment threw down its arms, and, with colors at its head, rushed over and surrendered. All along the field smaller detachments did the same. Webb's brigade brought in eight hundred; taken in as little time as it requires to write the simple sentence that tells it. Gibbon's old division took fifteen stand of colors.

"Over the fields the escaped fragments of the charging line fell back—the battle there was over. A single brigade, of which the Seventh Michigan is part, came out with fifty-four less officers, and seven hundred and ninety-three less men, than it took in! So the whole corps fought; so, too, they fought farther down the line.

"It was fruitless sacrifice. They gathered up their

broken fragments, formed their lines, and slowly marched away. It was not a rout; it *was* a bitter, crushing defeat. For once the Army of the Potomac had won a clean, honest, acknowledged victory."

General Pickett's division was nearly annihilated. One of his officers recounted that, as they were charging over the grassy plain, he threw himself down before a murderous discharge of grape and canister, which mowed the grass and men all around him, as though a scythe had been swung just above his prostrate form.

During the terrific cannonade and subsequent charges, our ammunition and other trains had been parked in rear of Round Top, which gave them splendid shelter. Partly to possess this train, but mainly to secure this commanding position, General Longstreet sent two strong divisions of infantry, with heavy artillery, to turn our flank, and to drive us from this ground. Kilpatrick, with his division, which had been strengthened by Merritt's Regular brigade, was watching this point and waiting for an opportunity to strike the foe. It came at last. Emerging from the woods in front of him came a strong battle-line, followed by others.

DEATH OF GENERAL FARNSWORTH.

To the young Farnsworth was committed the task of meeting infantry with cavalry in an open field. Placing the Fifth New York in support of Elder's battery, which was exposed to a galling fire, but made reply with characteristic rapidity, precision, and slaughter, Farnsworth quickly ordered the First

GETTYSBURG.

Virginia, the First Vermont, and Eighteenth Pennsylvania in line of battle, and galloped away and charged upon the flank of the advancing columns. The attack was sharp, brief, and successful, though attended with great slaughter. But the Rebels were driven upon their main lines and the flank movement was prevented. Thus the cavalry added another dearly earned laurel to its chaplet of honor—*dearly earned*, because many of their bravest champions fell upon that bloody field.

Kilpatrick, in his official report of this sanguinary contest, says: "In this charge fell the brave Farnsworth. Short and brilliant was his career. On the twenty-ninth of June a general; on the first of July he baptized his star in blood; and on the third, for the honor of his young brigade and the glory of his Corps, he yielded up his noble life."

Thus ended the battle of Gettysburg—the bloody turning-point of the Rebellion—the bloody baptism of the redeemed Republic. Nearly twenty thousand men from the Union ranks had been killed and wounded, and a larger number of the Rebels, making the enormous aggregate of at least forty thousand, whose blood was shed to fertilize the Tree of Liberty.

In the evening twilight of that eventful day, General Meade penned the following interesting despatch to the Government:

HEADQUARTERS ARMY OF THE POTOMAC,
Near Gettysburg, July 3, 8.30 P.M.

To Major-General Halleck, General-in-Chief:

The enemy opened at one o'clock, P.M., from about one hundred and fifty guns. They concentrated upon my left center, continuing without intermission for about three hours, at the expiration of which time he assaulted my left center twice, being, upon both occasions, handsomely repulsed with severe loss to them, leaving in our hands nearly three thousand prisoners. Among the prisoners are Major-General Armistead, and many colonels and officers of lesser note. The enemy left many dead upon the field, and a large number of wounded in our hands. The loss upon our side has been considerable Major-General Hancock and Brigadier-General Gibbon wer. wounded.

After the repelling of the assault, indications leading to the belief that the enemy might be withdrawing, an armed reconnoissance was pushed forward from the left, and the enemy found to be in force. At the present hour all is quiet.

The New York cavalry have been engaged all day on both flanks of the enemy, harassing and vigorously attacking him with great success, notwithstanding they encountered superior numbers, both of cavalry and artillery. The army is in fine spirits.

GEORGE G. MEADE,
Major-General Commanding.

On the morning of the Fourth of July, General Meade issued an address to the army:

HEADQUARTERS ARMY OF THE POTOMAC,
Near Gettysburg, July 4.

The commanding general, in behalf of the country, thanks the Army of the Potomac for the glorious result of the recent operations. Our enemy, superior in numbers and flushed with the pride of a successful invasion, attempted to overcome or destroy this army. Utterly baffled and defeated, he has now withdrawn from the contest.

The privations and fatigues the army has endured, and the heroic courage and gallantry it has displayed, will be matters of history to be ever remembered.

Our task is not yet accomplished, and the commanding general looks to the army for greater efforts to drive from our soil every vestige of the presence of the invader.

It is right and proper that we should, on suitable occasions, return our grateful thanks to the Almighty Disposer of events, that, in the goodness of His providence, He has thought fit to give victory to the cause of the just.

By command of MAJOR-GENERAL MEADE.

S. WILLIAMS, *A. A.-General.*

It is fitting that we should close this chapter with President Lincoln's brief yet comprehensive announcement to the country:

WASHINGTON, D. C., July 4, 1863, 10 A. M.

The President of the United States announces to the country that the news from the Army of the Potomac, up to ten o'clock P. M., of the third, is such as to cover the army with the highest honor—to promise great success to the cause of the Union—and to claim the condolence of all for the many gallant fallen; and that for this he especially desires that on this day, "He whose will, not ours, should ever be done," be everywhere remembered and reverenced with the profoundest gratitude. ABRAHAM LINCOLN.

CHAPTER XXIX.

VICKSBURG.

The Impregnable Stronghold.—The Batteries of the Bluff.—The Siege Begun.—A Reign of Terror.—Assault of the Nineteenth.—Distributing Rations.—Assault of the Twenty-second.—Desperate Work.—Sergeant Griffith and the Brave Eleven.—Union Colors on Enemy's Bastion.—McPherson's Losses.—Failure to Carry the Works.—Six Weeks' Siege.—The Enemy Starved Out.—The White Flag.—Surrender.—Grant's Triumphant Entrance into Vicksburg.—"Rally Round the Flag."—Close of the Campaign.—Lincoln's Letter.

AT a distance of three hundred and ninety-five miles above the mouth of the Mississippi River, on a high bluff, facing westward, and rising nearly a hundred feet above the level of the water, lies the city of Vicksburg—a stronghold which for the first two years of the war defied all assault. Its formidable defences united to its natural strength of position, rendered its reduction a work of difficulty and danger. But on our National Anniversary of 1863, this mighty citadel, so long secure on its embattled bluff, surrendered to superior strategy and skill, and the celebration of that "Glorious Fourth" by the soldiers of Vicksburg contained an element of patriotic fervor which only a fresh victory in the cause of freedom could give.

The rise of the river bank at that point is gradual for about two miles back, and on this inclined slope lies the town—cradled in a hollow of the bluff. On the bluff below the city, a fort mounting eight guns guarded the approach from beneath, while on the height above, a formidable, three-banked battery bristled with tiers of guns, rising one above the other, from a point half way down the slope to the summit. Each tier contained four heavy guns, and ditches and rifle-pits helped to make up the defences.

The combined forces of Pemberton and Price, estimated at fifty thousand men, were in possession of the city. Their guns were estimated at one hundred and sixty.

For six weeks previous to July fourth, 1863, General Grant had been occupied with the siege of Vicksburg, which he pressed energetically.

Every day further progress was made in digging and mining, and at length he reached a point where his batteries could send their screaming shells directly to the heart of the city. A reign of terror then took possession of the town, and its inhabitants dug for themselves caves in the earth, seeking protection against the missiles of destruction which daily and nightly dropped in their midst. Meantime, rumors were current that Johnston, with heavy reënforcements, was to attack our forces in the rear and if possible raise the seige. This, in connection with other reasons, determined Grant to try an assault at once. Accordingly, at two o'clock in the afternoon of May nineteenth, a general attack was ordered on the land-ward fortifications of Vicksburg.

General Grant, in his report of that attempt, gives his reasons for the movement. He says:—"I believed an assault from the position gained by this time could be made successfully. It was known that Johnston was at Canton with the force taken by him from Jackson, reënforced by other troops from the east, and that more were daily reaching him. With the force I had, a short time must have enabled him to attack me in the rear, and possibly to succeed in raising the siege. Possession of Vicksburg at that time would have enabled me to have turned upon Johnston and driven him from the State, and possess myself of all the railroads and practical military highways, thus effectually securing to ourselves all territory west of the Tombigbee—and this before the season was too far advanced for campaigning in this latitude. It would have saved Government sending large reënforcements much needed elsewhere; and finally, the troops themselves were impatient to possess Vicksburg, *and would not have worked in the trenches with the same zeal, believing it unnecessary, that they did after their failure to carry the enemy's works.*"

But the attack of the nineteenth only resulted in a slight advance of our besieging army towards the Confederate fortifications. Blair's division of Sherman's Corps succeeded in placing their colors on the enemy's ramparts,—the Thirteenth Regulars of Smith's brigade paying the terrible price of seventy-seven men out of two hundred and fifty, for the bloody attempt. The outer line of Confederate defences were also carried by the Eighty-third Indiana, Colonel

Spooner, and the One-hundred and Twenty-seventh Illinois, Colonel Eldridge. Though they were unable to enter the works they yet succeeded in holding their ground till night. The remaining regiments were only successful in gaining a closer position to the almost impregnable fortifications. General Sherman seeing his troops slaughtered to no purpose, ordered them to retire a short distance and take shelter behind the broken ground.

The two days succeeding this abortive attempt were occupied in artillery firing and in distributing an advance supply of rations; and on May twenty-second, at ten o'clock in the morning, a simultaneous assault by the entire besieging force, was made at all points. Five batteries poured their deadly fire on the Rebel bastion commanding our approach. The sharpshooters were in the advance, and a storming party carrying poles and boards to bridge the ditch, followed them.

Frank Blair's division led Sherman's attack—the brigade of General Hugh S. Ewing, Thirtieth Ohio, having the advance, followed by the regiments of Giles Smith and T. Kilby Smith.

The storming party of this corps pressed forward to the angle of the bastion in their front without attack and "passed towards the sally-port, when there shot up behind the parapet, a double rank of the enemy, who poured on the head of the column a fire that swept it down in an instant. No troops could or should persist in braving such utter, useless destruction. The rear of the column attempted to rush on; but it was madness; and soon, all had sought cover from that deadly fire." But notwithstanding this murderous work, the men of Ewing's command crossed the ditch on the left of the bastion, and clambering up its outer wall, planted their flag near the top.

Holes dug in the hill-side sheltered them from fire in their flank. The brigade of Giles Smith, further on the left, under cover of a ravine, re-formed in line of battle, ready to again make an assault, while Kilby Smith deployed his men on an eminence near by and kept up a fire on the parapet.

An attempt by the brigades of Giles Smith and Ransome, to take the parapet by assault resulted only in defeat and loss. Half a mile away on the right, the division of Steele was fighting splendidly, but without result. On our left, the efforts of McClernand were, for a time, at least, more successful. Within fifteen minutes after his assault, the ditch in front of the fort they attacked, was crossed and the slope and bastion carried. Sergeant Griffith of the Twenty-second Iowa, with eleven privates succeeded in effecting an entrance. But their desperate bravery was at the cost of their lives—every one falling within the fort except the sergeant, who brought thirteen prisoners. "The colors of the Forty-eighth Ohio and Seventy-seventh Illinois were planted on the bastion; and within the next quarter of an hour, the brigades of Benton and Burbridge, fired by this example, had carried the ditch and slope of another strong earthwork, planting their colors on the slope; while Captain White of the Chicago Mercantile Battery, carried forward one of his guns by hand to the ditch, double-shotted it and fired it into an embrasure, disabling a Rebel gun ready to be fired, and doubtless doing execution among its gunners. McClernand supposed his assault successful, and reported to Grant that he had carried two of the Rebel forts; and again, "We have gained the enemy's intrenchments at several points, but are brought to a stand;" at the same time asking for reënforcements. Grant, when he received the first despatch, immediately ordered the assault on Sherman's front (where he then was) to be renewed, while he started back to his original position with McPherson in the center, which he had not reached when he received from McClernand the further message above cited; whereupon, though distrusting its accuracy, he ordered Quinby's division of McPherson's corps to report to McClernand."

Mower's brigade having been sent up to carry the fort where Ewing's force had met with repulse, succeeded in planting the colors of the Eleventh Missouri regiment beside those of Blair's command, and until dark the National colors floated on the breeze under the guns of the beleaguered city. The command of Steele failed to carry the bastioned fort in their front, but gained possession of the hill-side below, remaining there until night, when they were withdrawn with the rest. The heavy losses in McPherson's command in the center, told the story of his daring bravery; but every effort was fruitless, save in carnage. The divisions of Osterhaus and Hovey had been driven behind the shelter of a ridge by the enfilading fire of the enemy.

McArthur's division, ordered to reinforce McClernand's, did not reach Vicksburg until next morning, and Quinby's two brigades did not come up until nearly dark. Colonel Boomer, commanding one of the brigades was killed while leading his men into action.

At eight o'clock in the evening our forces were recalled from their advanced positions after having suffered a loss of three thousand men.

General Grant in his report of the campaign speaks in the following language of the attack of the twenty-second :—" The assault of this day proved the quality of the soldiers of this army. Without entire success and with a heavy loss, there was no murmuring or complaining, no falling back, nor other evidence of demoralization. After the failure of the twenty-second, I determined upon a regular siege. The troops now being fully awake to the necessity of this, worked diligently and cheerfully. The work progressed rapidly and satisfactorily until the third of July, when all was about ready for a final assault."

To the citizens of the beleaguered city the scene as described by one of its inmates, was 'awfully sublime and terrific.' There had been no lull in the shelling all night; and as daylight approached, it grew more rapid and furious. Early in the morning too, the battle began to rage in the rear. A terrible onslaught was made on the center first, and then extended farther to the left, where a terrific struggle took place, resulting in the repulse of the attacking party. Four gunboats also came up to engage the batteries. * * Three points were attacked at once ; to wit, the rifle-pits by the enemy in the rear ; the city by the mortars opposite; and the batteries by the gun-boats. Such cannonading and shelling, has perhaps scarcely ever been equaled; and the city was entirely untenable though women and children were on the streets. It was not safe from behind or before, and every part of the city was alike within range of the Federal guns. The gun-boats withdrew after a short engagement; but the mortars kept up the shelling and the armies continued fighting all day. * * * * The incessant booming of cannon and the banging of small arms, intermingled with the howling of shells, and the whistling of Minie-balls, made the day truly most hideous."

Vicksburg was now surrounded and its downfall was only a question of time. Day by day the siege was pushed vigorously forward—the digging and mining going steadily on.

Porter's gunboats, with thirteen-inch mortars and one-hundred-pound Parrot guns, safely anchored under the high bank below Vicksburg, sentineled the river above and below. A three-gun battery on the peninsula opposite, played havoc with the Confederate garrison, burning up their shot and shell foundery. While the enemy's forts were being mined, counter mines were dug by them and the sound of their picks could be heard through the thin wall of earth which separated the hostile armies. For six weeks our batteries never ceased dropping their shot and shell on the doomed city. Food became scarce and the "inhabitants grew wan and thin in their narrow dens." At last the enemy's ammunition gave out, and Pemberton, despairing of Johnston's aid in raising the siege and believing that Grant was ready for another assault on his works, hung out a white flag in front of General A. J. Smith's division. This was on the third of July. On sending forward to learn the meaning of the white flag, they were informed that General Bowen and Colonel Montgomery of Pemberton's staff, were bearers of a communication to General Grant. The officers were then conducted blindfolded to the tent of General Burbridge and their message was delivered to General Grant. It proved to be an application for an armistice with a view to arranging terms of capitulation. But General Grant was prompt and decided in his response. He would have nothing but unconditional surrender. However, a meeting was arranged to take place between Grant and Pemberton at three o'clock in the afternoon of that day. They met "midway between the lines under a gigantic oak, while the two armies left their places of concealment and swarmed upon the ramparts to witness this extraordinary scene. Pemberton was the first to speak and asked Grant what terms he proposed. "Unconditional surrender," was the prompt reply. "Never," rejoined the haughty Rebel, "so long as I have a man left me."

"Then," said Grant, "you can continue the defence: my army was never in a better condition to continue the siege."

After some further conversation the interview terminated without coming to definite result, Grant saying he would confer with his officers. He did so, and sent a note saying that the entire surrender of the place and garrison would be required, but that the troops would be paroled and allowed to march out of the lines—the officers taking with them their regimental clothing, and the staff, and field, and cavalry officers a horse each. The proposal was accepted, and, on the morning of the Fourth of July, General McPherson met Pemberton half a mile within the lines to receive the surrender. General Grant soon rode up and the trio went together into the town where General Logan established a provost-guard. The enemy's flag was hauled down and the stars and stripes went up over the captured works amid the enthusiastic cheers of the boys in blue. At half past eleven o'clock of that eventful morning our National banner shook out its folds to the breeze from the top of the Court House, while the soldiers, standing beneath its emblematic colors, sang "Rally round the Flag," with a fervor which only a fresh victory for that banner of freedom could lend.

By three o'clock in the afternoon our forces had entire possession of the city and bluff, and the Confederate soldiers, after being paroled, and supplied with three day's rations, were escorted out of the town and across the Big Black, on their way to Jackson. The number of prisoners on parole from the capture of Vicksburg was estimated at twenty-seven thousand, —only fifteen thousand being fit for duty.

The surrender of Vicksburg ended one of the most brilliant and successful campaigns of the war, and the name of Grant, surrounded with a halo which had scarcely reached its zenith of brightness at the close of the rebellion, was already beloved of the nation. This chapter cannot more appropriately close than with the letter which President Lincoln wrote to the General of our armies after this campaign. It is dated at the

"EXECUTIVE MANSION, WASHINGTON,
July 13th, 1863.

"*Major General Grant:*

"My dear General:—I do not remember that you and I ever met personally. I write this now as a grateful acknowledgment for the almost inestimable service you have done the country. I wish to say a word further. When you first reached the vicinity of Vicksburg, I thought you should do what you finally did—march the troops across the neck, run the batteries with the transports and thus go below: and I never had any faith except a general hope that you knew better than I, that the Yazoo Pass expedition and the like could succeed. When you got below, and took Port Gibson, Grand Gulf and vicinity I thought you should go down the river and join General Banks, and when you turned northward, east of the Big Black, I feared it was a mistake. I now wish to make the personal acknowledgment that you were right and I was wrong.

A. LINCOLN."

CHAPTER XXX.

PORT HUDSON

The Citadel on the Bluffs.—Four Miles of Batteries.—The Pledge of the Northwest.—First Operations against Port Hudson.—The Stronghold Invested.—General Assault.—Repulse and Loss.—Bravery of Officers and Men.—Colonel Bartlett.—Heroic Conduct of Colored Troops.—The Siege Carried Forward.—Gloomy Outlook.—Another General Assault.—Heavy Losses.—The Enemy Starving.—The Delicacies of a Rat Stew.—Announcement of the Surrender of Vicksburg.—The Council of War in the Camp on the Bluffs.—Unconditional Surrender of Port Hudson.—"Flag of Union and Freedom Wave!"—The Promise of the Northwest Redeemed.

DURING the stormy days of the civil war, when Rebellion flaunted its red flag over our fair land, Port Hudson, on the Lower Mississippi, was one of its fastnesses. Situated at a point twenty-five miles north of Baton Rouge in Louisiana, and nearly a hundred and sixty miles by water above New Orleans, Port Hudson, secure behind its strong earthworks, grimly guarded all hostile approach—a very Gibralter of defence.

Along its bluffs, commanding four miles of river distance, a line of death-dealing batteries sentineled the shore. The approach to the little village from the landward side, back of the town, was like ascending the hill Difficulty. Ravines and swamps and other obstructions stubbornly contested every step of the way, while an army of thirteen thousand men garrisoned its strongly fortified heights. Before the capitulation of Vicksburg, the Confederates had exclusive control of the Mississippi River between that point and Port Hudson—a stretch of two hundred and fifty miles. Across this country, various essential articles of supply were transmitted from Texas, for the benefit of the Rebel armies, and by its occupation the great Northwest was robbed of one of its main avenues of outlet. Port Hudson, with threatening guns, barred the ascent of the river as Vicksburg barred its descent, and it was of the greatest importance to the country at large and to our armies, that this arterial channel should be opened from its source in the far north to its mouth at the gulf; and to this end the patriotic men of the northwest had pledged themselves.

As early as the month of March, 1863, operations against Port Hudson were in progress, and on the thirteenth, General Banks marched his command from Baton Rouge, Louisiana, towards that stronghold, his object being a diversion in favor of Farragut's fleet, then endeavoring to force a passage up the river. Three divisions under Generals Augur, Grover, and Emory bivouacked on the night of the thirteenth within sound of the guns on the bluff. A detachment under Colonel Molineaux, diverging on the Clinton road, encountered a Confederate force at Cypress Bayou Bridge, and a skirmish ensued which resulted in the retirement of the enemy with a loss of eleven killed and wounded. On the fourteenth the boats Hartford and Albatross of the fleet, passed up the river and General Banks ordered a return to Baton

Rouge, having accomplished the object of his movement.

On May twentieth—the day after Vicksburg was invested by Grant's besieging army, the troops under General Banks again marched on Port Hudson and two days afterwards drew their lines closely about it in regular seige.

On the twenty-fifth, Banks sent the Seventh Illinois Cavalry under Colonel Price, to destroy the boats Red Chief and Starlight, which were anchored just above Port Hudson in Big Sandy Creek, near its confluence with the Mississippi.

The object of this order was to cut off the water communication and encircle the place by land forces.

The troops of General Banks took position around this stronghold, beginning at the extreme northwestern end of the town and continuing in a southeasterly direction. General Augur had the center, General Grover the right, and General T. W. Sherman the left wing.

As the first red rays of morning shot athwart the sky on May twenty-seventh, the booming of cannon in a simultaneous burst from the batteries of the entire line, woke the echoes of the river bluffs and announced the assault of Port Hudson begun. The fire did not slacken until one o'clock in the afternoon, at which time an assault on the enemy's left was ordered, in which General Sherman was to co-operate, making an attack at the same time on the Union left. The field through which they were obliged to pass in order to make the attack was thickly strewn with trees recently felled, through whose obstructing branches our troops advanced in the face of shot and shell from the batteries of the enemy across the field. Mounted officers got down from their horses and led them through this difficult passage, for they could go forward in no other way ; while over them rained a furious storm of shot and shell. For two hours this deadly fire was braved by the heroic men struggling over the dangerous ground ; after which with repulse and loss they were withdrawn. " Colonel Bartlett of the Forty-ninth Massachusetts, having lost his leg, was compelled to go on horseback, or not at all. The enemy was so struck with his bravery that orders were issued not to shoot him." A little later in the day, Sherman's attack on the left was equally disastrous, the General losing a leg in the engagement and his command suffering heavy losses.

The attacking column on the right included the colored regiments raised by Banks. Of their bravery on that day their commanding general bears this testimony : " In many respects," said he, " their conduct was heroic ; no troops could be more determined or daring." "There had been so much incredulity avowed as to negro courage, so much wit lavished on the idea of negroes fighting to any purpose, that General Banks was justified in according especial commendation to these."

The Union loss in this assault was reported at one thousand and the enemy's loss at six hundred. Among the killed was Colonel Clarke of the Sixth Michigan, and Colonel D. S. Cowles of the One Hundred and Twenty-eighth New York—transfixed by a bayonet :—Colonel Payne, Second Louisiana and Colonel Chapin, Thirtieth Massachusetts. General T. W. Sherman was severely wounded and General Neal Dow slightly. On the twenty-eighth there was a cessation of hostilities for the purpose of burying the dead.

After this the work of digging their way to victory went earnestly forward. Zig-zag trenches were pushed up to the Rebel fortifications by the toilers in army blue, working under the relentless rays of a June sun; while our siege guns, co-operating with the artillery of the fleet, sent their thunders echoing along the shore. For two weeks this work went on; but the chances of bringing the siege to a successful conclusion were full of doubt. The outlook was gloomy. The small army of Banks—now dwindled down to twelve thousand—was isolated in a hostile country. A force of twenty-five hundred Rebel cavalry occupied a position in close proximity to the Union rear, and the well-garrisoned fortress of the bluff, nearly impregnable by assault, faced them with threatening batteries, in front. The concentration of forces for this siege had left most of the territory of Louisiana, from whence Dick Taylor had been lately driven, an open problem for him to solve, retracing his steps across the state if he liked, conscripting and raiding as he went, with the added possibility of capturing New Orleans as the sum of the problem.

Georgia and Alabama might supply force enough to raise the siege, while Joe Johnston was liable to come down from Jackson at any time with a command of sufficient strength to quench any hope of success. The Confederate line of defence extended for a distance of four miles around Port Hudson, while the Union lines, encircling theirs, were still longer, and a strategic concentration of their forces at any one point of the garrison must necessarily make it stronger at such a point than all the force that could be rallied against it. The Mississippi had fallen to the unusual depression of twenty-eight feet, which interfered with the "efficiency of the gun-boats and the means of obtaining supply." The capture of the garrison of Brashear City on the morning of June twenty-third, by a large Confederate force which had come up in rear of the Union army during the previous night, cut off the Federal occupation of Louisiana west of the Mississippi. The enemy, meantime, harrassing the communication between New Orleans and Port Hudson, had captured a quantity of supplies, fifty miles above the gulf, destined for the besieging army. Surrounded with such a combination of adverse probabilities—with Lee triumphant at Chancellorsville and Grant defied at Vicksburg, the prospect of continuing the siege at Port Hudson, looked exceedingly uncertain. Still, the besiegers worked steadily and earnestly on. After two weeks of digging and firing "a fresh attempt was made, under a heavy fire of artillery, to establish our lines within attacking distance of the enemy's works, so as to avoid the heavy losses incurred in moving over the ground in their front. Our men advanced at three o'clock in the morning, working their way through the difficult abattis; but the movement was promptly detected by the enemy, and defeated, with the loss on our side of some scores as prisoners." On June fourteenth—four days later—

another united assault was ordered. General Grover was to make the attack in front, while Dwight and Augur were ordered to make feints on the extreme left. The attacks were made, with a loss of three hundred men, and were successful only in advancing our position to an average distance of from fifty to two hundred yards nearer the Confederate batteries. At this point new intrenchments were dug and new batteries erected. On our left, a high position known as the "Citadel" was carried, by which Dwight was enabled to occupy the ground on the same ridge, within ten yards of the enemy's lines. An exploding shell was dropped into the mill of the garrison, and the building, with its two hundred bushels of corn burned to the ground.

The field over which the attacking column was obliged to pass, was "obstructed by an abattis of felled trees to which succeeded a ditch forty feet wide with six feet of water in it; and beyond that, a glacis about twenty feet high, sloping gradually to the parapet on which was a protection for the sharpshooters: behind this, one hundred yards distant, was another line of works, on which field and heavy artillery was mounted."

The attack commenced at daylight. Our skirmishers first went forward and deployed on both sides of the objective point, while the rest of the command followed. The Union troops suffered severely as they advanced from the sharp fire of the enemy, but undaunted and brave, they pushed on, in order to gain the ditch. The Seventy-Fifth New York reaching the ditch encountered a terrible enfilading fire which felled them like blades of grass under a hail storm. Nearly all were killed or wounded. The Ninety-first New-York, under Colonel Van Zandt, next came up, carrying their five-pound hand grenades which they threw over the Rebel breastworks. Meantime, General Weitzel's command moving up, assaulted the works of the enemy with desperate valor. But every attack was met with repulse. "Brigade after brigade followed in rapid succession, storming the works, until compelled to fall back under the terrible fire of the enemy."

At eleven o'clock in the morning the firing ceased, the most perceptible result of the battle being its dreadful carnage.

The soldiers of the respective commands dropped down behind the shelter of gullies, trees, and everything that could give them protection from the deadly storm of shot from the bluffs, and "waited for the day to pass and the darkness to come on. At nightfall, our troops commenced the burial of their dead and succeeded before morning in carrying most of their wounded from the battle-ground. Among the Union losses were General Paine and five colonels. The loss in killed and wounded was over two thousand." On the next day General Banks issued an order calling on a volunteer storming party for a last assault. He wanted a thousand men to lead in this column of victory. The Fourth Wisconsin and Sixth Michigan responded to the call and made the attack which resulted in their repulse and the capture of most of their number. And thus the tedious siege went on—the Union force daily losing some men, in addition to the bloody work of the assaults, by the accurate aim of the enemy's artillerists and sharpshooters. But slowly and surely, step by step, our troops pushed their works up to the very line of the enemy's defences, and on our left a mine calculated for thirty barrels of powder had been placed in a position to explode and destroy the "Citadel." The Confederate garrison had exhausted their stores to such an extent that rations of mule meat were served to the men, and rats were considered delicate eating. Their ammunition also began to fail and their guns had been disabled by the sure aim of our artillerists, until only fifteen out of fifty were fit for use. It was impossible that the garrison could hold out many days longer except by attacks which would raise the siege—and there was no hope of that.

"Suddenly, on July sixth, our batteries and gun-boats shook the heavens with one tremendous salute, while cheer upon cheer rose from behind our works, rolling from the gun-boats above, to those below the defenses, and back again, in billows of unmistakable exultation. It was not the 'glorious Fourth,' but two days after it: and the sinking hearts of the besieged anticipated the tidings before our men shouted across to them, "VICKSBURG HAS SURRENDERED!" No one needed to be told that, if such was the truth, further resistance was folly—that re-enforcements would soon be steaming down the river which would render holding out impossible."

That evening a council of war was held in the Confederate camp in which Gardner was chief, and the decision reached was that Port Hudson must be surrendered. Communication was opened with Banks, asking if the news shouted across the lines was true: whereupon, General Banks sent to General Gardner the letter of Grant announcing the surrender of Vicksburg. Application was then made by Gardner for a cessation of hostilities in order to arrange terms of capitulation; but this, Banks declined. Gardner then asserted his willingness to surrender, and an agreement was entered into, whereby the garrison became prisoners of war. On the next day—July ninth—at seven o'clock in the morning, formal possession was taken of the place by the army of Banks. The troops marched in, to the music of the "Star spangled Banner," and found the Confederate soldiers drawn up in line of battle with their arms stacked in front of them. The conquerors and conquered now met on fraternal ground, who had confronted each other in mortal combat before; and the Union General fed the hungry soldiers of the rebellious Confederacy. On the highest bluff of the battle-ground the old flag of freedom went up amid the thundered salute of the guns and the cheers of our brave soldiers. The loss on our side during the entire siege of forty-five days was estimated at three thousand men; while General Banks calculated the Rebel loss at eight hundred or one thousand. The number of prisoners captured was over six thousand, of whom four hundred and fifty-five were officers. Fifty guns and nearly forty thousand small arms were also captured.

The following dispatch was received at Washington:—

VICKSBURG, MISS., July 11th, 1863.

"*Major General Halleck, General-in-Chief*:—

"The following dispatch has been received from General Banks:—

BEFORE PORT HUDSON, July 8th, 1863.

" *General:*—

The Mississippi is now opened. I have the honor to inform you that the garrison at Port Hudson surrendered unconditionally this afternoon. We shall take formal possession at seven o'clock in the morning.

(Signed.) " N. P. BANKS, *Major-General.*

" U. S. GRANT, *Major-General.*"

Thus once more the noble Mississippi was opened for the free passage of vessels from the land of the Northwest down to the sea-board ; the guns of Vicksburg and Port Hudson no longer frowned threateningly on the National flag ; the Confederate occupation of the river ceased for ever and the promise of the men of the Northwest was redeemed.

CHAPTER XXXI.

FALLING WATERS.

Kilpatrick's Advance to Hagerstown.—Lee's Position.—Efforts to Cross the Swollen Potomac.—Meade Decides to Attack the Confederates.—The Escape by Night.—Kilpatrick's Discovery.—The Cavalry in Motion.—The Encounter at Falling Waters.—The Enemy Surprised.—Hard Fighting.—Death of Pettigrew.—Union Victory.—Capture of Battle-Flags and Prisoners.—Kilpatrick's Letter.

IN the early part of July, 1863, soon after the brilliant engagement at Boonsboro, in which our cavalry under Buford and Kilpatrick distinguished themselves by their splendid action, the cavalry force under Buford moved to Sharpsburg. This point was then the left wing of the Union line of battle. General Kilpatrick occupying the extreme right of this line, his position commanded the road from Hagerstown to Gettysburg. On the twelfth of July, Kilpatrick supported by an infantry force from Howard's Corps, under General Ames, advanced to Hagerstown, and sweeping down on the Confederates at that place, drove them from the town and established himself in their quarters. This movement shortened our lines by a distance of some miles.

Lee, after being driven from the soil of Pennsylvania at Gettysburg, occupied a strong natural position on the Maryland shore of the Potomac, near Falling

Waters. Here he fortified himself behind formidable earthworks, and for some days previous to the battle had been making strenuous efforts to bridge the swollen waters of the Potomac and cross over to the Virginia shore.

On the thirteenth, General Meade finally decided to assault the Rebel position. Orders to the various commands had been issued, the necessary dispositions completed, and the attack was to have been made on the fourteenth of July.

During the night of the thirteenth, General Kilpatrick, while examining his picket line, became convinced from certain well-known indications, that the enemy was leaving his front.

At once a courier was sent flying to Meade's headquarters, with the intelligence; but Kilpatrick, without waiting for orders, organized his command, and at three o'clock on the dark dawn of the fourteenth, the cavalry were in motion. At Williamsport, at seven o'clock, they encountered a portion of the rear-guard of the enemy and drove them into the Potomac. From this point they moved rapidly forward and came upon the remainder of the Confederate rear-guard one mile from Falling Waters.

The enemy's force consisted of an infantry division under Major-general Pettigrew. Like a whirlwind Kilpatrick swept down upon the Confederates, taking them utterly by surprise and capturing their artillery before it could be placed in position. General Pettigrew was killed in a sabre charge led by Major Webber, of the Sixth Michigan. Long and bravely did the enemy's infantry struggle to resist and hurl back the wild charges of our cavalry:—but in vain. Overpowered by the repeated and furious attacks of Kilpatrick they at last broke and fled in confused disorder, and the battle was ours. Pennington's artillery was very effective in coöperating with the cavalry in this engagement. Fifteen hundred prisoners, two guns, and three battle-flags were captured, and the dead and wounded of the enemy strewed the ground. The fight at Falling Waters gave the parting blow to Lee's invading army and sent them in rapid retreat through Virginia.

The following dispatch was sent to Washington by General Meade:—

HEADQUARTERS ARMY OF THE POTOMAC.
July 14, 3 P. M.

H. W. Halleck, General-in-Chief:

My cavalry now occupy Falling Waters, having overtaken and captured a brigade of infantry, fifteen hundred strong, two guns, two caissons, two battle-flags, and a large number of small-arms. The enemy are all across the Potomac.

GEORGE G. MEADE, *Major-General.*

Later in the day he sent the following:

HEADQUARTERS ARMY OF THE POTOMAC,
July 14, 8.30 P. M.

Major-General Halleck, General-in-Chief:

My cavalry have captured five hundred prisoners, in addition to those previously reported. General Pettigrew, of the Confederate army, was killed this morning in the attack on the enemy's rearguard. His body is in our hands.

G. G. MEADE, *Major-General.*

These dispatches were afterwards denied by General Lee in a letter to his authorities, as follows:

HEADQUARTERS ARMY OF NORTHERN VIRGINIA.
July ——, 1863.

General S. Cooper, Adjutant and Inspector-General C. S. A:

GENERAL: I have seen in the Northern papers what purports to be an official dispatch from General Meade, stating that he had captured a brigade of infantry, two pieces of artillery, two caissons, and a large number of small arms, as this army retired to the south bank of the Potomac on the thirteenth and fourteenth instant. This dispatch has been copied into the Richmond papers; and, as its official character may cause it to be believed, I desire to state that it is incorrect. The enemy did not capture any organized body of men on that occasion, but only stragglers, and such as were left asleep on the road, exhausted by the fatigue and exposure of one of the most inclement nights I have ever known at this season of the year. It rained without cessation, rendering the road by which our troops marched toward the bridge at Falling Waters very difficult to pass, and causing so much delay that the last of the troops did not cross the river at the bridge until one A. M. on the morning of the fourteenth.

While the column was thus detained on the road a number of men, worn down with fatigue, laid down in barns and by the roadside, and though officers were sent back to arouse them as the troops moved on, the darkness and rain prevented them from finding all, and many were in this way left behind. Two guns were left on the road; the horses that drew them became exhausted, and the officers went back to procure others. When they returned, the rear of the column had passed the guns so far that it was deemed unsafe to send back for them, and they were thus lost. No arms, cannon, or prisoners were taken by the enemy in battle, but only such as were left behind, as I have described, under the circumstances. The number of stragglers thus lost I am unable to state with accuracy, but it is greatly exaggerated in the dispatch referred to.

I am with great respect your obedient servant.

R. E. LEE, *General.*

This was evidently an attempt, on the part of the Rebel leader, to disparage our victories and to wipe out of his record, with a sort of legerdemain, the disgraceful and disastrous denoument of his invasion. In the following important statement General Meade confirms his position by incontestable facts, and shows how the matter stood:

HEADQUARTERS ARMY OF THE POTOMAC.
Aug ——, 1863.

Major-General Halleck, General-in-Chief:

My attention has been called to what purports to be an official dispatch of General R. E. Lee, commanding the Rebel army, to General S. Cooper, Adjutant and Inspector-General, denying the accuracy of my telegram to you, of July fourteenth, announcing the result of the cavalry affair at Falling Waters.

I have delayed taking any notice of Lee's report until the return of Brigadier-General Kilpatrick, absent on leave, who commanded the cavalry on the occasion referred to, and on whose report from the field my telegram was based. I now enclose the official report of Brigadier-General Kilpatrick, made after his attention had been called to Lee's report. You will see that he reiterates and confirms all that my dispatch averred, and proves most conclusively that General Lee has been deceived by his subordinates, or he would never, in the face of the facts now alleged, have made the assertion his report claims.

It appears that I was in error in stating that the body of General Pettigrew was left in our hands, although I did not communicate that fact until an officer from the field reported to me he had seen the body. It is now ascertained from the Richmond papers, that General Pettigrew, though mortally wounded in the affair, was taken to Winchester, where he subsequently died. The three battle-flags captured on this occasion, and sent to Washington, belonged to the Fortieth, Forty-seventh, and Fifty-fifth Virginia regiments of infantry.

General Lee will surely acknowledge these were not left in the hands of stragglers asleep in barns.

GEORGE G. MEADE, *Major-General Commanding.*

Kilpatrick, in his letter of explanation, referred to in the above despatch, gives the following graphic account of this last scene in the great drama of the invasion:

HEADQUARTERS THIRD DIVISION CAVALRY CORPS,
Warrenton Junction, Va., Aug. ——.

To Colonel A. J. Alexander, Chief of Staff of Cavalry Corps:

COLONEL: In compliance with a letter just received from the headquarters of the Cavalry Corps of the Army of the Potomac, directing me to give the facts connected with the fight at Falling Waters, I have the honor to state that, at three A. M. of the fourteenth ultimo, I learned that the enemy's pickets were retiring in my front. Having been previously ordered to attack at seven A. M., I was ready to move at once.

At daylight I had reached the crest of hills occupied by the enemy an hour before, and, a few minutes before six, General Custer drove the rear-guard of the enemy into the river at Williamsport. Learning from citizens that a portion of the enemy had retreated in the direction of Falling Waters, I at once moved rapidly for that point, and came upwith the rear-guard of the enemy at seven thirty A. M., at a point two miles distant from Falling Waters. We pressed on, driving them before us, capturing many prisoners and one gun. When within a mile and a half of Falling Waters, the enemy was found in large force, drawn up in line of battle on the crest of a hill, commanding the road on which I was advancing. His left was protected by earthworks, and his right extended to the woods on our left.

The enemy was, when first seen, in two lines of battle, with arms stacked within less than one thousand yards of the large force. A second piece of artillery, with its support, consisting of infantry, was captured while attempting to get into position. The gun was taken to the rear. A portion of the Sixth Michigan Cavalry, seeing only that portion of the enemy behind the earthworks charged. This charge was led by Major Webber, and was the most gallant ever made. At a trot he passed up the hill, received the fire from the whole line, and the next moment rode through and over the earthworks, and passed to the right, sabring the Rebels along the entire line, and returned with a loss of thirty killed, wounded, and missing, including the gallant Major Webber, killed.

I directed General Custer to send forward one regiment as skirmishers. They were repulsed before support could be sent them, and driven back, closely followed by the Rebels, until checked by the First Michigan and a squadron of the Eighth New York. The Second brigade having come up, it was quickly thrown into position, and, after a fight of two hours and thirty minutes, routed the enemy at all points and drove him toward the river.

When within a short distance of the bridge, General Buford's command came up and took the advance. We lost twenty-nine killed, thirty-six wounded, and forty missing. We found upon the field one hundred and twenty-five dead Rebels, and brought away upward of fifty wounded. A large number of the enemy's wounded were left upon the field in charge of their own surgeons. We captured two guns, three battle-flags, and upward of fifteen hundred prisoners.

To General Custer and his brigade, Lieutenant Pennington and his battery, and one squadron of the Eighth New York Cavalry, of General Buford's command, all praise is due.

Very respectfully, your obedient servant,

J. Kilpatrick, *Brigadier-General.*

CHAPTER XXXII.

CHICKAMAUGA.

Under the Shadow of Lookout Mountain.—Evacuation of Chattanooga.—The Long Battle-line.—Bragg Contests the Union Advance.—Disposition of Troops at Chickamauga Creek.—Attack of the Nineteenth.—Fierce Struggle for Position.—Bragg's Attack of the Twentieth.—Furious Fighting.—Buckner's Battery and its Deadly Work.—The Union Army Cut in Two.—Thomas on Missionary Ridge.—The Storm Breaks.—Desperate Assault of Longstreet.—Repulse of the Confederates.—Thomas, Master of the Field.—The Enemy in Retreat.—Occupation of Chattanooga.—Letter of Rosecrans.

THE battle fought under the shadow of Lookout Mountain on West Chickamauga Creek, September nineteenth and twentieth, 1863, secured to the Federal Government the possession of Chattanooga—a strong strategic point on the Tennessee River, and one of the three difficult passes in a mountain range of forty miles. The occupation of this point and of Cumberland Gap furnished a base which commanded the States of Tennessee and Kentucky, and also supplied a key for operations against Alabama, Georgia, and South Carolina.

Bragg had evacuated Chattanooga as a matter of necessity, in order to prevent the army of Rosecrans from coming between him and his expected reinforcements. It was an attempt to regain possession of the roads leading to Chattanooga, after being reinforced, and also of the town itself, that brought on the battle of Chickamauga.

Crittenden's Corps occupied a position on the Creek, near Gordon's Mill, with the entire Confederate army in his front. The corps of Thomas was at the eastern foot of Lookout Mountain, and McCook held Winston's Gap, forty miles away. The army of Rosecrans thus occupied all the passes of Lookout Mountain from Gordon's Mill to Alpine.

On the fourteenth of September Bragg had concentrated his forces at Lafayette, Georgia, to contest the Union advance,—his army having been reinforced by troops from Mississippi, and by the captured garrison of Vicksburg and Port Hudson, released on parole and declared exchanged by the Confederate authorities. The Union headquarters, meantime, had been established at a place called Crawfish Springs, the army being concentrated on West Chickamauga Creek.

When our troops attempted to advance southward through the passes of Pigeon Mountain, the enemy were discovered to be in force in our immediate front beyond the creek.

Rosecrans and his army occupied the rising ground west of the stream, while the enemy held a position east of it. On the seventeenth and eighteenth, reconnoissances were made which showed that Bragg was massing his troops in front of Rosecrans' left and center, with the evident purpose of placing himself between Chattanooga and the Union army. To counteract this movement, Rosecrans wheeled his whole army back down the creek.

On Saturday morning, the nineteenth, the Union line of battle stretched along the Lafayette and Rossville road, due north and south—the right resting at Gordon's Mills and the left at Kelly's House. "On the extreme left was Brannan, next Baird and Reynolds, with Johnston in reserve in the center, Palmer on the right of Reynolds, Van Cleve on his, and Wood at Gordon's Mills. The line completed by the divisions of Davis and Sheridan, faced a little south of east. Negley formed a defensive crotchet at Owen's Ford, higher up the valley. Detached from this line, covering the Ringgold approach to Rossville, the reserve corps under General Gordon Granger, was stationed, but not operating with the main column, can hardly be said to have formed part of the line of battle." The Confederate army reached Chickamauga Creek on the eighteenth, after a dusty march of four days, having increased their strength by three brigades under General Hood—Longstreet and his troops not having yet arrived. At ten o'clock on the morning of the nineteenth our left attacked the Confederates with the intention of driving them across the stream. The battle was a struggle for position, and though it lasted until nightfall neither army were successful in gaining the contested ground. The troops of Crittenden's corps on the Union side received the brunt of the attack, and on the Confederate side, the forces under the Irish Major Cleburn—once a private in the English army, and at that time risen to the rank of Major-General in the Confederate army—were the chief contestants.

"During the night of Saturday, General Rosecrans

made some changes in the disposition of his forces, by which the line was so far withdrawn that it rested along a crossroad running northeast and southwest, and connecting the Rossville with the Lafayette road. By this change the line was shortened one mile, and the right wing caused to rest on a strong position at Mission Ridge. Thomas held the left, Crittenden the center, and McCook the right. Upon the right of General Thomas' line, as held by Reynolds and Brannan, was a slight rise in the plain, and from the top of this the whole field could be commanded. It was the key to the position. During the night, the troops of Thomas had built a rude breastwork of logs and rails for their protection. General Lytle held Gordon's Mills.

General Longstreet joined the Confederate force on Chickamauga Creek late on the night of the nineteenth, and was placed in command of the Confederate left wing. At nine o'clock on the morning of the twentieth, the fighting was renewed.

An attack had been ordered at daybreak, but unforeseen obstacles delayed the movement until a later hour. Bragg pursued his usual plan of battle at Chickamauga, which was to make a successive attack along the whole line from right to left. Accordingly, a furious battle was soon raging around the Union left between the veteran troops of Thomas and the attacking lines of the enemy. Again and again the Confederates charged the Union ranks, behind their breastworks of logs and rails, with impetuous fury; but each time they met with repulse. A storm of fire and shot from our batteries mowed down the

Confederate ranks with bloody havoc and sent them reeling back upon their supports. At eleven o'clock, Longstreet had commenced his attack. "Steadily advancing, he swept away the head of every formation; though often checked and, for the moment, repulsed, again and again he rode to the head of his troops, and, hat in hand, rising in his stirrups, with voice and gesture animated his men. The Western troops were brave and hardy men, the material of as fine an army as ever shouldered musket, but could not check the attack of Longstreet, who was pressing right on for the possession of Chattanooga." Rosecrans saw the danger and quickly took measures to meet it. Wood was instantly ordered to the support of Reynolds, while Davis and Sheridan moved over to the left, and thus closed up the line. Wood, though fiercely assaulted, succeeded in reaching his destination. The Confederate General Walker dispatched a courier to Longstreet with intelligence of this movement, and Buckner's battery of twelve pieces was immediately ordered forward.

Davis, who was coming up to fill Wood's place, received the full force of this encounter and was driven to the right in disorder by the sudden fury of the attack. His command lost heavily in killed and wounded. On the right, the onset of the foe was equally severe, and the divisions of Van Cleve and Palmer were forced to give way in confusion. "The rout of the right and center was now complete, and after that fatal break the line of battle was not again re-formed during the day." The Union army was now cut in two, the disaster being largely due to the terrible work of Buckner's battery. McCook was hurled back to the right and, with the exception of one brigade of Wood's, Crittenden's corps was broken in pieces. Thomas had formed his line of battle in a semi-circular position, with the right at the Gap, as the arc of the circle, and a hill near its center forming the key to the position. His left rested on the Lafayette road. At this point the troops which had hurled back the Rebel right in the morning were rallied, together with portions of Sheriden's and other divisions.

Longstreet, sweeping onward with a career unchecked during the day, now hurled his battalions against this position. But Thomas, intrenched behind his earthworks, held the Ridge securely against every assault of the enemy and sent him back with terrible repulse. About mid-afternoon, the Confederate columns began pouring through a break in the Union right flank, but Granger with his reserves reaching the field at this time, succeeded in pushing them back.

The storm of battle now broke over Thomas and his stalwart men on Missionary Ridge with greater fury than before. His troops, formed in two battle-lines, advanced to the crest of the Ridge and delivered their volleys in rotation. As the deadly rifle-blast of one line blazed out on the air with terrible accuracy, the men, falling back a little, dropped on the ground to re-load, while the second line marched to the crest and discharged their fire into the ranks of the enemy. With desperate valor the Confederates came forward again and again to take by assault this strong position; but their efforts were in vain. The division of Preston succeeded in partly ascending the hill, but was swept back as the previous attacking divisions had been, with repulse and loss.

At last, as twilight darkened the bloody field, the enemy retired beyond the range of our artillery, and Thomas was master of the situation. The troops of McCook and Crittenden had by this time retired within the defences of Chattanooga, and during the night Thomas fell back to Rossville, "where, on the twenty-first, he offered battle to the enemy, who, however, declined to renew the contest. Accordingly, on the night of the twenty-first he withdrew his troops into Chattanooga." The total Union loss in this battle of Chickamauga, in killed, wounded, and missing, was fifteen thousand eight hundred and fifty-one men. Thirty-six guns, twenty caissons, and several thousand small arms and infantry accoutrements were also lost, besides two thousand prisoners captured. The Rebel loss, as stated by themselves, was over eighteen thousand.

In this bloody battle of Chickamauga, it was afterwards well known that the enemy largely outnumbered us. General Rosecrans, in a letter written concerning the battle, says:—"we fought against terrible odds," and estimates the number opposed to him in battle at ninety-three thousand. He also says that a "Union merchant of Chattanooga who was at Marietta when the foe were advancing on us, tried to send me word, and subsequently saw and told me that the enemy had reënforced Bragg with thirty thousand under Longstreet and twenty-five thousand under Joe Johnston, in addition to which Governor Brown had fifteen thousand Georgia militia; and so confident were they of overwhelming us that the Kentucky and Tennessee Rebel refugees at Marietta had hired conveyances and loaded their household goods, expecting to follow their victorious hosts back into Tennessee and Kentucky.

"I could add much more corroborative evidence to show that the brave and devoted Army of the Cumberland sustained and successfully resisted the utmost power of a veteran Rebel army, filled with the spirit of emulation and hope, and more than one-half larger than itself—inflicted on it much more damage than we received, and held the coveted objective point, Chattanooga.

"What we attempted, we accomplished. We took Chattanooga from a force nearly as large as our own, and held it after our enemy had been reënforced by as many men as we had in our whole command."

After the occupation of this point by the Union army, the passes of Lookout Mountain were taken possession of by the Confederates, which, together with the capture of McMinnville, almost completely cut off Rosecrans from his base.

Why Bragg left so many public buildings standing in Chattanooga—so many depots of supply, and all his hospitals, besides two steamboats, was cause for much speculation and wonder among the Union troops when they entered that city; but these things made it evident that his evacuation of Chattanooga was only a temporary movement.

Owing to faulty dispositions of troops, the battle

of Chickamauga lost to Rosecrans the confidence of his Government. He was shorn also of his former prestige, and the public dissatisfaction brought about a change of commanders. It is a difficult question to answer, whether he could have avoided a battle: or, having changed the scene of conflict to Chattanooga, whether a battle fought there would have brought about more favorable results.

Unlooked for contingencies sometimes arise in the best laid plans of men and mice which overturn their most reasonable calculations. To ask whether certain events, had they happened, would be more fruitful in good results than certain other events which *did* transpire, is like propounding the riddle of the Sphinx.

CHAPTER XXXIII.

BRISTOE.

Condition of Meade's Army.—"Going Home to Vote."—Lee's Advance.—Cavalry Encounter.—Roast Lamb and Coffee Left Behind.—Order for Retreat.—Fight at James City.—Incidents of the Day.—On to Washington.—Stuart Hemmed in at Catlett's Station.—The Pine Thicket.—The Concealed Force.—Hill Entangled.—Battle of Bristoe.—Sharp Fighting.—The Confederates Beaten.—Lee in Full Retreat.—The Campaign Ended.

AFTER the memorable battle of Gettysburg, Lee retired to the south bank of the Rapidan, where, from the first days of July until October tenth, he remained comparatively inactive save in strengthening his resources and recruiting his army. About a month previous to this date, some new dispositions of troops in the Army of the Potomac were supposed to indicate a forward movement on the part of General Meade; but all was quiet along the Potomac until the middle of the month of October.

Meantime, on account of important military movements in Tennessee, reënforcements from Meade's army had been sent to help Rosecrans in his Southwestern battles, and the autumn elections of Ohio and Pennsylvania caused a large number of troops to be furloughed in the interest of the freeman's right of elective franchise. Lee, taking advantage of this state of affairs, and despite the fact that Longstreet had been sent to reënforce Bragg in the West, determined on another attempt to accomplish the invasion of Maryland and Pennsylvania. Accordingly, on the ninth of October, 1863, the army of Lee was in motion and crossed the Rapidan with the design of bringing on an engagement with Meade, whose troops were encamped around Culpepper Court House and from that point to the Rapidan.

The cavalry of Fitzhugh Lee was ordered to remain and hold their lines south of the Rapidan, while General Imboden advanced by way of the Shenandoah valley to guard the passes of the mountain. Hampton's division of Stuart's cavalry, moving on the right of the column, encountered our cavalry under Kilpatrick near James City on October tenth.

It was early in the morning, and steaming breakfasts of roast lamb, sweet potatoes, bread, milk, and honey were left untasted as our pickets were driven in with the intelligence that an attack in force was being made in our front. A prompt retreat was ordered which was executed in good style, with columns unbroken and regiments closed up. At the river sharp skirmishing occurred, which deepened into a furious battle when we reached a point nearer James City. Here the enemy charged us with wild impetuosity, but our boys returned the attack with an equally vehement counter-charge, repelling their advancing legions with the same determined front that had won the day on many a previous battle-field. Nightfall at length put an end to the conflict which had raged ceaselessly since morning with alternate charges, counter-charges, and skirmishes. On that eventful day I was in command of a line of skirmishers deployed on one of the flanks, in front of some woods, near by. A second line was posted about forty rods behind us just inside the woods, and we had orders to hold the position at all hazards. From mid-day until sunset our boys gallantly obeyed the command, firmly maintaining their ground against all assaults.

At one time during this sharp cavalry engagement a solid shot came flying down the road just where Davies and his staff had halted—their position being directly in range of a section of the enemy's artillery. The concussion of the ball nearly threw the general's horse off his feet, but Davies maintained an exterior as calm and undisturbed as though cannon balls whizzing by were the most natural occurrences of life.

The fight at James City was the inaugural engagement, as Bristoe was the closing scene in the retreat of Meade and the advance of Lee towards Washington. On the morning of the eleventh, the retreat of the Army of the Potomac towards the Rappahannock was continued, the enemy following in close pursuit and keeping up constant skirmishing. At Culpepper the corps separated, Gregg taking the road to Sulphur Springs and Buford moving in the direction of Stevensburg, while Kilpatrick marched on the main thoroughfare, along the railroad. After leaving Culpepper, Hampton's cavalry made a fierce attack on the rear-guard of Kilpatrick, but were repelled by our forces without interrupting the order of retreat, until opposite the residence of John Miner Botts, when a few regiments wheeling about, dashed upon the Confederates in a handsome saber-charge, giving them an unexpected repulse. Arrived at Brandy Station, Kilpatrick found himself environed by combinations which threatened his destruction, but with the genius of a master, he cut the gordian knot of difficulties and increased his already glorious fame by the brilliant generalship displayed on this famous battle-ground.

On the evening of the thirteenth while bivouacking near Bealeton Station, an ammunition wagon took fire and caused a wide-spread alarm within the camp, sending its exploding shells and flying shot in every direction. Supposing the enemy to be upon us in force, every man rushed to his post ready for duty, but was relieved to find the supposed attack a false alarm.

During this retreat, Stuart, closely following the Union rear, was actively engaged in harrassing our troops and committing all the depredations in his power. When near Catlett's Station, by a flank movement, he inadvertently got ahead of our Second Corps under General Warren, and was completely hemmed in between the Union troops.

Long lines of infantry, cavalry, and artillery swept by on both sides of him and his only resource was to conceal his force in the pine thickets near by and await in silence the passage of the Union army. Accordingly, under cover of night he entered the thicket and orders were issued that "no sound should be uttered throughout the command."

The heavy tramp of the Union infantry and the rumble of our artillery sounded plainly in the ears of the concealed soldiers. The accidental report of a fire-arm would have disclosed their position and in view of the overwhelming force of the enemy, nothing awaited them but destruction or surrender. * * * Three scouts were disguised in the Federal uniform and instructed to cross the enemy's line of march, report the situation to General Lee, and request him to attack the enemy's left flank at the next daybreak, when Stuart, breaking cover, would attack in the opposite direction and complete the confusion. The adventure succeeded. At dawn Rodes opened on the enemy as suggested; and Stuart, hurling the thunders of his artillery from an opposite direction, in the very pitch of the confusion, limbered up his guns and dashed with cavalry and artillery through the hostile ranks, giving them a complete surprise and inflicting upon them a loss of several hundred in killed and wounded."

Early on the morning of the fourteenth, A. P. Hill's corps left Warrenton, with orders to strike our rear at Bristoe Station where the Second Corps under General Warren was encamped behind the railroad embankment.

The enemy advanced to Broad Run Church, on the Alexandria Turnpike, and deflecting on the Greenwich road, soon after struck our trail just behind the Third Corps. Preparations for an attack occupied them until about noon, when General Warren's Second Corps, bringing up the Union rear, appeared upon the scene.

Hill then discoverea the mistake into which his own indiscretion had led him. Sandwitched between the retreating Third Corps and the advancing Second, he turned upon the force under General Warren, hoping to fight his way out of the difficulty and drive back our opposing troops. But Warren, though surprised to find the enemy in his front, quickly comprehended the situation and instantly wheeled his batteries into position where they were soon blazing havoc into the ranks of the enemy. The telling musketry fire of their comrades in arms, was also very effective. The fighting was sharp and bloody, and the Confederates fell back terribly repulsed, leaving multitudes of their dead, wounded, and prisoners in our hands. Six guns were captured, five of which, still serviceable, were turned against the enemy with great effect. "Our loss in killed and wounded was about two hundred, including Colonel James E. Mallon, Forty-second New York, killed, and General Tile, of Pennsylvania, wounded; that of the enemy was probably four hundred (besides prisoners), including General Posey (mortally), Kirtland, and Cooke, wounded, and Colonels Ruffin, First North Carolina, and Thompson, Fifth North Carolina Cavalry, killed."

The battle of Bristoe was the last and only *general* engagement that grew out of Lee's last advance northward, and probably decided the issue of the campaign; for the severe check here given to the Confederate pursuit, prevented, it may be, a raid into Maryland and Pennsylvania. Immediately afterwards, Lee took up his retreat, his campaign of manœuvres having ended disastrously to the Confederate cause. His attempt to flank our army and get between Meade and Washington was anticipated, and the recoil in the fortunes of the South which began at Gettysburg rolled steadily on. Bristoe virtually ended the campaign of 1863, but another battle known sometimes as the "Buckland Races" occurred soon after, which was the closing action of the year and which vitally affected my career as a soldier. The strange vicissitudes of that day and the dark chapter it opened in my life, affecting all my future, are events which will be recounted in another chapter.

CHAPTER XXXIV.

NEW BALTIMORE.

Kilpatrick's First Defeat.—Stuart Covers the Retreat of Lee.—*En Route* for Warrenton.—Fitzhugh Lee's Attack.—Charge of Stuart's Cavalry.—Surrounded on All Sides.—Kilpatrick's Generalship.—The Desperate Charge.—Holocaust of Death.—The Author's Capture.—In Warrenton Jail.—A Specimen of Southern Chivalry.—Kilpatrick's Dinner Interrupted.—Case of the Campaign.

IN the closing engagement of the campaign of 1863, near New Baltimore, General Kilpatrick suffered his first defeat.

Overwhelmed by superior numbers, after a sharp struggle he was obliged to retire to Haymarket, leaving the attacking cavalry of Stuart in undisputed possession of the field.

After the Confederate defeat at Bristoe, where the confident advance of Lee's army had been suddenly checked and his legions hurled backward in retreat, the rear of the retiring army was covered by Stuart's cavalry, which fell slowly back towards Warrenton. The Union force followed in that direction in pursuit and thus gave Lee an opportunity for a flank attack at Buckland. On the night of the eighteenth of October, Kilpatrick's division, consisting of the brigades of Custer and Davies, bivouacked near Gainesville, posting their pickets along Cedar Run.

We reached Gainesville at about dark, having skirmished all day with the enemy's cavalry, who had sharply disputed our advance, from the time we left Sudley Church in the morning until we bivouacked at nightfall. The firing was kept up until a late hour, —the crack of carbines and pistols breaking the stillness of the night air along Warrenton turnpike, and lighting the darkness with fitful flashes. During the night, our regiment was drawn up in column of squadrons, ready for action at a moment's notice, and we were ordered to "Stand to horse."

A little after dawn the next morning the order to advance was given, and breaking camp, we were soon *en route* for Warrenton. Stuart's cavalry, in our immediate front, retired slowly before us, skirmishing as they fell back. The Harris Light, marching in column of platoons, led the van. Just after we had passed New Baltimore, on the Warrenton pike, we were startled by a sudden thunder of artillery which shook the air, and to our dismay we discovered that Fitzhugh Lee was making a furious attack on our rear-guard at Buckland Mills. A storm of shot and shell from the enemy's batteries swept our ranks, and at the same instant Stuart, in our front, wheeled about and charged the small brigades of Kilpatrick with wild fury. The onset was terrible and we were taken completely by surprise. Lee and his cavalry had been sent by a circuitous route with the design of falling upon our rear, and having come upon a small detachment of Union infantry at Thoroughfare Gap, he had cut his way through their lines and advanced by an unpicketed road upon our troops. Here by a preconcerted movement with Stuart, he begun the attack. Almost at the same moment, General Gordon, in command of a third division of cavalry, emerged from the woods on our left, and made an attack on the Union flank with determined fury. A less skillful commander than Kilpatrick, would have been overwhelmed by a crisis so unlooked-for and portentious. Surrounded on all sides by the swarming hordes of the enemy, and assaulted in front, flank and rear, by a force greatly outnumbering our own, certain destruction seemed to await us. It was a moment in which decisive action was imperative to save the command from utter annihilation. But Kilpatrick, with the genius of a master mind, rose to the exigencies of the hour, and led his men out of the trap about to spring upon them and seal their fate. Though unable to turn defeat into victory in the face of such terrible odds, he yet managed to extricate himself and them from the difficult environments of his situation. Quickly his plans were formed, and the order "Platoons right about wheel!' rung down the column. It was followed in an instant afterwards by the command, "gallop! march!" and at the head of his small brigades, he made a desperate charge upon the cavalry and artillery of Fitzhugh Lee, arrayed in line of battle along the banks of Cedar Run. Our boys obeyed the voice of their chief, with unflinching determination, as their desperate onset proved: but the three hundred slain left on the field, showed at what a cost the charge was made. It was a bloody alternative, but the command was saved and their road to escape made clear.

When we were in pursuit of the retreating foe, the

Harris Light Cavalry, had the advance, but by a sudden evolution of the regiment during the fight, we were thrown in the rear and compelled to defend ourselves as best we could from an attack on the flank. Reaching a slight elevation in the road, we made a stand and succeeded in holding the enemy in check for some time, by the deadly volleys from our carbines and pistols. Stuart, who was commanding the Confederate force in person, ordered an assault on our position and charged upon us amid wild yells with an entire division. A furious hand-to-hand conflict ensued which made the battle field a scene of confusion and distress. Numbers, it is said, were drowned in Cedar Run while endeavoring to effect their escape. At this crisis of affairs, a fatal bullet pierced my horse and we fell to the ground, trampled by the charging squadrons of the foe. For some time I lay in the mud, lost to all consciousness, while the roar of battle surged around me unheeded. Meantime, our brave troops, overpowered in the unequal contest, were forced to fall back, leaving their wounded and dead on the field. How long I lay insensible under the feet of the trampling horsemen, I do not know, but when I awoke to consciousness, I found myself in the hands of a Rebel guard who were hastily carrying me from the scene of action. Thus began the first chapter in the record of my long captivity. On the night of that fatal day of October nineteenth, we slept in Warrenton Jail and at daybreak the next morning started for Culpepper. During our first night's incarceration, most of the prisoners were robbed of their clothing and valuables by the guard—everything of the slightest value being taken. One of these specimens of Southern chivalry preferred the modest request for my entire wardrobe. His language was a trifle short of classic elegance as he told me to " come out of that ar hat and overcoat, and them ar boots too, you d——d blue jacket!"

In looking over my career as a soldier, I can see how vitally this day of capture affected my whole after life. Like the springs on high mountain ranges where a slight change of conformation decides whether their clear waters shall flow to the east or the west, so there are hours in the history of most men whose events, however slight, decide the direction of all their after lives. Out of the experience of which this day was the opening page, grew my first book, " Beyond the Lines," and " Soldiers of the Saddle,"—a record of three years of cavalry life in the Union service—followed in natural sequence.

Just before the cavalry action of New Baltimore began, Kilpatrick had stopped at the house of a citizen near Gainesville to whom he declared that "Stuart had been boasting of driving him from Culpepper, but now he was going to drive Stuart." General Kilpatrick, on that day, is described as having been as " furious as a wild boar." He was about to sit down to a well-cooked dinner when the sound of artillery from the direction of Buckland Mills, announced the tumult of coming battle. Kilpatrick sprang to his feet, threw himself into the saddle and almost immediately was galloping away like the wind, to lead his command. But the disastrous *denouement* of the battle dispersed his division and sent his men flying for dear life. The

General's race-horse 'Lively,' a thorough-bred mare, flew the track on this occasion, and fell into the hands of Moseby.

After the action of New Baltimore, Lee and his army resumed their march southward, and General Meade commenced a forward movement from the line of Cedar Run to the line of the Rappahannock. In November, the Army of the Potomac was located along the Upper Rappahannock, and the enemy occupied the south side of the Rapidan. Here both armies fortified their respective positions and active operations were suspended for the remainder of the year.

CHAPTER XXXV.

FORT FISHER.

Outer Defences of Wilmington.—Blockade-running.—Admiral Porter's Expedition.—Rough Weather.—The Attack.—The Torpedo Vessel. —The First Day's Bombardment. —Reconnoissance. —Strength of the Fort.—Return to Hampton Roads.—Renewed Preparations.—Attack of the Second Expedition.—Bivouac Fires.—Terrible Bombardment.—Desperate Assault of Union Troops.—They Effect a Lodgment.—The Attack goes on.—The Last Trenches Cleared.—Fort Fisher Ours.—Valor of Colored Troops.—Spoils of Victory.

AT the southernmost extremity of a narrow neck of land branching out from the North Carolina coast, and separating Cape Fear river from the tumultuous waters of the wide Atlantic, stands Fort Fisher, grimly guarding the approach to Wilmington twenty miles to the northward, up the river.

During the year of 1863, Wilmington was the great center of blockade-running, and owing to the vast difficulties of enforcing the blockade, the port had defied all effort to abridge its privileges, and in consequence an extensive trade was carried on between Wilmington and foreign ports.

Early in August, 1863, a joint naval and military expedition under Admiral Porter was organized with the avowed purpose of closing this port by capturing its outer defences. The squadron, however, did not start on its hazardous enterprise until December twelfth, owing to the difficulties of obtaining a sufficiently large co-operating land force to insure success. Leaving Hampton Roads, where they had remained since August, the squadron, numbering seventy-five vessels all told, sailed for their destination, having on board a land force of six and a half thousand men under General Butler. The fleet arrived off Wilmington on December fifteenth, but owing to rough weather, the vessels were unable to get into position to land the troops or to make an attack until noon of the twenty-fourth, when a furious fire was opened upon Fort Fisher. The storm of shot dropped at the rate of thirty per minute and continued until night.

On the day previous to the attack, a torpedo vessel, disguised as a blockade-runner, was towed to a point within four hundred yards of Fort Fisher, and two hundred yards of the beach, where she was securely anchored while preparations were made to blow her up.

She had on board an amount of powder supposed to be sufficient to explode the magazine of the fort. The enemy were completely deceived as to the character of the vessel, believing her to be a blockade-runner, and in consequence giving the signals customary with that class of craft. The party under Commander Rhind in charge of the torpedo vessel, set her on fire under the cabin and then getting into their boats, made good their escape to the Wilderness,—one of the boats belonging to the fleet. As soon as the torpedo party were on board, the Wilderness put out towards sea, to avoid the explosion.

"At forty-five minutes past one o'clock on the morning of the twenty-fourth, the explosion took place, but the shock was nothing like so severe as was expected. It shook the vessel somewhat and broke one or two glasses, but nothing more."

As the morning of the twenty-fourth dawned, the fleet got under way and was soon arrayed in battle line ready to make a grand attack on the almost impregnable walls of Fort Fisher.

At half-past eleven o'clock, the ship Ironsides begun the assault, the rest of the fleet following in succession and opening fire as soon as their guns were brought within range of the fort. The enemy were driven to their casemates by the iron hail, and for five long hours the terrible storm continued without intermission. But it was without result. The transports did not arrive off Wilmington until the twenty-fifth, having been delayed on the way by a storm which obliged them to put into Beaufort. A fresh attack was then ordered, under cover of which a force of three thousand men, General Weitzel commanding, was landed at a point five miles east of the fleet. General Weitzel made a reconnoissance and reported that an assault at that time would be butchery. As General Butler was of the same opinion, the troops were ordered to re-embark and the transports returned to Hampton Roads. General Butler, in a letter to Admiral Porter, written on the twenty-fifth, says that the strip of land up which the attacking party would be obliged to pass in order to assault the fort, was not wide enough for more than a thousand men in line of battle. Flag Pond Hill Battery and its garrison of sixty-five men and two commissioned officers were captured, as was also Half Moon Battery, including its force of seven officers and two hundred and eighteen men of the Third North Carolina Junior Reserves. General Butler in the letter mentioned, says :—" General Weitzel advanced his skirmish line within fifty yards of the fort, while the garrison was kept in their bomb-proof by the fire of the navy, and so closely that three or four men of the picket line ventured upon the parapet and through the sally-port of the work, capturing a horse which they brought off, killing the orderly who was the bearer of a dispatch from the chief of artillery of General Whiting, to bring a light battery within the fort, and also brought away from the parapet the flag of the fort.

" This was done while the shells of the navy were falling about the heads of the daring men who entered the work, and it was evident as soon as the fire of the navy ceased because of the darkness, that the fort was fully manned again, and opened with grape and canister upon our picket line.

" Finding that nothing but the operations of a regular siege, which did not come within my instructions, would reduce the fort, and in view of the threatening aspect of the weather, wind arising from the southeast, rendering it impossible to make further landing through the surf, I caused the troops with their prisoners to re-embark, and see nothing further that can be done by the land forces."

Some idea of the strength of the fort may be obtained from the fact that during one of the most terrific bombardments of modern warfare, the fort remained uninjured.

A Richmond paper in an issue of the time says:—"General Bragg has issued a congratulatory order on the defeat of the enemy's grand armada before Wilmington, paying a merited compliment to Generals Whiting and Kirkland, Colonel Lamb, and the officers and men engaged. The enemy's attack on the first day lasted five hours ; on the second day, seven hours,—firing altogether over twenty thousand shots from fifty kinds of vessels. The Confederates responded with six hundred and sixty-two shots on the first day and six hundred on the second. Our loss is three killed and fifty-five wounded. The ground in front and rear of the fort is covered with shells and is torn in deep pits. Two guns in the fort burst, two were dismounted by ourselves and two by the enemy's fire, yet the fort is unhurt."

But the effort to take Fort Fisher was not allowed to remain a failure. The returning troops were reënforced at Fortress Monroe, and immediate preparations were made for a renewed attack. General Terry succeeded General Butler in command of this second expedition, which comprised a land force of over eight thousand men, including a division of colored corps—the Twenty-fifth—and the batteries of Lee and Myrick. The troops embarked on board government transports and left Fortress Monroe on the sixth of January, 1864, to coöperate with Porter's fleet off Beaufort. Owing to wind and weather, the combined movement was delayed and the fleet did not reach the Wilmington coast until the thirteenth.

On that day, this formidable armada, arranged in five divisions, moved upon the grim and threatening works of Fort Fisher.

At seven and a half o'clock in the morning, a line of ironclads, headed by a vessel named the New Ironsides, moved up directly in front of Fort Fisher, taking a position one thousand yards distant. The guns of the fort opened on them as they approached, but the iron fleet did not return the enemy's fire until an hour afterwards. At nine o'clock the troops were landed—some of the men in their eagerness jumping into the water, waist deep. A skirmish line was immediately pushed out and the entire attacking force was ashore by three o'clock in the afternoon, at which time they took possession of Half Moon Battery. Very soon, the force advanced along the beach towards Fort Fisher, pausing at dusk out of range of the enemy's guns to wait until they could go forward under cover of the darkness. At ten o'clock, the bivouac fires of the attacking force shone through the darkness, two miles distant from the fort, where our troops were encamped, covered by a kind of lagoon extending between their right flank and the woods beyond. The gunboats of the enemy shelled our lines at this point from Cape Fear river. During the night of the thirteenth, the fort was strengthened and the enemy reënforced. The next day our troops constructed a line of breastworks between Cape Fear river and the sea, and on the fifteenth, at daybreak, the attack commenced. The Brooklyn and the eleven-inch gunboats—all of them iron clads—opened the bombardment with a terrible fire. Under cover of this cannonading, the division of Ames, drawn up to assault the west end of the fort, were marched up to within one hundred and fifty yards of the point of attack. Abbott's brigade occupied the intrenchments facing Wilmington in opposition to a force five thousand strong, under Hoke, which threatened our troops in that direction. "A column of fourteen hundred sailors and marines, under Captain Bresse, was detailed from the fleet to assault the sea front, which had been so terribly demolished by the bombardment that it was thought a lodgment might be effected there more easily." At ten o'clock a terrific cannonade from the entire fleet was opened on the fort, which lasted until three o'clock in the afternoon almost without intermission. At that time the ships changed the direction of their fire from the path of the charging columns to other works, and a half hour later a desperate assault was made on the sea front. The brave besiegers gained the parapet, but were subsequently repulsed and driven back in disorder.

When the column was re-formed it was sent to the intrenchments facing Wilmington, and Abbott's brigade joined the forces of Ames. This attack, though unsuccessful, diverted the enemy's attention from the main storming party and aided in the results of the day.

The men of the old Tenth Corps, three or four thousand strong, constituted principally the attacking party, and at the word of command they gallantly charged the enemy's works. A force of twenty-two hundred garrisoned the fort.

Colonel Curtis led our troops in a headlong charge and succeeded in effecting a lodgment on the west end of the land front. The brigades of Pennypacker and Bell immediately followed, and at five o'clock in the afternoon, after contesting every inch of ground with the most desperate fighting and the severest loss, our troops gained possession of about one-half of the land front; after which Abbott came up from the defensive line, and the attack went on. At ten o'clock the last trenches of the enemy were cleared, and Fort Fisher was ours. The fighting lasted six and a half hours, and a more splendid record of valor or brilliant action than was displayed in this assault can rarely be found. Curtis was severely wounded while leading his men in the attack, Bell received a mortal hurt, fighting at the head of his troops, and Pennypacker was dangerously injured. At midnight the fort was surrendered without condition into our hands—the force inside numbering about eighteen hundred, under command of General Whitney and Colonel Lamb. These Confederate officers were both wounded. The chain of earthworks surrounding Fort Fisher and all their contents fell into our hands. Seventy-two guns, including an Armstrong, the camp and garrison equipage, and sixteen days' rations, were of the spoil. Besides the loss of the garrison, of whom four hundred were killed and wounded, the enemy also suffered the loss of Cape Fear river and its facilities for blockade running. "On our side, not a ship nor a transport was lost, and but little damage was done to the fleet." Nine hundred in killed and wounded of the land force, and two hundred on the fleet, comprised our loss in the engagement of men and officers. By some mismanagement, the magazine of the fort exploded, killing three hundred of the garrison.

The capture of Fort Fisher was a splendid achievement, and its importance as a strategic point of operations could hardly be over-estimated. During a period of nearly two years, the trade carried on from Wilmington with foreign ports, despite the blockade, amounted in the aggregate to sixty-six millions of dollars,—an item which contributed largely to the resources of the Confederates. In the desperate assault which, after long continued fighting, conquered the works of Fort Fisher, the colored troops distinguished themselves by their unflinching bravery.

Thus, another stronghold of Rebellion tottered to its fall, and the port of Wilmington was once more in possession of the Federal Government.

CHAPTER XXXVI.

OLUSTEE.

Expedition to Florida.—Sailing of the Fleet.—John Hay.—Lincoln's Letter.—Objects of the Expedition.—The Camp at Jacksonville.—Seymour's Sudden Move.—Attempt to Checkmate the Enemy at Olustee.—Hemmed in by Swamps.—The Fatal Surprise.—Overwhelmed by Superior Numbers.—Decimated Ranks.—The Battle Lost.—Seymour's Bravery.—Patten Anderson.—Who was to blame?

TOWARDS the latter part of the year 1863, an expedition to the coast of Florida was determined upon by the Federal Government, for which purpose a portion of Gilmore's fleet in Charleston Harbor was assigned, and in January, 1864, the flotilla was under way. Twenty steamers and eight schooners, having on board a force of six thousand men under the immediate command of General Truman Seymour, sailed from Hilton head for Jacksonville, on the St. John's river.

President Lincoln, having good reason to suppose that Florida was ready to return to her allegiance to the Federal Government, sent his private secretary John Hay, commissioned as Major, with the expedition, bearing despatches to Gilmore with instructions to inaugurate measures looking towards a speedy restoration of Florida to the Union. In his letter, he said that "understanding that certain persons were endeavoring to construct a legal government in Florida and that Gilmore might possibly be there in person, he had dispatched Mr. Hay, one of his private secretaries, to aid in the proposed construction. "It is desirable," he said, "for all to co-operate; but if irreconcilable differences of opinion shall arise, you are master. I wish the thing done in the most speedy way possible, so that when done it will be within the range of the late proclamation on the subject. The detail labor will of course have to be done by others, but I shall be greatly obliged if you will give it such general supervision as you can find consistent with your more strictly military duties." The other avowed objects of the expedition were to procure an outlet for cotton, lumber, timber, &c., second, to cut off the enemy's sources of commissary supplies, &c., and third, to obtain recruits for colored regiments.

The troops embarked on February sixth, and on the seventh reached Jacksonville, where they went into camp.

It was designed to make Jacksonville a base of supplies from whence to advance into the interior. Accordingly, on the night of the eighth, the Union cavalry under Colonel Guy V. Henry, pushed forward towards Baldwin, reaching that place at daybreak on the ninth. During the night they had passed a Confederate camp and captured a battery three miles in its rear.

At Baldwin, one hundred prisoners, eight pieces of artillery and other valuable property fell into our hands. Gilmore, after going to Baldwin and superintending the preliminaries of this movement, returned to Jacksonville and Hilton Head, leaving Seymour in charge of the expedition. Meantime, Colonel Henry pushed on to Sanderson, a point forty miles distant, seizing and destroying considerable property at that place. Near Lake City the enemy was discovered to be in too great force to hazard an attack by the command of Colonel Henry, and consequently our cavalry "fell back five miles, bivouacked in a drenching rain-storm and telegraphed to Seymour for orders and food." A report that the enemy, under General Finnegan, had fallen back from Lake City that night, probably induced Seymour to make the sudden move which resulted so disastrously to our arms at Olustee. On the fifteenth, Gilmore was startled on receiving a letter from Seymour saying that he proposed to make an advance to the Suwanee river—Lake City being the objective point. Gilmore at once dispatched General Turner to Jacksonville with orders countermanding this mad attempt: but when Turner reached his destination, the Olustee blunder was already being enacted. Seymour had marched his force of five thousand men out of Jacksonville on the eighteenth, and the next day he reached Barber's Station, on the Florida Central Railroad, about thirty miles from his point of starting. Receiving information at this place which led him to believe that he would be able to defeat the enemy's plans and that great strategic advantages could be secured by a rapid advance to Lake City, he resumed his advance on the morning of the twentieth. His troops passed through Sanderson without halting and pushed forward towards Olustee, nine miles beyond, believing the enemy to be at that station. But upon arriving within three miles of Olustee, the head of the Union column unexpectedly stumbled into the trap set for them, just as the enemy anticipated. It was two o'clock in the afternoon, and our men, after a march of sixteen miles over difficult roads, were faint with hunger and fatigue. At the point of attack a long cypress swamp confronted them, through which the railroad passed, "while the wagon road, making a square turn to the right crossed the railroad in order to avoid and flank the swamp." The troops of the enemy, commanded by General Finnigan, were so disposed under cover of this swamp and the neighboring pine forest, that our men stumbled into the ambuscade before they were aware of its existence. The attack was sudden and furious, and our infantry, hastily forming in line of battle, returned the enemy's fire at great disadvantage. The Seventh Connecticut Infantry under Colonel J. R. Hawley, and the Fortieth Massachusetts under Col. Henry had the advance and received the first fire of the concealed foe. We had sixteen pieces of artillery, but its position was in such close proximity to the woods within which the Confederates were concealed, that their sharpshooters, with unerring aim, made targets of our gunners and horses with terrible results. In twenty minutes after the action began, Hamilton's battery had lost forty out of fifty horses, and forty-five out of eighty-two men. The Seventh New Hampshire was ordered up in support, but was soon demoralized. The Eighth United States colored regiment was then advanced, and for an hour and a half they bravely held their position, though at a loss of three hundred and fifty of its men. At this juncture "Colonel Barton led his brigade consisting of the Forty-eighth, Forty-ninth, and One-hundred-and-fifteenth New York into the hottest front of the battle. Colonel Sammons of the One-hundred-and-fifteenth, was among the first of his regiment disabled; seven of its captains or lieutenants were killed or wounded; one of its companies lost thirty-two out of fifty-nine men. Six captains or lieutenants of the Forty-seventh were killed or disabled and its colonel was also wounded." The column on our left, headed by the Fifty-fourth Massachusetts and First North Carolina, both colored, entered the arena of conflict "just in time to stop a Rebel charge." They were overpowered by the greatly superior numbers of the foe, but "it was admitted that these two regiments saved our little army from being "routed." Their charge enabled Seymour to re-form his batteries farther to the rear, and a retreat was ordered, which was covered by the Seventh Connecticut and executed in good order. The enemy did not effectively pursue us. One thousand of our wounded were brought off the field, but a large number were unavoidably left to the consideration of the enemy. The loss on the Confederate side was stated at eighty killed and six hundred and fifty wounded. Seymour went back to Jacksonville the next morning and thus the death blow to the restoration of Florida was given, for that time at least. During the battle, Seymour, who was everywhere present, was described as being recklessly brave, dashing into the thickest of the fight and doing what he could, after the ambuscade had been brought on, to avert its disastrous consequences. But bravery alone was impotent against such fearful odds and disadvantages of position.

Too late the affair at Olustee was discovered to be

a mistake. The country was greatly excited over it, and Gilmore, Seymour, John Hay, and the President were alternately blamed for the needless slaughter. The Seventh New Hampshire and a colored regiment were also accused of being responsible for the loss of the battle.

An act which reflects credit on the Confederate General Patten Anderson, in connection with Olustee, should not go unnoticed. Soon after the engagement he sent in a complete list of our prisoners and wounded, in his hands, with a description of the nature of the wounds received, of both black and white.

After the dark chapters of Fort Wagner and Fort Pillow, it is pleasant to chronicle an incident like this.

Olustee was the central and only action of importance which occurred in Florida during the year 1864, or from thenceforward until the close of the war of Rebellion.

I enjoyed a personal acquaintance with General Seymour, and do not agree with those who believe that he was incapable of directing the movements of an independent force. All concede to him a bravery verging on rashness, but I am unable to see that the surprise at Olustee proves him devoid of generalship. How far he may have been to blame in taking upon himself the responsibility of an advance, I do not know, as some writers claim that the presence of John Hay may have had something to do with the movement and with running counter to Gilmore's orders. But I am unwilling to play the part of detractor to a noble officer who fearlessly faced death for country's sake, inciting his men to brave endeavor, and displaying every quality which could win the admiration of a soldier.

Let the laurel wreath of glory which the heart ever accords to valor and patriotism, rest undisturbed upon the name of one whose daring, at least, remains unassailed.

CHAPTER XXXVII.

FORT PILLOW.

One of the Outgrowths of Slavery.—The Negro Soldiery.—Confederate Law.—The Black Flag.—Location of Fort Pillow.—Forrest Before the Defences.—Severe Fighting.—No Surrender.—Flags of Truce.—Treachery.—Surprise of the Fort.—Overwhelmed by the Enemy.—The Butchery Commenced.—Horrible Scenes.—The Inhumanity of Man.—Influence of Slavery.

THE massacre of Fort Pillow was one of the legitimate outgrowths of the institution of negro slavery, and the savage butcheries there perpetrated under the folds of the "black flag," disgrace the records of human civilization and stain the page of history. The soldiers who fought in defence of liberty at Fort Pillow were black soldiers, and that was their offence. The Confederacy, with strange inconsistency, while employing slaves for its own belligerent purposes, passed a law that if they were so employed by Union officers, no quarter might be expected, and that nothing less than extermination would be the fate meted out to them. The law referred to, found a place on their statute books in the early part of the year 1863, and contained the following clause:—"Every white person, being a commissioned officer, or acting as such, who, during the present war, shall command negroes or mulattoes in arms against the Confederate States, shall, if captured, be *put to death*, or otherwise punished, at the discretion of the court." But there was not found in the Confederacy an officer of any note, with qualities sufficiently fiendish to permit the "black flag" dispensation to be carried into effect, until Forrest appeared before Fort Pillow, and there, by his cold-blooded atrocities, covered his name with eternal infamy. Overlooking the surrounding country from a high and nearly inaccessible bluff on the Mississippi river, at a distance of about forty miles above Memphis, in Tennessee, stood the historic fort,—a work of moderate size, and mounting only six guns. In the early part of the last year of the war, the place was garrisoned by a force under Major L. F. Booth, numbering five hundred and fifty-seven men, two hundred and sixty-two of whom were colored troops belonging to the Sixth United States Heavy Artillery. The other battalion under Major Bradford, of the Thirteenth Tennessee Cavalry, was white.

On April twelfth, 1864, this fortress was wrested from the United States forces there garrisoned, by an act of treachery, under the leadership of Forrest, unparalleled during all the four years of fighting to which the Rebellion gave birth. The battle commenced at daybreak, when a furious assault on our troops was made by the enemy.

The Union forces fought at first in the outer defences, and for hours the contest raged with sharp severity. At nine o'clock in the morning, in the thickest of the fight, Major Booth was killed, after which Major Bradford withdrew his men to the inner fort, where from that time until three o'clock in the afternoon they bravely defied every attempt of the enemy to dislodge them. Their gallant defence was aided by the gunboat New Era, which sent a vigorous storm of shells into the ranks of the enemy.

At about mid-afternoon, under a flag of truce, Forrest sent a demand for the unconditional surrender of the fort, to which Bradford replied, asking one hour's time to consider the proposal. Very soon, Forrest, under a second flag of truce, sent the message that if the Union troops were not moved from the fort in twenty minutes, he would order an assault. Major Bradford replied that he would not surrender. While the flag of truce was flying, the Confederates, with unworthy treachery, gradually crept up to a position under the fort, from which they could overwhelm the garrison by a sudden attack.

Captain Marshall of the gun-boat, refrained from firing in order not to give an excuse for subsequent atrocities in case the fort should be captured by the enemy. Immediately after the second flag of truce retired, the rebels made a rush from the positions they had so treacherously gained, and obtained possession of the fort, raising the cry of "no quarter." But little opportunity was allowed for resistance. Our troops, black and white, threw down their arms and sought to escape by running down the steep bluff near the fort, and secreting themselves behind trees and logs in the bushes and under the brush; some even jumping into the river and leaving only their heads above the water as they crouched down under the bank. Then followed a scene of cruelty and murder without parallel in civilized warfare, which needed but the tomahawk and scalping-knife to exceed the worst atrocities ever committed by savages.

The Rebels commenced an indiscriminate slaughter, sparing neither age nor sex, white nor black, soldier nor civilian. The officers and men seemed to vie with each other in the devilish work. Men, women, and children wherever found, were deliberately shot down, beaten, and hacked with sabers. Some of the children, not more than ten years old, were forced to stand up and face their murderers while being shot. The sick and wounded were butchered without mercy, the rebels even entering the hospital buildings and dragging them out to be shot, or killing them as they lay there unable to offer the least resistance. All over the hillside the work of murder was going on. Numbers of our men were collected together in lines or groups and deliberately shot. Some were shot while in the river, while others on the bank were shot and their bodies kicked into the water; many of them still living, but unable to make exertions to save themselves from drowning. * * * * All around were heard the cries of "No quarter! No quarter!" "Kill the damned niggers!" "Shoot them down!" All who asked for mercy were answered by the most cruel taunts and sneers. Some were spared for a time only to be murdered under circumstances of greater cruelty. No cruelty which the most fiendish malignity could devise, was omitted by these murderers. One white soldier who was wounded in the leg so as to be unable to walk, was made to stand up while his tormentors shot him. One negro, who had been ordered by a Rebel officer to hold his horse, was killed by him when he remonstrated. Another, a mere child, whom an officer had taken up behind him on his horse, was seen by Chalmers, who at once ordered him to put the child down and shoot him, which was done. The huts and tents in which many of the wounded had sought shelter, were set on fire, both that night and the next morning while the wounded were still in them, those only escaping who were able to get themselves out, or who could prevail on others less injured to help them out, and even some of these thus seeking to escape the flames, were met by these ruffians, and shot down, or had their brains beaten out. One man was deliberately fastened down to the floor of a tent, face upward, by means of nails driven through his clothing and into the boards under him, so that he could not possibly escape, and then the tent was set on fire. Another was nailed to the side of a building outside of the fort and then the building was set on fire and burned. * * * * These deeds of murder and cruelty closed when night came on, only to be renewed the next morning, when the demons carefully sought among the dead lying about in all directions, for any other wounded yet alive, and those they found were deliberately shot. * * * The Rebels had made a pretence of burying a great number of their victims, but they had merely thrown them, without the least regard to care or decency, into the trenches and ditches about the fort, or the little hollows and ravines on the hillside, covering them but partially with earth. Portions of heads and faces, hands and feet were found protruding through the earth in every direction." And so the sickening recital goes on. A committee of investigation who visited the spot two weeks afterwards, reported that the ground at the foot of the bluff where most of the murders had been committed, was still stained with the blood of the slaughtered soldiers, although heavy rains had fallen in the meantime. Major Bradford, in command of the fort, who up to the moment of capture, was uninjured, was brutally murdered the day after he was taken prisoner. Only eternity will reveal how many of our troops there engaged, fell victims to the fiendish inhumanity of Forrest, in like manner. "The motive for the murder of Major Bradford seems to have been the simple fact that, although a native of the South, he remained loyal to his Government."

Both Forrest and his superior, Lieutenant-General S. D. Lee, attempted palliation and even denial of the dark deeds of this day; but they were too well authenticated by scores of unimpeached witnesses, some of whom were shot and left for dead long after the fighting had ceased, and who testified to the cold-blooded murders committed. The murderers declared that they shot the colored troops because they were "niggers," and the whites because they were "fighting with the niggers."

Forrest, giving his loss at twenty killed and sixty wounded, and stating that he buried two hundred and twenty-eight of our men on the night of the battle, not reckoning numbers that were buried next day, yet had the assurance to claim that this number was killed in fair fight.

Lee, in writing a defence of the case, asserts, in the face of all contradictory evidence, that their officers "endeavored to prevent the effusion of blood." Only three weeks before this, Forrest had summoned Paducah in unmistakable terms, closing with these words,—"If you surrender, you shall be treated as prisoners of war; *but if I have to storm your works you may expect no quarter.*

After the capture of Fort Pillow, Forrest made a rapid retreat into Mississippi unmolested,—the Union cavalry force at hand not being sufficiently strong to make an effective pursuit.

The news of the butchery of Fort Pillow sent a thrill of horror through the loyal North, and the outraged sense of the people, finding vent in bitter denunciation, produced a reactionary effect on the South.

It was not exactly pleasant for a section which boasted so much chivalry and refinement, to be catalogued with barbarians or held up to the view of the civilized world with the knife in one hand and the black flag in the other. It perhaps augured a returning sense of justice that even an attempt at palliation for the wholesale crime should be made, and it was well for the reputation of our country that this terrible precedent found no subsequent parallel in the history of our civil war.

Little by little the gigantic crime of American slavery, to whose brutalizing influence the dark deeds of Fort Pillow may be traced, was undermined until at last its doom was sealed and our country was able to make her claims of freedom consistent with her acts.

CHAPTER XXXVIII.

COLD HARBOR.

Cold Harbor Tavern.—The Historic Cross Roads.—Grant's Design of Forcing the Chickahominy.—Disposition of Troops.—Preliminary Fighting.—The Battle Inaugurated by a Thunder Storm.—The Grand Attack.—Gallant Dash of the Second Corps.—The Position Gained and Lost.—Vantage-ground of the Enemy.—Failure of Grant's *coup-de-main*.—The Heroic Brigade of Colonel McKean.—The New Thermopylæ.—The Enemy's Last Attack.—The Curtain Falls on Cold Harbor.

THE neighborhood of the Chickahominy river, first made historic by McClellan in 1862, was again baptized with the blood of contending armies two years later, when Grant fought the battle of Cold Harbor at such fearful cost of life.

An old inn, known as Cold Harbor, standing at a junction of cross roads leading out of Richmond, gave its name to the contest here waged. From this point the traveler may go to Dispatch Station and Bottom Bridge on the south, White House on the east, Hanovertown and Newcastle on the north, and Richmond, via Gaines' Mills on the west. At this point in the first days of June, 1864, Grant determined to force the Chickahominy, which constituted the outer line of defence for Richmond. It was nearly the same spot which McClellan had occupied two years before, when the renowned swamps south of the river were traversed by his army.

The right of the enemy's line covered the Chickahominy river and his left stretched along the Virginia Central Railroad, holding also the Cold Harbor road from Atlee's Station on the Fredericksburg Railroad to Gaines' Mill.

The cavalry of the enemy extended to Hanover on the left and Bottom Bridge on the south. This was the disposition of troops on Tuesday, May thirty-first, three days previous to the battle. Skirmishing between the two armies was kept up from the beginning of the week until Friday when the engagement became general.

On Tuesday, Lee, suspecting Grant's intention of concentrating his troops on the left, instituted a series of manœuvers for position which brought on some lively skirmishing.

Torbert's cavalry was sent to the right, to Cold Harbor, to take possession of the eminences in that direction, and succeeded in holding the ground after a sharp fight.

On Tuesday night the Sixth Corps marched to Cold Harbor where the Eighteenth Corps, after losing its way, joined it at three o'clock in the afternoon of June first, taking position on the right of the Sixth in four lines. A field of ploughed land fronted the two corps, beyond which, the enemy were intrenched, covered by a pine forest. The two center divisions of our line charged across the ploughed land at the double-quick, cheering as they went. A murderous fire met them as they advanced, but undeterred they pushed forward and gallantly carried the first Confederate line, taking six hundred prisoners. But the captured line was in a position where it could be enfiladed by the enemy's fire, and being also commanded by a redoubt the position was relinquished.

During the night the enemy endeavored in vain to regain their lost line. This day's action cost us two thousand men, but Cold Harbor remained in our possession. The left extremity of the Union line was located at this point while the right was at Bethesda Church, eight miles distant on the Hanovertown road. Late in the afternoon there was an attack along the whole line, but it was without noticeable results on either side. By Thursday noon, June second, a new disposition of troops for the attack had been completed, the Second Corps was shifted to the Union left and the advance was ordered. But just before the appointed hour, a heavy thunder storm obscured the heavens, and the battle of the elements inaugurated the contest below. The play of lightning was incessant, the rain fell in torrents and the waters of the Chickahominy foamed turbulently with the sudden flood. The attack which was to have been made at five o'clock that afternoon was postponed until four and a half o'clock the next morning, Friday, June third. Burnside held the extreme right, next to him came Warren, next Warren was the Eighteenth Corps under Smith, Wright's Corps came next and Hancock held the extreme left.

The two armies confronted each other from opposite sides of a low, swampy piece of ground which was destined to go down to history as the battle-field of

Cold Harbor. Behind the enemy's lines, which were drawn up for battle two deep, the turbulent Chickahominy raged, before them lay the swamp drenched with water from the rain of the previous night, and beyond that gleamed the bayonets of the Union front, ready for action. In the gloom of the early morning the skirmish lines of the two armies advanced, and soon irregular volleys of musketry announced their encounter.

The artillery then opened, and down the battle lines which stretched along the Chickahominy, the thunder of the guns resounded, scarcely less terrible than the thunder of the heavens on the preceding night.

Hancock, on the left, first came up to the Confederate works, and his extreme left under Barlow, followed by the division of Gibbon, dashed forward in the face of a galling fire straight up to the guns of the enemy. Then with a rush they scaled the parapets of the Rebel fortifications, capturing their guns and colors at that point, besides several hundred prisoners.

This position had been the key point of the battle of Gaines' Mills two years before and commanded the whole field from the bald top of a ridge named Watt's Hill.

It also covered the angle of the Dispatch road, and had the brilliant charge which captured this position received proper support, the battle of Cold Harbor would have had a different sequel. Lee, doubtless, would have been forced to retreat across the Chickahominy, and thus one of the gates to Richmond would have been seized. But Lee, in guarding against the possible catastrophes of battle, had not overlooked this one, and a heavy force under Hill was quickly dispatched to regain the lost eminence. Our brave boys under Barlow had rushed onward so far in advance that the enemy's artillery raked their ranks with a terrible enfilading fire, while Hill fell upon them with overwhelming numbers. It was impossible to withstand an onset with such fearful odds, and the shattered ranks were compelled to fall back, though still keeping in charge part of their prisoners. The desperate efforts of the Second Corps to carry the Confederate works were without success. The Sixth Corps carried the first line of rifle pits in its front, gaining a point within two hundred and fifty yards of the enemy, but all the fury of its five batteries did not noticeably damage their main works.

The action of the right of our line under Warren and Burnside was confined principally to heavy artillery firing.

The Second corps bore the brunt of the battle, and the advantage which their valor gained was only temporary. Again and again did Grant, massing a heavy force, hurl it against a single point of the enemy's line: but the position lost and gained by the Confederates during the first ten minutes of fighting secured such strength of vantage ground that all our efforts to dislodge them were rendered of no avail. Although the battle lasted for five long hours, this first ten minutes decided its issue. Seven times did the valiant Sixth corps sweep down upon the right-center of the enemy, and as many times did the enemy defy its assaults.

Our entire line was drawn up in close proximity to the Confederate position, and at one point on the extreme left the contending forces were reported to be only *fifteen* yards distant! During a lull in the fury of conflict, the two central figures in the Union army, Grant and Meade, were seen on an eminence in anxious consultation, and the question, "Will the assault be renewed?" was asked along the lines. A writer for the New York Times speaks as follows concerning the relative positions of the fighting hosts:

"One portion of our line retained all day a position within fifteen yards of the Rebel works. This heroic band was the brigade of Colonel McKean, a brigade of Gibbon's division of Hancock's corps, and numbering about eight hundred men. The conduct of these eight hundred is as splendid a stroke of heroism as ever lit up the story of the 'glory we call Greece, and the grandeur we call Rome.' Through the livelong day, these men held their line, within fifteen yards of the enemy, and all his forces could not dislodge them. Repeatedly during the day the Rebels formed double columns of attack to come over the work and assail them, and the officers could be heard encouraging their troops, saying to them, 'There are only four or five hundred of them—come on!' But the moment the Rebels showed themselves above their parapet, a line of fire flashed out from behind the earthen mound, where those eight hundred heroes stood in a new Thermopylæ, and many a Rebel threw up his arms and fell prone under their swift avenging bullets.

"The sequel of this bit of history is as curious as the deed itself—for while the Rebels dared not venture out to assail McKean's men, neither could he nor his command recede from the perilous position. He could not get back to us—we could not go forward to him. In this dilemma, the ingenious device was hit upon of running a 'sap,' or zigzag trench, up from our line to his. In this way a working party were able to dig up to where they lay, begrimed with powder and worn down with fatigue, and a few hours ago they were brought safely away, —'all that was left of them, left of six hundred!' But McKean, their gallant leader, he came not away alive. Since eleven in the morning, he had lain behind the bulwark his valor defended, a corpse, While preparing to resist a Rebel assault, he fell. pierced by the bullet of a sharpshooter, and after living for an hour or two in an agonizing death-in-life, begging his staff officers to put an end to his misery, his heroic soul forsook the turmoil of this weary, warring world."

All day this position was retained, neither army making any decided demonstrations of attack. Just after dark, however, a fierce charge was made by the enemy on Hancock's Corps; but the brave boys of the Second dealt them such deadly volleys from musketry and artillery that the charge, though desperate, resulted only in terrible loss of life. The enemy evinced a bravery in this charge which could not fail to call forth the admiration of those who witnessed it. Their ranks, torn open at every discharge from our guns, closed steadily up and pressed forward to our very breastworks, some even scaling the parapets, though only to fall dead in the act. But their most desperate efforts to carry the intrenchments were in vain, and their broken ranks fell back through the gloom of the night to their old position.

Thus the curtain fell on the last act in the battle of Cold Harbor—a fight neither lost nor won: for Cold Harbor remained ours in defiance of every endeavor of the enemy to take it; but the Chickahominy, at that point, remained their's, defying in turn all our valor and skill.

CHAPTER XXXIX.

FORT WAGNER.

Site of the Fort.—First Assault.—Bombardment from the Fleet.—Heaven's Artillery.—The Advance at Night.—The Colored Regiment.—Furious Assault and Terrible Slaughter.—Bravery of Colored Troops.—Death of Colonel Shaw.—Waiting under a Hailstorm of Death.—The Possession of an Hour.—Repulse and Losses.—Wagner Impervious to Assault.—Progress of the Siege.—The "Swamp Angel."—Fort Sumter in Ruins.—Calcium Lights.—The Enemy Driven to the Wall.—Wagner Evacuated.—Spoils of Victory.

THE story of Fort Wagner possesses for me a peculiar and personal interest, on account of having first listened to its recital in detail from the lips of one of the colored participants, while I was held a prisoner in Charleston jail yard. Sergeant Johnson was a full-blooded and intelligent negro, and gave me an interesting history of the captivity of himself and comrades after the final bloody assault of the eighteenth. They were free negroes living in the state of Massachusetts, but were tried on a charge of leaving their masters and joining the Union army. Happily, the abolition of slavery renders such mockeries in the name of justice no longer possible, and gradually the long-suffering and down-trodden race is being placed on the merit of character instead of color.

On the south side of the entrance to Charleston Harbor lies Morris Island—a sand formation washed up by long accumulations of debris swept outward from the beach, and inward from the wide ocean. Cumming's Point is at the northern extremity of this island, and southward, down the beach, on a narrow peninsula of sand, Fort Wagner faces the sea. Early in July, 1863, a combined military and naval expedition was organized by the Federal Government for the purpose of taking possession of Morris Island, and reducing Fort Wagner.

On July tenth, a lodgment on Morris Island was effected, and the infantry of the attacking force was pushed forward to within six hundred yards of Fort Wagner. In a dispatch to General Halleck, from Morris Island, dated July twelfth, General Gilmore says:—"We now hold all the Island except about one mile on the north end, which includes Fort Wagner, and a battery on Cumming's Point. * * * * On the morning of the eleventh instant, at daybreak, an effort was made to carry Fort Wagner by assault. The parapet was gained, but the supports recoiled under the fire to which they were exposed, and could not be got up. Our loss in both actions will not vary much from one hundred and fifty in killed, wounded, and prisoners."

But the effort to reduce Fort Wagner by assault was not thus easily relinquished, and another attack was determined upon, which took place on the eighteenth of July. A bombardment from the fleet was to have opened at dawn on that day, but a terrible storm which burst over land and sea, dampened our powder and caused a delay of six hours. At half past twelve o'clock the attack began, and a rain of fire fell upon

Fort Wagner from six iron-clad gunboats, stationed at short range from Morris Island, and also from a semi-circular line of batteries ranged across the island a mile distant, to the southward. Several wooden gunboats farther away, also sent their shells into the ramparts of the fort. The bombardment, though raging severely, from noon until nightfall, was without apparent effect. As the sun went down, the boom of cannon died away over the bay, and from the depths of a black thunder cloud which now unrolled itself over the sky, the jagged lightnings leaped in angry flashes. The roar of the artillery of the sky, mingling with the fierce tempest which now broke over Charleston Harbor, succeeded the thunder of the fleet. In the midst of the storm, arrangements were perfected to carry the fort by assault—an impression having been received that the works were evacuated. Our iron-clads, with the exception of the Montauk, returned to their anchorage. General Strong, Colonel Putnam, and General Stevenson, led three brigades respectively in this perilous undertaking, the Fifty-fourth Massachusetts (colored) having the advance. The troops, forming in line, moved forward over the hard beach, from which the tide had retired, towards the fort. The hour of low tide had been chosen on account of the narrowness of the strip of land along which the attacking force were obliged to pass in order to reach the fort. The Fifty-fourth Massachusetts regiment was commanded by Colonel Robert G. Shaw, and was the first colored force organized in a free State. Anxious to prove their bravery, the regiment, in order to be on the battle-ground in season, marched for two days " through heavy sands, working its way across creeks and inlets, unsheltered through the pelting rains of the intervening nights; only reaching at six in the afternoon General Strong's headquarters, about midway of the island, where it was halted five minutes: but there was now no time for rest and food, and it went forward hungry and weary to take its place in the front line of the assaulting columns. * * * Advancing a few hundred yards under a random fire from two or three great guns, halted half an hour during which the Fifty-fourth was addressed by General Strong and by its colonel: and then, as the dusk was deepening rapidly into darkness, the order to advance was given, and under a storm of shot and shell from Wagner, Sumter, and Cumming's Point, our soldiers moved swiftly on." Silently they advanced until when within two hundred yards of the fort the silence was broken by a great shout and with a wild rush the troops swept forward up the glacis, the other regiments following closely. The furious storm of grape and canister which greeted then from the fort, decimated their ranks with terrible havoc; but the colored troops plunged boldly on, numbers of them crossing the ditch, though the water in it was four feet deep, and gaining the parapet. But they were driven back by hand grenades, though not until half their number were left dead on the field. Their brave young colonel was among the number whose lives paid the forfeit of this terrible charge. "The Sixth Connecticut Regiment, under Lieutenant Colonel Rodman, was next in support of the Fifty-fourth and they also suffered terribly, being compelled to retire after a stubborn contest.

The Ninth Maine, which was next in line, was broken up by the passage of the remnant of the repulsed colored regiment through its lines, and retired in confusion, excepting three companies, which stood their ground." The Third New Hampshire now rushed into the contest and three companies waded the water of the ditch and found shelter under the embankment.

The Second Brigade being unaccountably delayed in coming up, General Strong ordered the men to fall back and lie down on the glacis. Here, while waiting for their supports and while exposed to a galling fire, General Strong was wounded. The Second Brigade not yet arriving, the order to retire was given and the men left the field in perfect order. The other regiments soon afterwards coming up, rushed with impetuous valor up the glacis, undeterred by the steady fire of the enemy, and climbing over the parapet descended into the fort, where a desperate hand-to-hand encounter took place. For over an hour our gallant troops held possession of the fort, obliging the garrison to seek the shelter of the traverses at one side of the works. But re-enforcements arriving for them, our gallant boys were at last driven from the fort, overpowered by superior numbers.

The Forty-eighth New York regiment under Colonel Barton, having been among the first to reach the fort, was fired upon by mistake, by a regiment that gained the parapet a few moments later, supposing it to belong to the Confederate garrison.

The brave Forty-eighth came out of the fight with decimated ranks.

At midnight the order to retire was given and the

troops fell back to the rifle pits outside their own works.

As the Union force retired, a "Rebel yell of triumph from Wagner rose above the thunder of their guns from Sumter and Cumming's Point." The Union loss in this desperate assault was fifteen hundred, while the Rebel loss in killed and wounded was not much over one hundred. Only the severely wounded on our side, were taken prisoners, but six hundred Union dead, according to Confederate authority, were buried on this woeful battle-field.

"Among these was Colonel Shaw—a hereditary Abolitionist—on whom they vainly thought to heap indignity by 'burying him in the same pit with his niggers.' His relatives and friends gratefully accepted the fitting tribute." General Strong received a mortal wound near the spot where the young Colonel met his death, and the lives of many other brave officers were here laid down, a noble sacrifice for the cause they loved.

Fort Wagner having thus been proven impregnable to assault, General Gilmore began the reduction of the place by regular siege. The cross fires from Fort Sumter, Battery Gregg and several other batteries on James Island, rendered this work one of difficulty, and the narrow land approach to the fort, complicated it still further.

But steadily, night after night, under cover of the darkness, and in the face of all obstacles, the beseigers worked on.

Trenches were dug, batteries erected and mortars and siege guns placed in position to do their deadly work. Row after row of inclined palisading was pushed forward towards the doomed fort, until there was no longer room to advance parallels, on account of the proximity of fort and beach. But the approach was now continued by zig-zag trenches at acute angles with each other. Torpedo mines also filled the ground from this point forward. Meantime, while the work of the seige went on, the guns of our fleet continued to belch their thunders over the bay, bombarding the defences of the harbor, with little intermission.

In the soft, black mud westward of Morris Island, on a platform of logs supported by piles driven down to the hard sand-bed below, the 'Marsh Battery' was erected, mounting a single eight-inch rifled Parrott, protected by a sand-bag parapet. This was the celebrated "Swamp Angel" of soldier nomenclature, and its design was to shell Charleston unless Morris Island surrendered. It carried a projectile of one hundred and fifty pounds weight, but at its thirty-sixth discharge it burst, and its work was thus brought suddenly to an end.

The steady storm of shot and shell which was continuously poured upon Fort Sumter from our batteries and iron-clads, began to take effect, dismounting its guns, and crumbling its walls, until at length, it was reduced to a mass of shapeless ruins, and on the twenty-third of the month, General Gilmore ceased firing in that direction, and reported to Halleck that "Fort Sumter as an offensive work was now practically demolished."

And thus the siege went on, from the time of the final assault on the eighteenth of July, through all the month of August and the opening days of autumn. Towards the last of the siege, all our light mortars had been brought to the front and placed in battery, and powerful calcium lights were used by night to blind the enemy and "assist the operations of our cannoneers and sharpshooters."

On September fifth, at daybreak, our batteries, after a temporary check, re-opened on the enemy's works, aided by the "New Ironsides," which dropped its exploding shells into the fort, from a broadside of eight guns. The calcium lights "turned night into day, blinding the garrison, and rendering visible to the besiegers everything connected with the fort." Under this terrible attack, the enemy were compelled to remain under the shelter of their bomb-proofs, thus leaving our sappers free to push forward their work under the very wall of the fort. On the evening of September sixth, everything was ready for another grand assault, and General Terry was ordered to lead the attack in three columns, at nine o'clock on the morning of the seventh. But at midnight on the sixth the garrison were discovered to be escaping, and so quickly did they move, that only seventy-five prisoners were captured. Eighteen guns were left in Fort Wagner and seven in Battery Gregg. The bomb-proof shelter of Fort Wagner was found to be not seriously injured, thus proving that sand—of which it was constructed—is possessed of far greater power of resistance than stone or brick.

In a dispatch from Gilmore to Halleck, dated September seventh, he says:—"About ten o'clock last night the enemy commenced evacuating the island and all but seventy-five of them made their escape from Cumming's Point, in small boats.

"Captured dispatches show that Fort Wagner was commanded by Colonel Keitt of South Carolina, and garrisoned by one thousand four hundred effective men, and Battery Gregg by between one hundred and two hundred men.

"Fort Wagner is a work of the most formidable kind. Its bomb-proof shelter, capable of containing one thousand eight hundred men, remains intact after the most terrific bombardment to which any work was ever subjected.

"We have captured nineteen pieces of artillery, and a large supply of excellent ammunition."

New batteries were erected upon Morris Island after its capture, with the design of commanding Fort Sumter and aiding any naval attack which might storm Charleston. The city which recklessly, and without counting the cost, had sown the seeds of disunion, was yet doomed to reap the fruits thereof in war's merciless desolation. Her ocean defences were now forced and the guns of Liberty thundered at her gates. Soon, the shriek of exploding shells resounded through her streets and her people abandoned their dwellings, seeking places of safety. The "cradle of secession" was violently rocked, and the progeny which, fathered by injustice, had been nursed therein, was soon to struggle in death's fatal throes.

CHAPTER XL.

CEDAR CREEK.

Sheridan in the Shenandoah Valley.—Pursuit of Early.—Cedar Creek Encampment.—The Enemy Re-enforced.—The Determined Attack.—The Silent March.—The Slumbering Army Surprised.—The Wild Yell through the Fog.—The Union Army a Mass of Fugitives.—The Nineteenth Corps Forced Back by the Wave of Retreat.—Efforts of the Brave Sixth.—The Fight Near Middletown.—Sheridan at Winchester.—His Wild Ride.—The Stream of Fugitives Arrested. The Union Battle-line Re-formed.—Our Victorious Charge.—The Enemy Routed in Confusion.—Honor to Sheridan.

THE renown with which the battle of Cedar Creek covered the name of Sheridan, will live while history is written or has power to survive the wreck of time. No more eloquent theme could be furnished the pen of the historian or the inspiration of the poet than the battle of Cedar Creek, with Sheridan's ride from Winchester and its glorious sequel. No single event of the late war presents stronger claims for our hero-worship than this. None more clearly evidences the wonderful power of a magnetic *will* force, to control circumstances and subdue even the reverses of battle.

After the complete surprise that Early had given our army at Cedar Creek, and its consequent terrible rout and defeat, it seems little less than a miracle that the presence of one man should stem the retreat, turn the tide of battle, and lead a shattered army back to conquest and glory.

When Sheridan had returned from his pursuit of Early up the Shenandoah Valley in the autumn of 1864, he retired to the north bank of Cedar Creek, near Strasburg. Supposing the enemy too severely crippled by defeat and by the wholesale destruction of property in the valley, to attempt an attack at that time, Sheridan left his army and went up to Washington for a little visit.

General Early, having been re-enforced by twelve thousand men, and hearing that Sheridan had gone to Washington, determined to attack the Army of the Shenandoah, before its general could have a chance to return.

His own army was short of supplies, and the rich spoils which he knew were in possession of the Union troops was too tempting a prize to be lightly passed by. "Our force at this time, was posted on three moderate hills extending for three miles across the country, each one a little back of the other."

The Army of West Virginia, under Crook, held the first hill; the second was occupied by the Nineteenth Corps under Emory, and the Sixth Corps, with Torbet's cavalry covering its right flank, held the third eminence. Early crossed the mountains between the two forks of the Shenandoah River on the night of October eighteenth, 1864, and forded the north branch, —marching in five columns. His design was to surprise the Union camp, and that the march might be noiseless, he ordered the canteens of the soldiers to be left behind, to prevent any alarm from being given to the Union pickets, by their clanking against the bayonets. His march was towards our left, and notwithstanding the fact that at about two o'clock in the morning, the heavy muffled tramp of Early's army of between twenty and thirty thousand was heard by some of our pickets, few precautions were taken and no reconnoisance was sent out. Not dreaming of the contemplated attack, on the eve of a great surprise, our army, unconscious of its danger, slumbered peacefully on. Meantime, the enemy pushing on through the gray gloom of the early morning and marching on the borders of our position for miles, halted at last when they were within six hundred yards of our camps.

A reconnoitering force from Crook's army was just preparing to go out, when suddenly a wild yell burst through the fog which hid from their view the Confederate army, which was quickly followed by a withering musketry fire and the clash of arms. Before our surprised and panic-stricken troops could be formed in battle array, the enemy were upon them, and after a short and sharp encounter, the Army of Western Virginia was thrown in utter rout—a mass of fugitives flying before the pursuing foe back towards the second hill where the Nineteenth Corps was encamped.

The few regiments of Crook's force which endeavored to make a stand, were swept back before the swelling tide of fugitives in full and disordered retreat.

The Nineteenth Corps attempted to arrest the Confederate advance, but the enemy getting in our rear and enfilading us with our captured batteries, the troops broke rank and fell back in confusion towards the encampment of the Sixth Corps on the third hill in the rear.

A new line of battle was formed by Wright, who was making desperate attempts to stay the onward tide of fugitives which steadily poured to the rear. Early's hungry troops now began to leave their ranks in large numbers to plunder the two deserted camps of their rich booty. Had Wright been aware of this fact, perhaps he could have successfully resisted the Confederate advance. As it was, after having hurled back a fierce onset of the enemy and covered the retreat of the disordered crowd in his rear, he began to fear that his communications might be endangered and therefore fell back towards Middletown. Wright had thus heroically interposed himself and his command between our army and its threatened destruction.

Merritt and Custer with two divisions of cavalry were ordered to our left to check the murderous fire assailing it, and a severe fight ensued in the fields near Middletown. The enemy endeavored to gain possession of the turnpike, in order to seize our trains and get between our forces and Winchester. A concentrated fire from Middletown Heights where Early had planted his batteries, was poured upon the left, and unable to withstand its force, they were compelled to retreat in the direction of Newtown, five miles distant. As they slowly retired, their ranks were exposed to the cannonade of the enemy from the heights.

While the brave Sixth Corps was firmly covering the retreat of the routed army, General Rickets commanding received a severe wound in the breast.

But while his army was struggling for four anxious hours on the brink of destruction, where in the meantime, was Sheridan? He had arrived at Winchester, twenty miles from his camp, on the night of the eighteenth, intending to go on to Cedar Creek the next morning. He sipped his coffee leisurely at Winchester on the morning of the nineteenth, never dreaming of the maelstrom of rout into which his army had been thrown, and with which they were at that moment contending. It was about eight o'clock, when with his escort, he rode out of Winchester towards camp. As he went onward, the vibrations of the ground, trembling under the heavy discharges of artillery in the unseen distance, gave him his first intimation of the battle that raged in his front. Nothing alarmed, however, he proceeded on his way though at a quickened pace, thinking that if Early had dared to attack our strong position at Cedar Creek, he could not fail to meet with terrible punishment for his temerity. But as the thunder of the cannon grew louder until at last it deepened into one continuous roar, the terrible conviction was forced upon him that his army was retreating northward.

Startled from his composure as the truth flashed over him, he dashed the spurs into his horse and was soon far ahead of his escort, tearing madly along the road.

> "And there through the flush of the morning light
> A steed as black as the steeds of night
> Was seen to pass on with eagle flight;
> As if he knew the terrible need
> He stretched away with his utmost speed.
> Hills rose and fell; but his heart was gay
> With Sheridan fifteen miles away."

Wildly, with distended nostrils and fiery eye-balls

and foam-flecked sides, the black horse of Sheridan galloped onward like the wind, yet all too slow for the anxious heart of the leader, impatient to be on the battle-field.

"Under his spurning feet, the road
Like an arrowy Alpine river flowed,
And the landscape sped away behind,
Like an ocean flying before the wind;
And the steed like a bark fed with furnace ire,
Swept on with his wild eye full of fire.
But lo! he is nearing his heart's desire,
He is snuffing the smoke of the roaring fray
With Sheridan only five miles away."

Soon he encountered the stream of fugitives surging northward, but they paused and turned about as they saw their brave leader flying towards the front, and even the wounded men lying by the roadside cheered him. Swinging his cap above his head, he shouted as he dashed onward, "Face the other way boys, face the other way; we are going back to our camps; we are going to lick them out of their boots!"

It was about ten o'clock when he galloped up to the front, with his horse covered with foam, and by his voice and magnetic presence, stopped the retreat and infused new life and energy into the panic-stricken army.

Every effort was now directed to re-forming his men, which a pause in the pursuit favored—the army taking a position out of range of the enemy's fire. A new line of battle was arranged with the Sixth Corps in the center, Crook's command on the left, and

ARRIVAL OF SHERIDAN AT THE BATTLE OF CEDAR CREEK.

the Nineteenth on the right, with Custer's cavalry on the extreme right, and Merritt's cavalry on the extreme left.

While the line was forming, Sheridan seemed to be everywhere at once, attending to the work of re-organization, dashing up and down the front and imbuing the men with his own wonderful enthusiasm and courage.

"Boys," said he, "If I had been here this never should have happened. I tell you it never should have happened. And now we are going back to our camps. We are going to get a twist on them. We are going to lick them out of their boots."

Shouts and cheers followed him, and though they had eaten nothing since the night before, and had been fighting for five hours, the excited soldiers felt a new strength given them by the confidant bearing and language of their heroic commander.

The Confederates, meantime, had placed their artillery in range of our new position and then a grand charge was made across the fields, directly on the Nineteenth Corps.

Emory had orders to stop the enemy's advance at all hazards, and the terrible repulse which hurled back Early's men showed how well the order was obeyed.

When the news of the repulse was despatched to Sheridan, "Thank God for that," said he, "Now then tell General Emory if they attack him again, to go after them and follow them up, and to sock it into them, and to give them the devil!" And with almost every word, bringing his right hand down into the palm of his left, with a sharp blow, he added, "We'll get the tightest twist on them yet, you ever saw,—we'll have all those camps and cannon back again."

And Sheridan kept his word.

Early, compelled to relinquish the offensive, retired a short distance and began throwing up breast-works. Their wagon-trains were brought across Cedar Run, with the evident intention of retaining their position during the night. But Sheridan did not propose to stop short of putting the enemy to rout and regaining the lost camps on Cedar Creek. At half-past three o'clock, therefore, the re-organized troops dashed forward in a bold charge, Getty's Second Division having the advance.

A murderous fire from artillery and musketry greeted them as they rushed towards the foe, and under its withering blaze the lines broke and fell back.

"The sight roused Sheridan almost to frenzy, and galloping amid the broken ranks, he, by his thrilling appeals and almost superhuman efforts, restored order, and although his few remaining cannon could make but a feeble response to the overwhelming batteries of the enemy, he ordered the advance to be resumed.

"The next moment came a prolonged roar of musketry, mingled with the long-drawn yell of our charge —then the artillery ceased—the musketry died into spattering bursts, and over all the yell triumphant.

"Everything on the first line, the stone walls, the advanced crest, the tangled wood, and the half-finished breast-works had been carried."

Where shot and shell crashed thickest, there rode Sheridan, heedless of the storm, dashing along the front and giving his orders in person to the various division and corps commanders. It was a fearful crisis, but Sheridan, with the grandeur of a hero, rose master of the situation, and as our brave boys responded to his appeals, they swept everything before them with resistless valor and sent the panic-stricken enemy flying in utter confusion and rout.

On through Middletown and beyond it, the pursuing army of the Shenandoah chased the flying foe. The squadrons of Custer and Merritt charged the flanks of the enemy right and left, "taking prisoners, slashing, killing, driving as they went."

The road was strewn with knapsacks, muskets, clothing, and everything that could retard the flight of the panic-stricken foe, the guns they had captured from us and their own artillery falling into our hands.

The pursuit did not cease until the Confederates had been driven through Strasburg to Fisher's Hill and beyond to Woodstock, sixteen miles distant.

The victorious army that night bivouacked in their old camps along Cedar Creek, and though they had not yet tasted food and though the dead and wounded lay all around them, nothing could repress their enthusiasm over the great victory; as the news of the capture of prisoners and guns from the pursuing cavalry in the advance, came to them, the air was rent with their cheers.

Thus ends the record of one of the most wonderful contests of the war, of which Sheridan was pre-eminently the savior. It is a battle scene which stands out like a picture on the page of history, and over the central figure of Sheridan and his black charger, there hovers a cloud of glory whose light outlines the splendid spectacle of the hero on his "eagle flight" and before which all hearts yield willing homage.

"Hurrah! hurrah for Sheridan!
Hurrah! hurrah for horse and man!
And when their statues are placed on high,
Under the dome of the Union sky,
The American soldier's Temple of Fame,
There, with the glorious General's name,
Be it said in letters both bold and bright;
'Here is the steed that saved the day
By carrying Sheridan into the fight
From Winchester—twenty miles away.'"

CHAPTER XLI.

WAYNESBORO.

Personal Experiences.—Concealed in a Cypress Swamp.—The Union Guns.—Wheeler at Waynesboro.—The Enemy's Attack on Atkins. Repulse.—Kilpatrick Charges the Barricades, Everything Swept before Them.—Valor of Union Soldiers.—Wheeler in Disordered Flight.—Union Pursuit.—Kilpatrick's Report.—Sherman's Complimentary Letter.—Incidents in the Author's Escape.

THE name of Waynesboro summons back to remembrance, with all the vivid power attributed to Aladdin's wonderful lamp, the perilous days of my escape from southern prisons.

Skirting the Savannah River, within hearing of the railroad trains which rolled heavily by with their loads of yelling Confederate soldiers, we heard, with a thrill of joy, the heavy boom of cannon which told us our friends were near.

No voice of welcome, greeting the return of the wanderer from foreign lands, ever sounded sweeter to home-sick hearts than did the roar of Union guns to my companion and myself on that December day. But the Savannah River flowed between us and liberty, and had we ventured from our place of concealment in the daytime, certain capture would have awaited us.

We did not then know that Sherman was making his grand march to the sea, and that our own Kilpatrick was contributing his brilliant generalship to the movement.

The enemy had been steadily driven before our advancing army, and on the second of December, 1864, the Union cavalry, in order to cover the movements of the infantry, advanced on the Waynesboro Road. Waynesboro is a station about thirty miles south of Augusta, Georgia, on the railway connecting that place with Millen, where a junction is made with the Macon and Savannah line.

On the evening of the second, Wheeler moved towards Waynesboro, making a furious attack on Colonel Atkins' regiment, three miles south of the station. The attack was bravely repulsed, and Kilpatrick receiving orders to make a reconnoisance in force towards Waynesboro, and to fight Wheeler's cavalry wherever found, began the advance the next morning. Colonel Atkins, Second Brigade, led the column, and Wheeler's skirmishers were soon encountered and driven in. Our boys then advanced to take a long line of barricades, behind which the dismounted cavalry of the enemy were posted. But the attack, though bold and brave, failed of success, owing to a greater number being massed behind the defence than was at first supposed.

The second attack was made with the Tenth Ohio and Ninth Michigan Cavalry in column of fours on the right, and the Ninth Ohio on the left. The Ninety-second Illinois Mounted Infantry went into the fight dismounted. Captain Beebe's Battery, Tenth Wisconsin, opened fire on the barricades at a distance of six hundred yards and compelled the enemy's artillery to withdraw. At this opportune moment, the order to charge was given, and in splendid battle array the line moved forward upon the enemy's works. The contest was short and sharp, but the Union arms were victorious and the enemy fled from their defences.

The Confederates fell back for a hundred yards or so and endeavored to check our progress by counter charges. At one time during the fight there seemed to be a prospect of their success, but Colonel Heath with the Fifth Ohio Cavalry made a spirited attack on the Confederate flank which forced them to give away. They then fell back to Waynesboro and intrenched themselves in a new and strong position behind double lines of barricades.

General Kilpatrick then determined to break the Confederate center, and ordered Colonel Murray, commanding the advance, to "make his disposition of troops accordingly, which was immediately done. The Eighth Indiana Cavalry, commanded by Colonel Jones, was at once dismounted and sent forward as skirmishers; the Ninth Pennsylvania Cavalry, commanded by Colonel Jordan, held the left in columns of four by battalion; the Third Kentucky Cavalry, commanded by Lieutenant-Colonel King, had the center, while Colonel Baldwin, with the Fifth Kentucky Cavalry, and Captain Foreman with the Second Kentucky Cavalry held the right." The notes of the bugle pealed forth the well-known charge, and Kilpatrick's trusty squadrons dashed forward with resistless valor, driving the Confederates from their position and taking possession of the town. Through Waynesboro and beyond it to Brier Creek, eight miles away, the panic-stricken foe fled, and the hot pursuit was kept up. The railroad bridge was burned and the track destroyed, after which the Union forces moved to Alexander, where they bivouacked for the night. The enemy was completely routed, and Wheeler, never afterwards able to rally his demoralized troops, no longer molested our Cavalry, which continued its glorious march to the sea. In his official report of this action, Kilpatrick says:

"The men of my command fought most bravely throughout this day, and it is impossible to single out from among the officers, individual cases of gallantry where all did so well. * * * Judging from the enemy's killed and wounded, left on the field, his loss must have been severe, as upwards of two hundred, left in our hands, were wounded by the sabre alone."

In a letter from General Sherman which Kilpatrick received on New Year's Day, 1865, the following complimentary allusions occur:

"But the fact that to you, in a great measure, we owe the march of four strong infantry columns, with heavy trains and wagons, over three hundred miles, through an enemy's country, without the loss of a single wagon, and without the annoyance of cavalry dashes on our flanks, is honor enough for any cavalry commander."

Had my comrade and myself been on the other side of the Savannah River at that time, we should have made our way to the Union lines and thenceforward shared the fortunes and glory of Kilpatrick's command, in its march to the sea. But instead of fighting for country, we were doomed to days of frightful silence in Cypress swamps, and to nights of weary travel, with bruised and bleeding feet, guided only by the stars above and urged on by the very desperation of hope, despite the dangers confronting us at almost every step.

When on the fourth night after the battle of Waynesboro, we succeeded in crossing the Savannah, and landed on the Georgia shore, our conquering armies had swept onward towards the coast, beyond the hope of our joining them. But we soon struck the Union trail and followed it until at last we reached our lines at Savannah. Not unfrequently, we breakfasted or dined on the remains of rations thrown aside in their vacated camps, and the country was full of evidences that Sherman's army had passed that way.

The battle of Waynesboro baptized with new light the silver star of Kilpatrick, blazing always "in the front of war," and the soldiers of his command must ever feel a just pride in the glory accorded to their beloved commander.

CHAPTER XLII.

BENTONVILLE.

The Hostile Country of the Carolinas.—Sherman's Five Hundred Mile March.—The Country Desolated.—A Carnival of fire.—Arrival at Bentonville.—Johnston Encountered.—Battle of Bentonville.—The Enemy Repulsed.—Bravery of Slocum's Men.—Sherman's Army Intrenched.—Entrance into Goldsboro.—The Goal Won.—Glorious Success.—Congratulatory Order of General Sherman.

WHEN Sherman made his famous march through the hostile Carolinas, the most important battle of the campaign was fought near Bentonville.

Sherman's army, numbering about sixty-five thousand men, was divided into four corps with a wagon train of forty-five hundred vehicles, all told.

This immense train, if placed in a single line, would have been forty-five miles long.

After resting and recuperating at Savannah from the fatigue of the march through Georgia, Sherman began the vast enterprise of moving his army through the heart of two hostile states—Goldsboro, on the Neuse river, in North Carolina, being the objective point of the contemplated campaign. Goldsboro was five hundred miles to the northward from Savannah, but in order to take possession of it and its two railroads leading to Wilmington and Beaufort, a march unprecedented in military history was undertaken by the intrepid General who had just accomplished a journey of scarcely less magnitude across the state of Georgia. "One Rebel army lay at Charleston on his right, another at Augusta, on his left—North Carolina swarmed with troops, while every step he advanced took him nearer to Lee's gathered forces at Richmond. Large rivers were to be crossed, swamps traversed and battles fought, before he could reach the goal of his wishes." A tract of country forty miles wide and reaching from the sea-board at Savannah, to the center of North Carolina, was swept by the desolating tread of armies, harboring a special bitterness for the state where Rebellion was cradled and nursed. "In Georgia, few houses were burned; here, few escaped; the country was converted into one vast bonfire. The pine forests were fired, the resin factories were fired, the public buildings and private dwellings were fired. The middle of the finest day looked black and gloomy, for a dense smoke arose on all sides, clouding the very heavens. At night, the tall pine trees seemed so many huge pillars of fire. The flames hissed and screeched as they fed on the fat resin and dry branches, imparting to the forests a most fearful appearance."

Let it be said to the credit of our generals that this kind of work was not encouraged by them.

On the eighteenth of March, 1865, the two wings of Sherman's army under Howard and Slocum, had arrived within a short distance of Goldsboro where their long march was to end. Sherman supposing that after the repulse of the enemy near Ayresboro, a few days previous, no further opposition would be encountered, struck across the country from Slocum's command, to visit the other wing of his army, ten miles distant, under Howard, who was marching towards Goldsboro by way of Bentonville. Not many miles had been traversed, however, before he heard the thunder of guns behind him, in the direction of Slocum's camp, and couriers soon came riding up with the intelligence that the Confederate forces under Johnston were in Slocum's front near Bentonville. General Sherman immediately sent word to Slocum to act on the defensive until reënforcements could arrive, and aids were dispatched across the country to Blair and Howard. Blair, who was at that time near Olive Station, was ordered to come up in the enemy's rear, by way of Cox's Bridge on the Neuse, while Howard was directed to march on Bentonville, leaving his wagon train behind him.

Slocum, nothing alarmed by the sudden appearance of the enemy in his front, had his forces well posted, his artillery commanding the entire front. A second line of battle, established half a mile in advance, by the division of Morgan, received the first onset of the foe. The Confederate cavalry was first encountered, but their infantry and artillery soon blocked the way—Johnston having come up from Smithfield in the night, with the intention of overwhelming Sherman's left wing before the other columns of his army could come to its assistance.

The first dash of the enemy on our advance line, sent it back with the loss of three guns and caissons. Two divisions of the Fourteenth Corps were promptly deployed, and the same number of divisions of the Twentieth Corps were brought up in support on their left. A line of barricades was also hastily constructed.

The thunder of artillery, in the meantime, had summoned the dashing squadrons of Kilpatrick to the rescue and his troopers were massed on the left.

At four o'clock in the afternoon, the enemy in three columns, rushed forward on our line in a wild charge. But the fire from our artillery and the steady blaze of musketry which Sherman's men poured into the enemy's ranks sent their first column reeling back. Unmindful of the repulse of their comrades, the second column of the enemy rushed forward charging us with a yell. But the corps of Davis stood like a rock in the path of this living wave and sent it discomfited back. Six times in the space of an hour did the gallant left wing withstand the assaults of the foe led by Johnston in person. Not an inch of ground was yielded. The last charge broke Slocum's line, but quickly re-forming, a brilliant counter charge was executed, which drove the enemy back. "So close and desperate was the combat that many of the Rebel dead lay within our lines and even around the headquarters of the Generals."

Orders were sent Slocum that night to call up the two divisions guarding his wagon trains and Hazen's Divison of the Fifteenth Corps—these reënforcements enabling him to hold his ground, as he thought, in spite of the greatly outnumbering force of the Confederates. Dispatches from Schofield and Terry announced the former in possession of Kinston and able to reach Goldsboro on the twenty-first, the latter being near Faison's Depot.

Schofield was ordered to push for Goldsboro, and Terry to lay a pontoon bridge over the Neuse River at Cox's Bridge.

"At daybreak, on the morning of the twentieth, Hazen's division of the Fifteenth Corps, Geary's of the Twentieth and Baird's of the Fourteenth, reported on the field, having marched all night from the new Goldsboro road where the trains were moving."

Howard succeeded in effecting a junction with Slocum, on his left, and by four o'clock in the afternoon a strong line of battle faced the enemy. Johnston, therefore, did not find his coveted opportunity of fighting Sherman's army in detail, and his well-formed plans were thus rendered abortive.

On the rainy day of the twenty-first, Schofield entered Goldsboro with little opposition, and at the same time Terry was effecting a passage of the Neuse, ten miles above at Cox's Bridge. Mower's division of the Seventeenth Corps, on the extreme right, nearly succeeded in cutting off the enemy's only line of retreat at Mill Creek.

At this juncture of affairs, Sherman ordered the skirmish line forward in a general attack and the concluding engagement of the campaign took place. Johnston retreated to Smithfield that night and the Union army went into camp around Goldsboro—the goal of its desires. Here ended the wonderful march begun two months before at the southermost limit of the Carolinas. The losses of the left wing at Bentonville were one thousand two hundred and forty-seven in killed and wounded, one hundred and forty-five of this number being killed, exclusive of nine officers who met their death on that heroic field.

The right wing under Howard lost three hundred and ninety-nine men, thirty-seven of whom were killed. Slocum took three hundred and thirty-eight prisoners. Kilpatrick's cavalry, being held in reserve, experienced few if any losses. The object of the great march having been accomplished, Sherman turned his army over to Schofield and went to City Point, ready for the next move on the chess-board of military operations. Before leaving he issued the following congratulatory order to his army:—

"HEAD-QUARTERS MILITARY DIVISION OF THE MISSISSIPPI,
"IN THE FIELD, NEAR BENTONVILLE, N. C.,
"*March* 22, 1865.

"SPECIAL FIELD ORDERS—No. 35.

"The General Commanding announces to the army that yesterday it beat, on its chosen ground, the concentrated armies of our enemy, who has fled in disorder, leaving his dead, wounded, and prisoners in our hands, and burning his bridges on his retreat.

"On the same day, Major-General Schofield, from Newbern, entered and occupied Goldsboro', and Major-General Terry, from Wilmington, secured Cox's Bridge crossing, and laid a pontoon bridge across Neuse River, so that our campaign has resulted in a glorious success. After a march of the most extraordinary character, nearly five hundred miles, over swamps and rivers deemed impassable to others, at the most inclement season of the year, and drawing our chief supplies from a poor and wasted country, we reach our destination in good health and condition.

"I thank the army, and assure it that our Government and people honor them for this new display of the physical and moral qualities which reflect honor upon the whole nation.

"You shall now have rest, and all the supplies that can be brought from the rich granaries and store-houses of our magnificent country, before again embarking on new and untried dangers.

"W. T. SHERMAN, *Major-General Commanding.*"

CHAPTER XLIII.

FIVE FORKS.

Grant and Sherman in Consultation.—The End Drawing Near.—Grand Combination of Movements.—Sheridan *En route* for Five Forks.—Importance of Holding Five Forks.—The March Through the Rain.—Engagement on the White Oak Road.—The Union Ranks Victorious.—The Sunday Fight.—Grant Takes Advantage of His Victory.—Captured Prisoners.—Davis Flying from Richmond.—Evacuation of Richmond and Petersburg.—The End Drawing Near.

WHEN Sherman left Goldsboro for City Point after the conquering sweep of his armies through the Carolinas, it was on no less a mission than to consult with Grant concerning the next great move on the chess-board of war.

At City Point the two generals met and held anxious consultation. President Lincoln was there, also, and cordially welcomed the hero of the "Great March." On the deliberations of these men hung the fate of a nation; but when their council was ended, the last battle of the war had been planned. Every sign in the military heavens indicated a speedy termination of the war, but a false move at this crisis might overthrow the good results already obtained and prolong the contest indefinitely. Well might the great Chiefs of the nation be full of anxiety. But though the emergency was vast their genius mastered it.

While Sherman was destroying railroads and crippling military resources in South Carolina, General Stoneman was doing the same work in the direction of Lynchburg, Virginia, and Thomas was marching a cavalry force of ten thousand men into the heart of Alabama. At the same time, Sheridan, after having driven Early out of Waynesboro and making large captures of prisoners and munitions of war, was sweeping forward toward Richmond, "sending consternation into the Rebel Capital." Demolished railroads, broken canal-locks and burned bridges marked the path of his army.

With this grand combination of movements, Grant thought that the "Rebellion would have nothing left to stand on," but he did not know that the battle he was preparing, would end our four years of fighting.

On March twenty-seventh, 1865, Sheridan joined the army of the Potomac and was immediately sent around the Confederate left, to take possession of the Southside and Danville railroads, thus holding Lee's line of retreat in case of the evacuation of Richmond. But Grant wished to strike the enemy before he could have a chance to retreat.

Two days before the commencement of Sheridan's movement, the enemy made a sudden dash on Fort Stedman in front of the Ninth Corps, and carried it by assault. It was a bold and unexpected stroke, and the enemy seizing our guns, turned them upon us.

But the Union artillery blazed upon the victors from all quarters with such persistent energy, that they were obliged to abandon their newly-captured prize. In this assault, our loss was nine hundred and nineteen, and we took nineteen hundred prisoners. The other Corps were ordered to advance, which they did, capturing the Rebel picket-line in front of the Second and Sixth Corps, and taking eight hundred and thirty-four prisoners.

After the consultation between Grant and Sherman, it was decided that "Sherman should return to his army, and, making a feint as if to move up the Neuse to Raleigh, march rapidly north to the line of the Roanoke. This would be closing the last door on Lee, and Grant knew that the moment Sherman approached the river, the former would evacute Richmond."

It is a matter of wonder that Lee remained so long in the Confederate Capital. Perhaps he feared that his army might melt away through its large proportion of desertions, should he leave his defences at Richmond. Or perhaps he thought Johnston quite able to cope with Sherman and arrest his progress in the north. But Grant was full of anxiety lest the enemy should slip from his grasp, by effecting a junction with Johnston, thus compelling new plans and a new campaign.

On the morning of March twenty-ninth, Sheridan commenced his advance, and reached Dinwiddie Court House the same night. Sheridan held our extreme left, Parke the Union right, while Wright, Ord, Humphreys, and Warren occupied the intermediate positions. On the thirtieth, Sheridan pushed forward towards Five Forks, in a drenching rain which made the roads impassible for wagon-trains and artillery.

Five Forks is a point in the woods where five roads meet, three of which lead back to the Southside railroad. The possession of the junction would give our forces a choice of advance, and the point was therefore a strong strategic one. The White Oak road was filled with defences, constructed of logs and earth, and the approaches to it were blocked by felled trees, behind which sharpshooters were stationed.

On the morning of the thirty-first, Sheridan took possession of Five Forks, and Warren advanced on the enemy's fortifications down the White Oak Road. Ayres' division had the advance, and drove the Confederates back upon their main works a mile and a half below the White Oak Road. At this point the enemy made a grand rally and rushed with such impetuous force on the Union advance, that Ayres' division, though making stubborn resistance, was compelled to give way. The commands of Crawford and Griffin, which came next, were also driven back. But now, Warren being re-enforced by a division of the Second Corps, rallied his broken lines and charging the enemy, gained possession of the White Oak Road. At this juncture, however, the enemy, advancing in heavy force against Sheridan, drove him from his position back to Dinwiddie Court-House.

Here, Sheridan, instead of falling back on the main army, "deployed his cavalry on foot, leaving only mounted men enough to take charge of the horses. This compelled the enemy to deploy over a vast extent of woods and broken country, and made his progress slow." Sheridan sent word to Grant how affairs stood, and the Fifth Corps with General McKenzie's cavalry was at once ordered to his aid. The re-enforcements reached him at midnight on the thirty-first, and in the morning he again marched on Five Forks. After driving the Confederates into their intrenchments, a general attack was ordered. "The Fifth Corps on reaching the White Oak Road, made a left wheel, and burst on the enemy's left flank and rear like a tornado, and pushed rapidly on—orders having been given that if the enemy was routed, there should be no halt to reform broken lines. As stated before, the firing of the Fifth Corps was the signal to General Merritt to assault, which was promptly responded to, and the works of the enemy were soon carried at several points by our brave infantrymen. The Confederates were driven from their strong line of works and completely routed; the Fifth Corps doubling up their left flank in confusion, and the cavalry of General Merritt dashing on to the White Oak Road, capturing and turning their artillery upon them, and riding into their broken ranks, so demoralized them, that they made no serious stand after their line was carried, but took to flight in disorder. Between five and six thousand prisoners fell into our hands, and the fugitives were driven westward and were pursued until long after dark by Merritt's and McKenzie's cavalry, for a distance of six miles."

General Grant received the report of this victorious assault just after dark and in order to retain the position, immediately ordered Miles' division of Humphrey's Corps to re-enforce Sheridan at Five Forks. A "heavy bombardment of the enemy's lines" was ordered to be kept up during the night.

As the first hint of dawn began to streak the sky on the next morning, our army swept forward in a general attack, and the battle of the previous day was renewed. Wright carried his whole corps through the enemy's lines in his front, capturing thousands of prisoners and a large number of guns. Pushing forward, he met the corps of Ord, and making a junction with him, hemmed the enemy in Petersburg on that side of them, while Humphreys joined Wright on the left, and Gibbon's Corps captured the works south of Petersburg.

The battle now raged furiously along the entire line, the Confederates fighting with great desperation. But at this juncture, Sheridan charged down upon the enemy's flank and rear with such force as to drive them from their defences panic-striken. Large numbers of prisoners and guns fell into our hands.

While the battle was raging, President Lincoln and the President of the Confederacy were both awaiting the result of the contest within a few miles of each other. Lincoln was at Grant's headquarters before Petersburg, thoughtful and anxious. Davis was attending church in Richmond. "In the midst of the services, an orderly splashed with mud strode up the aisle and handed him a paper. Glancing at its contents, he saw that all was over, and a few hours afterwards, he had left behind him his Capital forever, and was fleeing towards Danville." That night the Confederate army withdrew from Richmond and Petersburg and commenced the retreat which ended in Lee's surrender.

CHAPTER XLIV.

THE SURRENDER.

The Last Act in the Drama.—The Historic Farm-House.—Events Succeeding the Battle of Five Forks.—Lee's Army Hemmed in.—Engagement at Barnesville.—The Enemy Hopelessly Surrounded.—Extermination or Surrender.—Triumphant Entrance into Richmond.—Lincoln's Levee in the Confederate Capital.—The Last Act.—Palm Sunday Anniversary.—Universal Rejoicing.

THE last act in the great drama of the war took place without dramatic accessory. There was no startling tableau, with the chief actors grouped in effective attitudes, surrounded by their attendants. No spreading tree lent its romance to the occasion, as some artists have fondly supposed.

A plain farm house between the lines was selected by General Lee for the surrender, and the ceremony of that act was short and simple. The noble victor did not complete the humiliation of the brave vanquished by any triumphal display or blare of trumpets. In his magnanimity he even omitted the customary usage of allowing the victorious troops to pass through the enemy's lines and witness their surrender. The two great commanders met with courteous salutation. General Lee being attended only by one of his aides. General Grant sat down at a table in the barely furnished room and wrote in lead pencil the terms of capitulation to which Lee dictated an agreement in writing. His secretary, Colonel Marshall, and Colonel Badeau, the secretary of General Grant, made copies of the agreement from the same bottle of ink.

"The exchange of these notes terminated the interview. It was singularly simple; utterly bald of all rhetorical flourishes and ceremonies; but its very simplicity gives it an interest and dignity that the most excessive formalities might fail to furnish. * * * * The manners of both commanders were easy, self-possessed, those of plain gentlemen in ordinary intercourse, and it is remarkable that no two men of important station could be found within the limits of America who so equally abhored the theatrical as General Ulysses S. Grant and General Robert E. Lee."

The final situation of the Confederate army before its surrender, was indeed desperate—its environment hopeless. Hemmed in at Appomattox Court House, on a strip of land between the Appomattox and James Rivers, the Union army nearly surrounded it on all sides. Sheridan was in front, Meade in the rear, and Ord south of the Court House. Lee had no alternative other than the wholesale slaughter of his reduced army or its surrender to Federal authority. He wisely chose the latter.

The decisive battle of Five Forks had put his army to rout and sent it in rapid retreat towards the junction of the Southside and Danville railroads at Burkesville. The Union troops pressed forward in pursuit, and it became a vital question which would reach the Junction first. Between Petersburg, their point of starting, and their destination at Burkesville the distance was fifty-three miles. The roads were bad and the troops tired with two days fighting ; but they pushed on with determination in this race which was destined to decide the fate of two armies.

On the fourth, Lee was at Amelia Court House, while Sheridan, pushing towards the Danville railroad struck it at Jettersville on the fifth, whither Meade with the Second and Sixth Corps followed him. Two divisions of the Ninth Corps, moving on the Cox Road, reached Wellesville, twenty-one miles from Burkesville, on the same day. "On the night of the fifth, the army lay in line of battle, stretched across three or four miles of country, and facing substantially northward. Custer's division of cavalry lay on the right flank, and McKenzie's on the left. The infantry line was formed with the Sixth Corps on the right, the Fifth in the center and the Second on the left. On the next day the Sixth Corps was transferred from the right to the left, and the whole army had, before noon, marched about five miles in the direction of Amelia Court House." At this point, learning that the enemy was moving in the direction of Farmville, the course of the Second and Fifth Corps was immediately changed to a northwesterly direction. At about four o'clock in the afternoon of April sixth, the Second and Sixth Corps engaged the enemy, putting him to rout and capturing many prisoners. Generals Ewell and Custis were among the number. On the seventh, the Second Corps encountered Lee at Barnesville sixteen miles west of Burkesville, where a sharp contest took place and Lee was again forced to retire. He retreated in the direction of Lynchburg but Hancock's, column had marched from Winchester on the fourth and stood ready to meet the enemy at Lynchburg, should occasion require. The remnant of Lee's once proud army was now hopelessly environed. In a few days it had been reduced from a force of fifty thousand to one of twenty, through its large numbers of desertions and the losses inflicted in battle. It took no prophet to foretell now the fate of Lee's army. Everyone could see that its doom was sealed.

Meantime, on the night of that eventful Sunday when Davis left his church services to take refuge in flight, Petersburg and the boasted Capital of the Confederacy were both evacuated. At daybreak on Monday morning General Weitzel marched the Army of the James into the streets of Richmond, and "was greeted with hearty welcome from the mass of the people." The Mayor went out to meet him in order to surrender the city, but missed him on the road. The city had been fired and the principal part of Main street was in ruins. The bridges also were destroyed. One thousand prisoners were taken besides five thousand wounded lying in hospitals. With a kind of poetic justice, Libby Prison and Castle Thunder were immediately filled with Confederate prisoners of war.

Two days after Davis fled from Richmond, President Lincoln made a triumphal entry into the city and held a levee in the Confederate Presidential mansion. When Grant had reached Farmville, on the seventh, in his pursuit of Lee, he addressed him the following note:

"APRIL 7.

"*General R. E. Lee, Commanding S. C. A:*

"General:—The result of the last week must convince you of the hopelessness of further resistance on the part of the Army of Northern Virginia in this struggle. I feel that it is so, and regard it as my duty to shift from myself the responsibility of any further effusion of blood, by asking of you the surrender of that portion of the C. S. army known as the Army of Northern Virginia.

"Very respectfully, your obedient servant,

"U. S. GRANT,

"Lieutenant-General Commanding Armies of the United States."

Early on the morning of the eighth, before leaving Farmville, Grant received the accompanying response to which he immediately replied:

"APRIL 7.

"General:—I have received your note of this date. Though not entertaining the opinion you express of the hopelessness of further resistance on the part of the Army of Northern Virginia, I reciprocate your desire to avoid useless effusion of blood, and therefore, before considering your proposition, ask the terms you will offer, on condition of its surrender.

"R. E. LEE, General.

"To Lieutenant-General U. S. GRANT, Commanding Armies of the United States."

"APRIL 8.

"*To General R. E. Lee, Commanding Confederate States Army:*

"General:—Your note of last evening, in reply to mine of the same date, asking the conditions on which I will accept the surrender of the Army of Northern Virginia, is just received.

"In reply, I would say that peace being my first desire, there is but one condition that I insist upon, viz:

"That the men surrendered shall be disqualified for taking up arms against the Government of the United States until properly exchanged.

"I will meet you, or designate officers to meet any officers you may name for the same purpose, at any point agreeable to you, for the purpose of arranging definitely the terms upon which the surrender of the Army of Northern Virginia will be received.

Very respectfully, your obedient servant,

U. S. GRANT.

"Lieutenant-General Commanding the Armies of the United States."

The pursuit was resumed on the eighth, and about midnight of that date General Grant, who was with Meade's column, received the following communication from General Lee:

"APRIL 8.

GENERAL:—I received at a late hour your note of to-day in answer to mine of yesterday.

"I did not intend to propose the surrender of the Army of Northern Virginia, but to ask the terms of your proposition. To be frank, I do not think the emergency has arisen to call for the surrender. But as the restoration of peace should be the sole object of all, I desire to know whether your proposals would tend to that end.

"I cannot, therefore, meet you with a view to surrender the Army of Northern Virginia, but so far as your proposition may affect the Confederate States forces under my command, and lead to the restoration of peace, I should be pleased to meet you at ten A. M., to-morrow, on the old stage-road to Richmond, between the picket lines of the two armies. Very respectfully, your obedient servant,

"R. E. LEE,

"*General Confederate States Armies.*

"To Lieutenant-General GRANT,

Commanding Armies of the United States."

In Grant's official report he says,—"Early on the morning of the ninth I returned him an answer as follows, and immediately started to join the column south of the Appomattox:—

"APRIL 9.

"*General R. E. Lee, Commanding C. S. A:*

"GENERAL:—Your note of yesterday is received. As I have no authority to treat on the subject of peace, the meeting proposed at ten A. M., to-day, could lead to no good. I will state however, General, that I am equally anxious for peace with yourself; and the whole North entertain the same feeling. The terms upon which peace can be had are well understood. By the South laying down their arms they will hasten that most desirable event, save thousands of human lives, and hundreds of millions of property not yet destroyed.

"Sincerely hoping that all our difficulties may be settled without the loss of another life, I subscribe myself, very respectfully, your obedient servant,

"U. S. GRANT,
"*Lieutenant-General U. S. A.*"

"On the morning of the ninth, General Ord's command and the Fifth Corps, reached Appomattox Station, just as the enemy was making a desperate effort to break through our cavalry. The infantry was at once thrown in. Soon after, a white flag was received requesting a suspension of hostilities pending negotiations for a surrender.

"Before reaching General Sheridan's head-quarters, I received the following from General Lee:—

"APRIL 9, 1865.

"GENERAL:—I received your note of this morning on the picket line, whither I had come to meet you and ascertain definitely what terms were embraced in your proposition of yesterday with reference to the surrender of this army.

"I now request an interview in accordance with the offer contained in your letter of yesterday for that purpose. Very respectfully, your obedient servant,

"R. E. LEE, *General.*

"To Lieutenant-General GRANT,
Commanding United States Armies."

To which communication this answer was returned:

"April 9.

"*General R. E. Lee, Commanding Confederate States Armies:*

"Your note of this date is but this moment (11.50 A. M.,) received.

"In consequence of my having passed from the Richmond and Lynchburg road to the Farmville and Lynchburg road, I am at this writing, about four miles west of Walter's Church, and will push forward to the front for the purpose of meeting you.

"Notice sent to me on this road where you wish the interview to take place will meet me. Very respectfully your obedient servant,

U. S. GRANT, *Lieutenant General.*"

"The interview was held at Appomattox Court House, the result of which is set forth in the following correspondence:—

"Appomattox Court House, Va., April 9.

"*General R. E. Lee, Commanding C. S. A.:*

"In accordance with the substance of my letter to you of the 8th instant, I propose to receive the surrender of the Army of Northern Virginia, on the following terms, to wit:

"Rolls of all the officers and men to be made in duplicate, one copy to be given to an officer designated by me, the other to be detained by such officers as you may designate.

"The officers to give their individual paroles not to take arms against the United States until properly exchanged, and each company or regimental commander sign a like parole for the men of their commands.

"The arms, artillery, and public property to be packed and stacked, and turned over to the officers appointed by me to receive them. This will not embrace the side-arms of the officers, nor their private horses or baggage.

"This done, each officer and man will be allowed to return to their homes, not to be disturbed by United States authority so long as they observe their parole and the laws in force where they may reside.

Very respectfully,

"U. S. GRANT, *Lieutenant-General.*"

"HEAD-QUARTERS, ARMY OF NORTHERN VIRGINIA,
April 9, 1865.

GENERAL:—I received your letter of this date, containing the terms of the surrender of the Army of Northern Virginia, as proposed by you. As they are substantially the same as those expressed in your letter of the 8th instant, they are accepted. I will proceed to designate the proper officers to carry the stipulations into effect.

"R. E. LEE, *General.*

"Lieutenant-General U. S. GRANT."

When the last letter was received, "Grant hastened to the front where Lee was awaiting him," and the concluding scene in the drama of Rebellion was then rehearsed. From the beginning of the last forward movement until the surrender, about ten thousand of the enemy's force had been killed and wounded in battle, over twenty thousand prisoners had been taken or had deserted, and one hundred and seventy pieces of artillery were captured.

It was Palm Sunday, April ninth, 1865, when the capitulation was signed, in the plain, frame dwelling near Appomattox Court House.

One is often struck with the curious coincidences—the apparent sympathy between nature and important human events. The dying hours of Cromwell and Napoleon were marked by violent storms. Omens in earth and sky were the precursors of the death of Julius Cæsar and King Duncan. A great comet heralded the opening of the war, and Palm Sunday—the day which commemorates the victorious entry of Christ into Jerusalem, ushered in the welcome reign of peace. The time was auspicious; the elements were rocked to sleep in a kind of Sunday repose. The two armies so long in deadly hostility, were now facing each other with guns strangely hushed. An expectant silence pervaded the air. Every heart was anxiously awaiting the result of the conference in the historic farm house.

When at last, the news of the surrender flashed along the lines, deafening cheers rose and fell for more than half an hour, over the victorious Union army. Other than this, there was no undue, triumphal display of the victors over the conquered foe. "There was a Federal column waving the white flag, and lines of troops fringing a distant hill. There was nothing visible in front but these; no crash of music disturbed the evening air. * * * On the Confederate side, the disbanded lines of attack moved across the field with the slow step of mourners."

The shout of joy which was sent up that day from Appomattox Court House, echoed through the entire North. Cannon boomed forth their iron peans of victory; the glad clash of bells was heard ringing "peace and freedom in," and bonfires flamed high their attestation of the unbounded delight everywhere exhibited. The day of jubilee seemed to have come and rejoicing was the order of the hour. The storm of war which had rocked the country for four long years, was now rolling away, and the sunlight of peace fell athwart the National horizon. The country for which Washington fought and Warren fell, was once more safe from Treason's hands, and Liberty was again the heritage of the people.

www.ingramcontent.com/pod-product-compliance
Lightning Source LLC
LaVergne TN
LVHW020058110826
845151LV00001B/19